D0916717

Python, PyGame, and Raspberry Pi Game Development

Second Edition

Sloan Kelly

Apress®

Python, PyGame, and Raspberry Pi Game Development

Sloan Kelly
Niagara Falls, ON, Canada

ISBN-13 (pbk): 978-1-4842-4532-3   ISBN-13 (electronic): 978-1-4842-4533-0
https://doi.org/10.1007/978-1-4842-4533-0

Copyright © 2019 by Sloan Kelly

This work is subject to copyright. All rights are reserved by the Publisher, whether the whole or part of the material is concerned, specifically the rights of translation, reprinting, reuse of illustrations, recitation, broadcasting, reproduction on microfilms or in any other physical way, and transmission or information storage and retrieval, electronic adaptation, computer software, or by similar or dissimilar methodology now known or hereafter developed.

Trademarked names, logos, and images may appear in this book. Rather than use a trademark symbol with every occurrence of a trademarked name, logo, or image we use the names, logos, and images only in an editorial fashion and to the benefit of the trademark owner, with no intention of infringement of the trademark.

The use in this publication of trade names, trademarks, service marks, and similar terms, even if they are not identified as such, is not to be taken as an expression of opinion as to whether or not they are subject to proprietary rights.

While the advice and information in this book are believed to be true and accurate at the date of publication, neither the authors nor the editors nor the publisher can accept any legal responsibility for any errors or omissions that may be made. The publisher makes no warranty, express or implied, with respect to the material contained herein.

Managing Director, Apress Media LLC: Welmoed Spahr
Acquisitions Editor: Spandana Chatterjee
Development Editor: James Markham
Coordinating Editor: Divya Modi

Cover designed by eStudioCalamar

Cover image designed by Freepik (www.freepik.com)

Distributed to the book trade worldwide by Springer Science+Business Media New York, 233 Spring Street, 6th Floor, New York, NY 10013. Phone 1-800-SPRINGER, fax (201) 348-4505, e-mail orders-ny@springer-sbm.com, or visit www.springeronline.com. Apress Media, LLC is a California LLC and the sole member (owner) is Springer Science + Business Media Finance Inc (SSBM Finance Inc). SSBM Finance Inc is a **Delaware** corporation.

For information on translations, please e-mail rights@apress.com, or visit http://www.apress.com/rights-permissions.

Apress titles may be purchased in bulk for academic, corporate, or promotional use. eBook versions and licenses are also available for most titles. For more information, reference our Print and eBook Bulk Sales web page at http://www.apress.com/bulk-sales.

Any source code or other supplementary material referenced by the author in this book is available to readers on GitHub via the book's product page, located at www.apress.com/978-1-4842-4532-3. For more detailed information, please visit http://www.apress.com/source-code.

For Annamarie

Table of Contents

About the Author

Sloan Kelly has worked in the games industry for nearly 12 years. He has worked on a number of AAA and indie titles and currently works for an educational game company. He lives in Ontario, Canada, with his wife and children. Sloan is on Twitter @codehoose and makes YouTube videos in his spare time.

About the Technical Reviewer

John Watson is a game developer, artist, guitar player, husband, and father. Among John's many software-powered side projects, he's building a Raspberry Pi–powered device that generates interactive music in live modern dance performances. He's also developing a retro-inspired 2D twin-stick arcade shooter called Gravity Ace. You can follow his progress on Twitter @yafd or at gravityace.com. Stop by and say hi!

Acknowledgments

I would like to thank Divya Modi, Spandana Chatterjee, and the entire team at Apress for giving me the opportunity to write the second edition of this book. A special thank you to Divya for keeping me in the loop throughout this process. I would also like to thank John Watson for the feedback that he gave while reviewing the text.

Thank you also to Eben Upton who gave us the little machine we will use to make games and explore electronics with and to Pete Shinners for starting PyGame and the community for keeping it going. Finally, a huge thank you to Guido van Rossum for designing the excellent Python language that you, dear reader, are about to learn and enjoy.

Introduction

This book is intended for anyone who wants to learn how to program games. It is ideally suited to students who want to learn Python and PyGame on their Raspberry Pi. While not necessary, this book has been oriented toward the Raspberry Pi computer.

The Python programming language is ideally suited to beginners and experts alike. The skills you will learn in this book are easily transferable to other computer languages too.

If you are unfamiliar with the Raspberry Pi, there are several good eBook guides on getting started including mine called *A Slice of Raspberry Pi*, available from all good eBook retailers.

This book assumes that you are familiar with the Raspberry Pi computer and that you have the Raspberry Pi Foundation's recommended Raspbian operating system installed. Raspbian is a distribution of the Debian Linux operating system built specifically for the Raspberry Pi. This distribution contains all the Software Development Kits (SDKs) including one for Python that includes PyGame. If you don't have Raspbian installed, you will have to ensure that you have Python and PyGame installed on your system.

Don't have a Raspberry Pi? Not to worry, you can still learn Python and PyGame. The code in this book will work on other OSs with Python and PyGame installed; Python is a platform-independent language.

You can obtain more information and download versions of Python from `www.python.org`. PyGame can be obtained from `www.pygame.org/`.

Sprites from Ari Feldman's SpriteLib have been used for the projects contained in this book.

How This Book Is Organized

The book is organized into chapters covering the following:

- Introduction to the Python language
- Containers in Python
- The IDLE IDE
- Introduction to PyGame library
- Designing your game
- User-defined functions
- File input/output
- Object-oriented design and programming
- Model View Controller design pattern
- Finite state machines
- Interfacing with electronics

There are five projects that produce complete games, all the code and resources for which are on the web site `www.sloankelly.net/`. The five games are

- Bricks
- Snake
- Invaders
- Copycat
- Couch quiz

Throughout the book are lines of code that you can type in to tell the computer to perform actions, or to add text to a file. In the book, these lines will appear like this:

```
print 'hello world'
```

Python uses white space characters, notably tabs, to denote blocks of code. Because this is an eBook and it is not possible to know how tabs will be rendered on your device, white space is very important to Python, so remember to use the "tab" key to indent the lines exactly as written like so:

```
name='Sloan'
if (name=='Sloan'):
    print ('Hello', name)
```

The line that starts with "print" has been indented using the "tab" key.

OS commands that are to be typed into a command window like Terminal will be preceded with a "$" sign:

```
$ ls -al
```

There are screenshots and other graphics throughout the text to illustrate output, but when it is just text it will appear in a box like this:

This is output from a command.

It can appear on one or more lines.

Finally, anything important will appear in a note formatted like this:

Take note of this message

CHAPTER 1

What Is a Programming Language?

A computer program is a list of statements that a computer must carry out in order to complete a task, usually a repetitive task that would take a human a long time to calculate. A computer language describes the arrangement or syntax of those statements. There are various computer languages out there, each suitable to one or more tasks.

Each language has its own unique syntax and set of commands, but they all have constructs that perform roughly the same types of actions:

- Input

- Output

- Branching (making decisions based on data)

- Loops

A command or keyword is a special phrase that is used by the language to perform an action whether it is to get input from the user or display text on the screen. These commands are reserved words that cannot be used

© Sloan Kelly 2019
S. Kelly, *Python, PyGame, and Raspberry Pi Game Development*,
https://doi.org/10.1007/978-1-4842-4533-0_1

for any other purpose in your program. We'll dive deeper into them later in this book, but examples of keywords in Python are

- for

- if

- pass

What Does a Computer Program Do?

A computer program performs a series of tasks over and over again manipulating the user's input and delivering output in a feedback loop. When you move your mouse (input), the arrow on the screen moves along with it (output).

The old definition of a computer program was a basic mathematical formula:

$$Program = Algorithm + Data$$

An algorithm is the step-by-step procedure for processing data. The algorithm solves a problem with the data that it has been supplied. What kind of problem? It could be anything from calculating the area of a rectangle or the volume of a room, where to move a player's avatar based on the input from a joystick, or deciding how an enemy should react to a player who just obtained a power up.

Are all computer programs written the same way? Is there a standard way to approach a given problem? Well, no. Not really. There are many ways to achieve the same result in computer programming! There is no correct way of solving a problem. So long as your program does what it is supposed to, that's just fine! You may want to 'tweak' your code later to speed it up, but any optimization happens once you have the algorithm right. Your program must function as expected. This is of paramount importance.

Conclusion

Computer programs are used to perform laborious tasks on a series of data elements that are input by users. For games, that means updating the player avatar location and maintaining the game world while displaying it to the player.

It is not advisable to stick to one language but rather experience as many languages as you can. This will enable you, the programmer, to decide which language is best for a given situation. Your first language is a great choice; Python is a very powerful language that can be used for a variety of purposes and is perfect for the first-time programmer.

CHAPTER 2

What Is Python?

Python is a modern programming language that supports object-oriented, functional, and imperative programming styles. It is ideal for the beginner because of its readability and ease of use. The upside to all of this is that you can write programs in less lines of code than an equivalent C/C++ or Java program.

What on earth did I just say? Let's break that last paragraph down and make it a little more readable.

Programming Styles

Python is suitable for programming in the following styles:

- Imperative
- Object-oriented
- Functional

Imperative programming was for the longest time the most common way to write computer code. It describes step by step how to perform changes to the data in a very linear manner.

For example, we have the following items:

- Tea bag
- Milk

© Sloan Kelly 2019
S. Kelly, *Python, PyGame, and Raspberry Pi Game Development*,
https://doi.org/10.1007/978-1-4842-4533-0_2

- Cup

- Spoon

- Kettle

- Water

These are the things we use and manipulate in our 'program'; this is our data. We want to change this data to a different state. What state? Well, we want a cup of milky tea. How do we do that? We prescribe a series of operations that will transform this data into some other data like so:

- Place tea bag in cup

- Pour water into kettle

- Boil the kettle

- While the kettle is boiling, watch TV

- Pour the water from the kettle to the cup

- Pour milk into the cup

- Stir the tea with the spoon

- Serve

In code (not specifically Python code), this could be written as

```
addTo(cup, tea_bag)
addTo(kettle, water)
boil(kettle)
while isBoiling(kettle):
    watchTV()
addTo(cup, getWaterFrom(kettle))
addTo(cup, milk)
stir(cup)
serve(cup)
```

These are the prescribed steps (process) to change our initial data (our input) and transform it into our output. See Figure 2-1.

Figure 2-1. *Input, process, output block diagram*

Object-Oriented

Imperative programs separate the functionality (the algorithm) from the data. Object-oriented languages keep the functionality with the data. Objects contain the data and the instructions used to manipulate that data in one place.

There is an advantage to this; algorithms stored with it process your data. Let's take a pencil as an example. It has certain attributes that describe it:

- Color
- Hardness
- Nib size
- Length

It also has certain actions or methods that can be applied to it:

- Write
- Erase
- Sharpen

These methods change the state of the object; remember that state is determined by the data. For example, when you write using a pencil, the nib length gets smaller and smaller. When you sharpen the pencil, its overall length gets shorter, but the nib size is reset to its maximum.

Functional

Functional programming is not new and was first developed in the 1930s. It has its roots in lambda calculus. Functional programming uses mathematical functions to perform calculations. No data is changed in these calculations; instead new values are calculated. This means that functional programs have no state.

Functional programming tends to be used for recursion (calling the same function from itself) and iteration through items.

In Python, Fibonacci numbers can be calculated with the following one line:

```
fib = lambda n: n if n < 2 else fib(n-1) + fib(n-2)
```

This was taken from a discussion on StackOverflow (http://bit.ly/FibonacciPython).

To calculate a value, the programmer simply passes in an integer value:

```
fib(5)
```

What Is Pygame?

Pygame was started by Pete Shinners as a wrapper around the Simple DirectMedia Library (SDL). It has been maintained by the community since 2000 and is released under the GNU Lesser General Public License. Which means you are free to look at the source code if you so choose.

Pygame was created to allow for the development of games without resorting to using programming languages like C or C++.

Pygame can be used to write fast-paced 2D games in a retro style, or modern casual and hyper-casual games. It handles the difficulties of loading in images, displaying sprites, playing sounds, etc., for you.

For more details about Pygame, please visit their web site: `www.pygame.org/news`.

Conclusion

Python is a modern, multiparadigm programming language. It can be used for imperative, object-oriented, and functional programming.

In addition, Pygame is a framework that allows you to create fast-paced action games in 2D.

So, now that we know what Python is capable of, it's time we looked at the language itself.

CHAPTER 3

Introducing Python

In this chapter we will introduce the Python language. At this stage we're only interested in understanding the format or syntax of the Python language and its keywords. Python is an interpreted language, meaning that it requires another program called an interpreter to run any code that we write.

The Python interpreter program is called Python and is an executable program. When you run Python from the command line by itself then you will see the following:

```
pi@raspberrypi ~ $ python
Python 2.7.9 (default, Jan 13 2013, 11:20:46)
[GCC 4.9.2] on linux2
Type "help", "copyright", "credits" or "license" for more info
>>>
```

This is the Python interpreter and will run each command block as you type it in.

The Terminal Window

For our first few Python experiments we will use the Terminal window in Raspbian. To open a terminal window, click the icon on the top left of the screen that looks a bit like >_. This will open a window with some text that looks like this:

```
pi@raspberrypi:~ $
```

© Sloan Kelly 2019
S. Kelly, *Python, PyGame, and Raspberry Pi Game Development*,
https://doi.org/10.1007/978-1-4842-4533-0_3

This is a very friendly prompt because the computer is telling some important information. It shows that you are logged in as (pi@raspberrypi) and where you are in the directory structure. In this case it's ~ which is shorthand for your home directory.

To the right of that text is the cursor. This is where the text that you type will appear.

Running the Python Interpreter

To start the Python interpreter, type the following in the terminal window:

```
$ python
```

A command block in Python is a list of commands at least one line long. Let's try one now:

```
print 'Hello, world!'
```

This will instruct Python to display the phrase 'Hello, world!' onscreen. Notice that Python doesn't display the quotation marks:

```
Hello, world!
```

This is because 'Hello, world!' is a string literal. A string is any phrase containing alphanumeric or symbol characters that is enclosed between 'and' or "and". You can't mix and match the quotes. Being able to use both becomes quite handy at times.

Let's try this:

```
print "It's going to rain on Saturday."
```

With double quotes used to mark where our string literal starts and ends, we can use the single quote as an apostrophe:

```
It's going to rain on Saturday.
```

If we used single quotes, we would have had to add a special escape character to the line:

```
print 'It\'s going to rain on Saturday.'
```

We'll get to escape characters later, but that's a little messy for just wanting to put an apostrophe in a sentence!

Let's break down the print statement that we've just used. print is a keyword used by Python to output information to the screen. The second part, the string literal, is a parameter of the print command. Parameters are also called arguments.

Python Is Interpreted

Every line of Python is interpreted. This means that the computer takes each line of code that you type and converts it one at a time to code that the computer can understand. The other type of language is compiled. When a language requires compilation to translate your source code into a language the computer can understand, that processing is done by another program called a compiler. This is a separate program that you run after you have written all your code.

Because the Python language is interpreted, you only need one program to run it: Python. When we are in the interactive Python shell, anything we type is immediately interpreted by the program and the result displayed onscreen, if there is a result.

Python As a Calculator

Say we want to add two numbers together, for argument's sake, 2 and 2. Type the following into the Python interpreter and press return:

```
2+2
```

What you will see onscreen is what you were (hopefully) expecting to see:

```
4
```

We will see later that all the arithmetic operations (add, subtract, multiply, and divide) are available as well as others that you might not have seen before. They'll be introduced as you go through the text.

Examples:

```
5 * 4
10 / 2
7 + 2
9 - 4
```

What about something more complex like

```
2 + 2 * 6
```

What did you expect to see? 24? Why is it 14? That's because arithmetic operators work on an order of precedence, or put another way, some operators are more important than other operators. The operators '*' for multiplication and '/' for divide are more important than + and – used for addition and subtraction respectively.

If you want to ensure the order of operation, you can use parenthesis marks '(' and ')' like so:

```
(2 + 2) * 6
```

Which will now give 24 because the addition of 2 and 2 will be performed first, then its product will be multiplied by 6. Watch your brackets! Ensure that they match up. If you don't you'll get a continuation marker '...') as shown in the following:

```
>>> (2 + 2 * 6
...
```

Let's say you want to calculate the area of a floor (width × length) in meters and convert that value to square feet. Assume that the room is 2 meters by 4 meters. You could use something like

```
(2 * 4) * (3.28 * 3.28)
```

This is because there are 3.28 feet in a meter; to get a square meter in feet, we multiply the 3.28 feet by itself which gives us 10.7584. Multiplying that by 2 * 4 gives us

```
86.0672
```

Or approximately 86 square feet.

We'll go into this next bit in depth later, but for now we should take a moment to discuss what has been typed so far.

The numeric values that you have entered are called constants. They can never change. 1 will always be 1 and 24.234 will always be 24.234. We can store constants in memory for safekeeping and refer to them later on in our program. These slots in the computer's memory are called variables. They are called this because the value that we store can vary over the course of the program. Let's say we wanted to store the 10.76 constant. We have to assign it a name. This action is called variable assignment and looks like this:

```
squareFeet = 10.76
```

You can read that as 'assign the value 10.76 to squareFeet' or 'give squareFeet the value 10.76,' or (as I like to call it) 'squareFeet equals 10.76.' That's more of a "say what you see mentality" though!

Any time we want to use this variable, we use it in much the same way as we'd use a constant. To calculate the area of that 2 × 4 meter room

```
(2 * 4) * squareFeet
```

Python is cAsE sEnsItIve! Note that the name of the variable is 'squareFeet' and not 'squarefeet' or 'Squarefeet.'

Keywords

Python has a very small number of built-in keywords, 31 in total. From these though we can make any program you want to make from a simple bat and ball game to a spreadsheet application, if you fancy making one of them. Python's keywords are the following:

- and
- as
- assert
- break
- class
- continue
- def
- del
- elif
- else
- except
- exec
- finally
- for
- from
- global
- if
- import
- in

- is

- lambda

- not

- or

- pass

- print

- raise

- return

- try

- while

- with

- yield

These are the building blocks of the language, the Lego bricks if you like. From all of these words you can create anything from simple calculations to games to application software. Sometimes, most of the really hard work is done for you and is supplied as a Python module. This is a library of commands, routines, and objects that are packaged together to provide a common functionality. PyGame is an example of a collection of modules. Each module in PyGame makes it easier for you the programmer to make a game by providing you with prewritten code to draw images on the screen, get input from the player, or play background music.

Printing

We've seen how to display simple results on the screen, but you can get much fancier with how those messages are formatted (how they look). For example, you can use escape sequences to add white space characters like tabs and returns to the text using the print command. For example:

```
print("these\nare\non\nseparate\nlines")
print("tab over\tto here")
```

The backslash character "\" is used to generate an 'escape' code for the next character. Escape characters or control sequences date back to the teletype days and are used to control the output to the device we're printing to: in this case the screen.

There are various control sequences and these are listed in Table 3-1 with their descriptions.

Table 3-1. *Control Sequences*

Escape Sequence	Description
\\	Outputs a backslash
\'	Outputs a single quote mark (')
\"	Outputs a double quote mark (")
\a	Bell
\b	Performs a backspace
\f	Performs a form feed
\n	Performs a line feed
\N(name)	Character named name in the UNICODE database
\r	Performs a carriage return
\t	Performs a horizontal tab
\uxxxx	Character with 16-bit hex value xxxx
\Uxxxxxxxx	Character with 32-bit hex value xxxxxxxx
\v	Performs a vertical tab
\ooo	Character with the octal value ooo
\xhh	Character with the hex value hh

From these escape characters you can create complex output. This can be used to display tabular information, for example:

```
print("Team\t\tWon\tLost\nLeafs\t\t1\t1\nSabres\t\t0\t2")
```

Will display the following table:

```
Team            Won     Lost
Leafs           1       1
Sabres          0       2
```

Which is pretty, but what if we want to do a better job? Say we wanted to align the numbers to the right instead of to the left? That means moving the numbers to the same column as the last character of "won" and "lost." This is where string formatting comes into play.

String Formatting

String formatting allows you to decide how information will be displayed to the user as text. We've already seen how we can manipulate the visual portion of the text by deciding where the text will be placed; we'll now examine at how the data can look to the user. We don't need to change the data: we're just altering how the user sees the data.

Formatting is achieved by using placeholders in the text for information you want to insert. These are shown in Table 3-2.

Table 3-2. *String Formatting Placeholders*

Placeholder	Description
%s	String
%d	Whole number
%f	Floating point number
%r	Raw value

The raw value isn't particularly helpful for end users of your program, but it can be handy when you are debugging the code trying to find out what went wrong. More of that later in the debugging chapter.

If we want to display three numbers, for example, the x-, y-, and z-coordinates of an object, then we could use something like

```python
print("{%d, %d, %d}" % (1, 2, 3))
```

The '%' inside the string literal denotes that the following item is a placeholder and it is of type 'd' for a whole number. The '%' outside the string literal is used to say 'fill in those placeholders with' and then the last bit in parentheses '(' and ')' is called a tuple. Those are the values that are placed in the string in the order that they appear. The text that appears when you enter that line is

```
{1, 2, 3}
```

Let's try it again, but this time with the player's name, their score, and percentage completed:

```python
print("%s scored %d and completed %f of the quest" % ('Sloan', 15, 55))
```

This will output

```
Sloan scored 15 and completed 55.000000 of the quest
```

You'll notice that the output is a little over the top; the floating point number is showing a lot of zeros. We can minimize this by specifying how many points there should be to the right of the decimal point.

Let's change the line to show only two decimal points:

```python
print("%s scored %d and completed %.2f of the quest" % ('Sloan', 15, 55))
```

Now the output of the statement is

```
Sloan scored 15 and completed 55.00 of the quest
```

We can also use the numbers after the '%' symbol to space out the values. For example:

```
print("%20s%20d" % ('Sloan', 15))
```

This displays the values 'Sloan' and '15' in columns of width 20:

```
Sloan                  15
```

The values are right-aligned to their positions and they both take up 20 columns. What if we wanted to left-align the name of the player though? We would use a negative value:

```
print("%-20s%20d" % ('Sloan', 15))
```

By using the negative value, you are specifying that you want 20 spaces but the text must be aligned to the left:

```
Sloan                              15
```

Going back to our hockey team example, we can now use this information to better place the text and data. Rather than relying on tabs that can vary depending on the size of the text, we can make the table use fixed values like so:

```
print("%s%s%s\n%s%d%d\n%s%d%d" % ('Team', 'Won', 'Lost',
'Leafs',1,1,'Sabres',0,2))
```

This shows how it appears without the values before the placeholder. And now with the column width of each item:

```
print("%-10s%10s%10s\n%-10s%10d%10d\n%-10s%10d%10d" % ('Team',
'Won', 'Lost', 'Leafs',1,1,'Sabres',0,2))
```

That's a lot of '%' symbols, isn't it! This is a rather severe case, and not one that would be particularly common. In fact, you would use something called variable assignment to make this a lot easier to read. We will now look at that in detail now.

Variables

Variables are used to store the data in memory while we are processing it. We access the data using names. Each variable can be assigned a value. This value represents our data that we want processed. Let's say we want to store the player's name so that we could retrieve it later.

This is called variable assignment. When we assign a value to a name, we are saying that that name now contains the assigned value:

```
>>> player = 'Sloan'
>>> print(player)
Sloan
>>>
```

Our variable assignment is

```
player='Sloan'
```

The left-hand side of the equals sign (=) is the name and the right-hand side of the equals sign is the value. The value can be anything from a string literal, a whole or floating point number, to a complex mathematical formula.

Naming Variables

You can call variables whatever you want, but I would suggest that they reflect the data that you are expecting to store in them. There are a couple of caveats to the characters you can use for a name. They can be alphanumeric characters and can contain the underscore character (_), but the name can't start with a number. You should also be wary of starting names with the underscore character because this is sometimes used for internal names used by Python itself, and other special cases that will be discussed later.

These are valid variable names:

```
playerName
player1
numOfLives
_arg1
this_is_a_long_name_hope_its_worth__it__555
```

These are invalid variable names. The reasons given are shown to the right of the '#'. The '#' is used as a comment character in Python. Everything after the '#' is ignored on a line:

```
123Fred # starts with a number
Fr*d # contains an illegal character '*'
player$ # contains an illegal character '$'
the Player # contains a space. Spaces are not allowed
```

Python variable names are case sensitive! Be careful:

```
thisVariable
```

is not the same as

```
Thisvariable
```

You have been warned! Watch your cases!

PYTHON IS CASE SENSITIVE!

Python As a Calculator, Part II

Remember that a computer program takes information from the user, processes it, and gives feedback to the user as output. We are going to turn

Python into a calculator for this section. Say we set the price of a can of soda as 55 cents, let's remember that by putting the value 55 inside a variable:

```
canOfSoda = .55
```

We can recall the price of a can of soda using this variable name. Now, suppose we have been told to buy 12 cans of soda, let's remember that too in another variable:

```
numCans = 12
```

We can now print out the value of 12 cans of soda using a simple formula:

```
canOfSoda * numCans
```

But wait! What is this?! You don't get 6.6, you actually get this:

```
6.600000000000005
```

This seems a little strange, doesn't it? Why should this happen? This is all to do with precision. When computers calculate a fractional number, they have to use binary numbers (base 2, 0, or 1) to calculate those fractions. When translating them back into decimal values, it doesn't quite add up. We can tidy it up ourselves using string formatting:

```
"%2.2f" % (canOfSoda * numCans)
```

That's better! And we can further tidy it up to show the dollar (or local currency symbol) amount:

```
"$%2.2f" % (canOfSoda * numCans)
```

Which will display

```
'$6.60'
```

Notice that our values have '' around them; that's because we're doing raw output to the Python terminal, so anything we type in immediately gets processed and output. If we want to print out the string without the quotes, we need to add the print command:

```python
print("$%2.2f" % (canOfSoda * numCans))
```

Outputs:

```
$6.60
```

Bad news though, the price of a can of soda has now risen to 70 cents. No problem though, because we can just tell Python to remember the new value:

```python
canOfSoda = .7
```

Now when we calculate 12 cans of soda we'll get a new value.

The output from the following session shows the previous value, the assignment, and the new value:

```
>>> canOfSoda
0.55
>>> canOfSoda = .7
>>> canOfSoda
0.7
>>>
```

If we want to see how much a dozen cans cost, we use the same line as before:

```python
print("$%2.2f" % (canOfSoda * numCans))
```

Did you know that you can use the up and down cursor (arrow) keys on your keyboard to move forward and back through the history of the Python statements you typed in the interactive Python program? When you step through your statements, you can use the left and right cursor keys to move along the line and the delete/backspace keys to remove unwanted characters. Could save you some typing time!

Arithmetic Operators

Arithmetic operators are short-form symbols used to perform arithmetic on numbers. You will have used the majority of them at school; Python uses some different symbols compared to the ones used in school (Table 3-3).

Table 3-3. *Python Arithmetic Operators*

Operator	Description	Example
+	Addition; the two values either side of the operator are added together	4 + 5 will give 9
-	Subtraction; the value on the right-hand side of the operator is subtracted from the value on the left-hand side	5 − 4 will give 1
*	Multiplication; the two values on either side of the operator are multiplied together	2 × 3 will give 6
/	Division; divides the value on the left-hand side of the operator with the value on the right-hand side	10 / 5 will give 2
%	Modulus; divides the value on the left-hand side of the operator with the value on the right-hand side to produce the remainder	5 / 2 will give 1
**	Exponent; raises the value on the left-hand side by the power supplied on the right-hand side	2 ** 4 will give 16. This is written in mathematics as 24 or 2 * 2 * 2 * 2
/	Floor division; divides the value on the left-hand side of the operator with the value on the right-hand side to produce the integer lower value	5 / 2 will give 2.0

Data Types

Python uses something called duck typing. Duck typing ensures that as long as a method or functionality exists for a particular named value (a variable), then Python will perform that action upon it. The poet James Whitcomb Riley came up with this phrase to describe inductive reasoning:

If it looks like a duck, swims like a duck, and quacks like a duck, then it probably is a duck.

Python does have specific data types as well, and these are used to describe the contents of a variable. Python has the following built-in data types:

- Numerics

- Sequences

- Mappings

- Files

- Classes

- Instances

- Exceptions

Numeric Types

Numbers in Python can be represented as whole or fractional. Whole numbers are called *integers* and they are numbers without a fractional component like –256, –5, 1, 5, 9, 17, 2048. Fractional numbers have a decimal point and some values after it, for example, 0.5, 0.333, –0.1.

Whole numbers are represented by two data types: 'int' which is short for integer and 'long.' Fractional numbers are represented by 'float.' There is another type of number called 'complex' that we don't really use in games, but Python can handle it.

The numeric data types are described in detail in Table 3-4.

27

Table 3-4. *Numeric Data Types*

Numeric Type	Description
int	Integers are at least 32 bits in size (4 bytes), which means you can store any whole number up to and including 4,294,967,295. However, this is usually a signed value, which means that the range of values actually goes from −2,147,483,648 to +2,147,483,647.
float	A floating point number is a number with a fractional component like 2.4 or 1.49387.
long	Long integers have an unlimited precision and therefore no upper limit on the number of bits that can be used to store them.
complex	Complex numbers have real and imaginary parts. These parts are floating point numbers.

In addition, the operators shown in Table 3-5 might come in handy. These aren't used in normal everyday arithmetic, but you might want to negate a value or convert it from an integer to a floating point or vice versa.

Table 3-5. *Additional Operators*

Operator	Description	Example
−x	Negate the value 'x'	−2 gives −2
+x	Leave the value 'x' unchanged	+2 gives 2
abs(x)	Absolute value of 'x'	abs(−5) gives 5
int(x)	Convert 'x' to an integer	int(5.44) gives 5
long(x)	Convert 'x' to an integer	long(5) gives 5
float(x)	Convert 'x' to an integer	float(5) gives 5.0
complex(real, imaginary)	Creates a complex number with the real part 'real' and the imaginary part 'imaginary'	complex(1,5) gives (1+5j)

For example, to calculate the area of the side of a building that is 5 meters along by 10 meters high:

```
width = 5
height = 10
area = width * height
```

To display the value, type in

```
area
```

This will display the answer to 5 × 10:

```
50
```

String Formatting Again

Let's go back to our hockey score table:

```
print("%-10s%10s%10s\n%-10s%10d%10d\n%-10s%10d%10d" % ('Team',
'Won', 'Lost', 'Leafs',1,1,'Sabres',0,2))
```

We can break this down into smaller, more readable chunks of data. Don't be afraid to do just that; making your program readable is preferable over speed. You should strive to get the code right rather than fast. Optimization can come later.

> *MAKE YOUR CODE READABLE! WHEN YOU RETURN TO IT AT A LATER DATE, YOU WILL STILL BE ABLE TO MAKE SENSE OF IT!*

There is common formatting used throughout the table; each team is allotted ten characters for their name and won and lost numbers. At the end of each is a new line character. We can set a variable up to remember this format:

```
formatter="%-10s%10s%10s\n"
```

Then it's a simple matter of assigning variables that use this format for each header and team:

```
header=formatter % ("Team", "Won", "Lost")
leafs=formatter % ("Leafs", 1, 1)
sabres=formatter % ("Sabres", 0, 2)
```

Now that we have our header and team data stored in variables, we can combine them all in one line to draw our table:

```
print("%s%s%s" % (header, leafs, sabres))
```

If we wanted we could assign this to a variable and print that out later. Our variable assignment would look like this:

```
table = "%s%s%s" % (header, leafs, sabres)
```

If we just type in the table in the Python interpreter program we get this displayed:

```
'Team Won Lost\nLeafs 1 1\nSabres 0 2\n'
```

This is the raw output of the contents of the name table. This shows us what the name table contains, but not how it will be displayed. To display the table correctly

```
print(table)
```

Will display

```
Team            Won     Lost
Leafs            1       1
Sabres           0       2
```

Conclusion

Python can be used interactively through the Python interpreter by typing python in a terminal window. While this is handy for one-off calculations and simple text output, we shall now be delving deeper into the world of Python by creating actual programs using a tool like a text editor.

CHAPTER 4

Breaking Free from the Interpreter

Up until now we have used the interpreter to write our code. As each line is entered, the Python program interprets it and the processed line's output is displayed onscreen. From now on we will use IDLE.

To quit the interpreter, if you haven't already done so, press Ctrl+D or enter quit(). Keep the terminal window open though! We will need that shortly.

What Is IDLE?

Throughout this book we will use the Integrated Development Environment (IDE) that is included with the Raspbian IDLE, which is short for Integrated Development and Learning Environment.

Starting IDLE

To start IDLE, click the Raspberry Pi logo, open the "Programming" entry, and click "Python 3 (IDLE)". The Python shell will open in a new window, as shown in Figure 4-1.

© Sloan Kelly 2019
S. Kelly, *Python, PyGame, and Raspberry Pi Game Development*,
https://doi.org/10.1007/978-1-4842-4533-0_4

Figure 4-1. *Starting the IDLE IDE*

Starting a New File

To start a new file click File ➤ New File or press Ctrl+N on your keyboard (Figure 4-2).

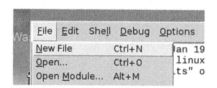

Figure 4-2. *Create a new editor window by choosing New File from the File menu*

This will open a new text editor window that we can enter the code that makes up our program (Figure 4-3).

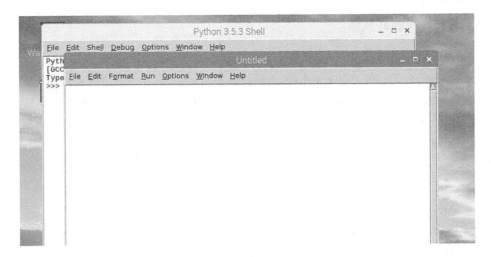

Figure 4 3. *A blank editor window that will be used to write a Python program*

It is a good idea to organize your work and know where to find it easily. Some basic project management will be shown here. We will first create a folder in the current user's home directory (usually /home/pi) and call this new folder "pygamebook" (without the quotes). We will place all the programs we write inside this folder. We may make subfolders for each project, but the "pygamebook" is our main folder.

In the terminal window/command prompt, enter the following commands pressing enter after each line to create the pygamebook folder:

```
$ cd
$ mkdir pygamebook
```

The first line will ensure that the 'pygamebook' folder will be created in your home (~) directory. The second line creates (mkdir is short for 'make directory') a directory called 'pygamebook.' Use this folder to keep all the files that you create from this book together.

Hello, World!

The first computer program most people write is one that displays the message 'Hello, World!' on the screen. This book will be no different! Type in the code below to the blank window, each line is described as we go.

The first line of any Python script file is the location of the Python interpreter. This is called a hash-bang and looks like this:

```
#!/usr/bin/python
```

All programs are run by the shell. This is a part of the computer's operating system that controls program's access to resources like memory, disk drives, etc.

Because source files are just text files, this hash-bang lets the shell know that it is a script that should be run by the Python interpreter located at /usr/bin/python.

Now that we have that in place, we can start our program. In this instance, it's super simple; our standard "Hello World!" program:

```
print("Hello, World!")
```

You should now have the following lines in the editor window:

```
#!/usr/bin/python
print("Hello, World!")
```

Save the file by clicking File ➤ Save or by pressing Ctrl+S on your keyboard. When prompted, save the file as "hello.py" (without quotes) to the "pygamebook" folder we created earlier.

Running from the Command Line

If you want to run your program from the command prompt, you will have to perform one more step. By default, Raspbian does not make files executable; we have to do that. In a terminal window, move to the 'pygamebook' folder and make the program executable by using the chmod command. The following sequence of command will do this:

```
$ cd
$ cd pygamebook
$ chmod +x hello.py
```

This adds the executable flag to the file's attributes. Without this attribute, the operating system will not be able to run our program. To run the program in a terminal window, type

```
$ ./hello.py
```

You will only have to add the executable flag attribute ONCE per script!

Why do we add the './'? It is because in Raspbian executable files are searched through a series of paths. Our new folder isn't part of the system path, so we must tell it where it is. Luckily there's a shortcut for this; the current directory is called '.'

You can omit this step if you want; in fact the hash-bang line is only required if you are running the program on its own as shown previously. If you omit the line, the Raspbian shell doesn't know what program to use to run the script. In this case, you can use

```
$ python hello.py
```

This will launch python and run the 'hello.py' script (Figure 4-4).

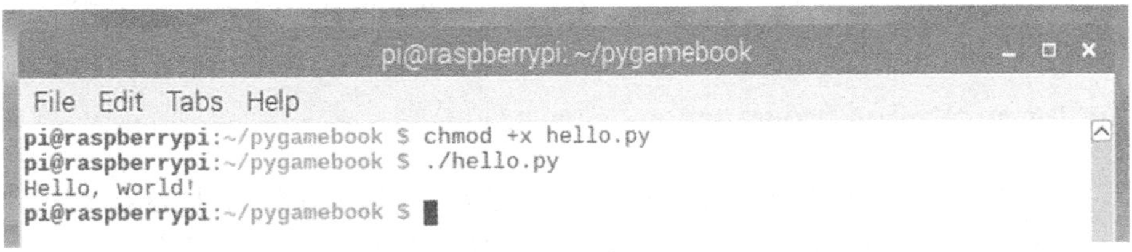

Figure 4-4. *Adding the executable attribute and running hello.py from the command line*

Running from Inside IDLE

To run the program from within IDLE, press F5 on the keyboard or click Run ➤ Run Module from the menu (Figure 4-5).

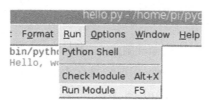

Figure 4-5. *Run the program by selecting Run Module from the Run menu or pressing F5 on the keyboard*

When the program runs you should see "Hello, World!" displayed in the window (Figure 4-6).

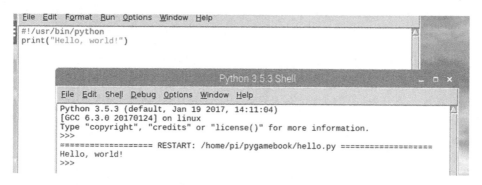

Figure 4-6. *Running hello.py inside the IDLE*

From now on in this text, instead of using the Python interpreter like we did in the first few chapters, this book will concentrate on writing script files for our Python programs.

> *WHEN CREATING A PYTHON SCRIPT FILE THAT WILL BE RUN FROM THE COMMAND LINE ALWAYS PLACE THE PATH TO THE INTERPRETER AS THE FIRST LINE IN A HASH-BANG: #!/usr/bin/python*

For the most part I will omit this line from the example programs and assume that we will be running from within IDLE or launching our programs with python.

Conclusion

Raspbian includes a Python IDE called IDLE that can be used to edit and run Python programs without resorting to using the terminal window. You can still run Python scripts that you create using IDLE in a terminal window, just make sure that you add the hash-bang line to show what Python interpreter program should be run when executing that script.

Throughout the text I will use script and program interchangeably. A script is a text file that is interpreted by a program to execute the instructions within it. A program is similar, but it is usually (but not always) compiled to machine code. Because of those similarities I'm not going to quibble about whether a Python source file is called a program or a script in this text.

CHAPTER 5

Making Decisions

Up until now we have seen very linear programs. These programs follow from one statement to the next, never deviating. They're just a linear shopping list; you get the vegetables first, then bread, then canned vegetables, and finally cat food. Why? Because that's the order that those items typically appear in a supermarket.

But what if you wanted to make simple changes? What if your program could decide what to do, based upon the input it was given?

In computer science this is called branching. Essentially, a decision is made based upon the given data, and one block of code is executed over another block of code. Let's look at a diagram in Figure 5-1.

© Sloan Kelly 2019

S. Kelly, *Python, PyGame, and Raspberry Pi Game Development*,
https://doi.org/10.1007/978-1-4842-4533-0_5

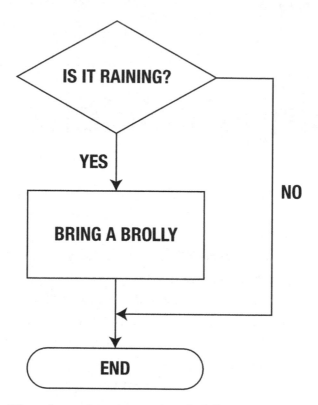

Figure 5-1. *Flowchart showing a simple 'if' statement*

This is called a flowchart and shows the route taken (process) through a series of decisions based on our input that we use to generate our output. In the diagram, we're asking a question: "Is it raining?" Our data is either a "YES" or a "NO." If the answer to the question is "YES" then we bring a brolly (umbrella). Otherwise? We do nothing.

Computers are excellent at these types of decisions; it's either YES or NO; on or off; true or false.

In fact, computers only really understand these binary decisions.

BINARY MEANS THAT SOMETHING IS EITHER OFF OR ON, TRUE OR FALSE.

In Python, we don't have "YES" or "NO" values, but we do have similar values; 'True' and 'False.' That's the 'On' and 'Off' values respectively.

So how do we write this in Python? We use the 'if' keyword. In English, we'd say, "If it's raining, I'll bring my brolly"; in Python that's written as

```
isRaining = True
if isRaining:
    print("I will take my umbrella to work today")
```

The first line assigns the 'True' constant to 'isRaining.' True is a special keyword (along with False) that is used in Python to denote the result of a Boolean test.

The second line checks the value contained within 'isRaining' and if it is set to True (which it is), it will print out the string of text. Notice that you will have to press the tab key at the start of the print statement. This is because it forms the list of statements that will execute if 'isRaining' is true. In this case, we have one statement, but if we had more statements to execute if 'isRaining' was true they would all be indented using the tab key.

   IF conditions always equate to one of two values: True or False.

We could also have written that 'if' statement as

```
if isRaining == True:
```

This is much more explicit but is not the preferred use. When you have a variable that begins with 'is' or 'has,' the assumption is that it contains a Boolean value. ALWAYS! ALWAYS! – check that this is the case before you use the variable.

The format of the 'if' statement is

```
if condition: {statement}
```

or

```
if condition:
    {block}
```

The second method is preferred because you may want to go back and add more lines to the code that is to execute inside the 'if' block. Not that for each line in the block, you will have to indent that line the same amount each time.

A Note About Blocks

A block of code is one or more lines of Python code. When contained within a controlling statement like an 'if,' 'for,' or a 'while,' for example, the statements that make up the block MUST be shifted one tab across. This is because Python does not use syntactic sugar or extra characters to denote the start and end of a block. Languages based upon the C language use '{' and '}' to indicate blocks. Python does not. For example, see Figure 5-2; this is the C language-style equivalent beside the Python version.

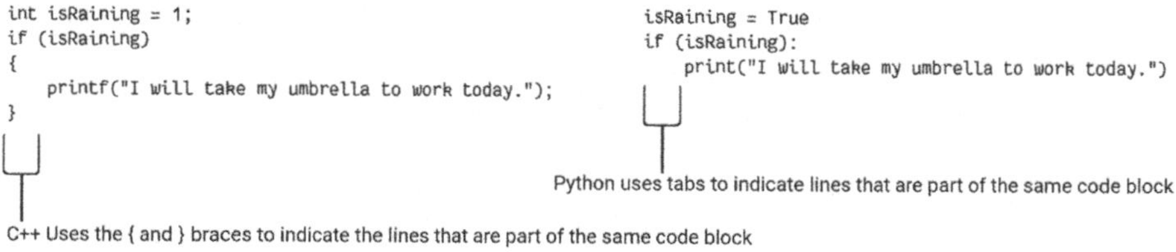

```
int isRaining = 1;
if (isRaining)
{
    printf("I will take my umbrella to work today.");
}
```

```
isRaining = True
if (isRaining):
    print("I will take my umbrella to work today.")
```

Python uses tabs to indicate lines that are part of the same code block

C++ Uses the { and } braces to indicate the lines that are part of the same code block

Figure 5-2. *Showing the difference between explicit block characters and Python's implicit indentation method*

We can also place more than one line after the ':' as shown in the following example:

```
isSunny = True
if isSunny:
    print("It is sunny outside")
    print("I won't need my umbrella")
```

Both lines inside the 'if' block are executed only if 'isSunny' is 'True'. What if we wanted to display something if isRaining wasn't true? Could we do this:

```
isRaining = True
if isRaining:
    print("I will take my umbrella to work today")
    print("It is nice and sunny")
```

The program displays the following output when it is run:

```
I will take my umbrella to work today.
It is nice and sunny
```

This is not an ideal situation because we were only looking for one line to be output. The second line is always going to be executed because as we know, programs run blindly step by step through a program until they get to the end and there are no more lines to process. What we need to do is this:

```
isRaining = True
if isRaining:
    print("I will take my umbrella to work today")
else:
    print("It is nice and sunny")
```

Notice the extra keyword 'else'. This allows us to better control what we expect to do if 'isRaining' turns out to be false. You don't have to put in an 'else' for each 'if'. Sometimes there will be no alternatives and you only want to run a particular set of statements for a particular condition.

Testing for Equality

Python allows the programmer to test for equality – we have seen this insofar as we were testing that a particular variable is equal to true. We know that IF conditions have to equate to one of two values: TRUE or FALSE, so how can we test for (in)equality? We use one of the following range operators:

- Equals (==)

- Less than (<)

- Greater than (>)

- Less than or equal to (<=)

- Greater than or equal to (>=)

- Not equal to (!=)

These are mathematical symbols. For those of you unfamiliar with them, especially the less-than and greater-than symbols, the small pointy end points to the lesser value. You cannot use these operators against variables that contain Boolean True or False; equality operators can only work against numbers or character strings.

The following program prompts the user to enter two string values and then checks which string is greater. We'll cover the finer details in just a second, but the program does have some shortcomings. Can you see what they are?

print "This program will take two strings and decide which one is greater"

```
first = input("First string: ")
second = input("Second string: ")
if first > second:
    tup = (first, second)
else:
    tup = (second, first)
print("%s is greater than %s" % tup)
```

The first line displays a message indicating what the program will do. The next two lines prompt the user to enter two separate string values and place them in 'first' and 'second' variables. The 'if' statement condition is

```
if first > second:
```

This checks to see if the first string is greater than the second. If it is, a tuple called 'tup' is created and first and second are stored. Note the order; first is before second. We'll discuss tuples in length later, but for now let's just say they're a collection of one or more values.

If the second string is greater than the first, then the tup variable is also created, but the order is reversed; 'second' appears before 'first.'

Type in the preceding program and run it. Enter the values in Table 5-1.

Table 5-1. *Values for Two String Program*

Run # of Program	'first'	'second'
1	Lowercase a	Uppercase A
2	Aaa	Zzz
3	9	100

What do you notice about the results? Were you expecting that?

The problem with our little example is that unless 'first' is absolutely greater than 'second,' the 'else' block is executed. We can remedy this by changing the program to

```
print("This program will take two strings and decide which one
is greater")
tup = None
first = input("First string: ")
second = input("Second string: ")
if first > second:
    tup = (first, second)
```

```
elif second > first:
    tup = (second, first)
if tup != None:
    print("%s is greater than %s" % tup)
else:
    print("The strings were equal")
```

The keyword 'None' is used to initially assign a value to 'tup.' None means that a value has not been assigned to the variable. We still want to have a variable called 'tup' and assign it a value later. So in this case we set 'tup' to equal 'None' initially because it might not get set at all in the logic of the program. If we don't set it, then trying to access it will cause a 'not defined' error.

> *If you see a "name 'variable name' not defined" error it usually means you have not assigned it a value before using it OR you have misspelt the variable name!*

Change the preceding program to use an equality sign (==) in the second 'if.' Will you need to change the text of the 'print' statements? If so, what would you change them to?

More common than text equality is numeric equality. Equality tests for numbers are used for collision detection, deciding if a player or enemy is dead, how much fuel is remaining, etc.

Say, for example, we wanted to check and see if the player's character was within a certain boundary on the screen. This involves checking both the x- and y-coordinates of the player. We can combine our conditions in one statement using Boolean logic.

In this example we are testing the player's x- and y-coordinates to determine if they are inside a rectangular area that is 100 units across and 225 units tall and placed at (0, 25) as shown in Figure 5-3:

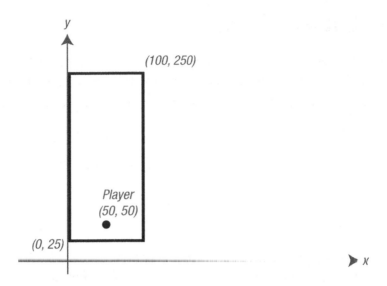

Figure 5-3. *Position of the player within a rectangular area*

From the diagram it is clear to us that the player is inside the rectangle. How can we get the computer to check if the player is inside the rectangle and respond accordingly? This is in 2D space – two dimensions; a horizontal and a vertical component to the player's position, that is, their x- and y-coordinates. The easiest way is to split this into two separate 1D checks and combine the results to both. In English:

If the player's x-coordinate is between 0 and 100 inclusive AND the player's y-coordinate is between 25 and 250 inclusive, they are inside the area.

In code this looks like

```
x = 50
y = 50
if x >= 0 and x <= 100 and y >= 25 and y <= 250:
    print("Player is inside the area. Sound the alarm!")
else:
    print("Player is outside the area. Do nothing")
```

Using Boolean Logic

As we saw in the previous chapter, computers use Boolean logic: any question so long as it results in a TRUE or FALSE answer. The following Boolean keywords can be used to make more complex If conditions:

- And

- Or

- Not

And

And in an 'if' statement will equate to true only if both conditions are true:

```
isRaining = True
isSunny = True
if isRaining and isSunny:
    print("Sun showers")
```

In the context of a game you might have a condition to test that if the player has a key and he or she hits a door, and then opens the door:

```
if playerHasKey and playerHitDoor:
    OpenTheDoor()
    RemoveKeyFromInventory()
```

The two methods OpenTheDoor() and RemoveKeyFromInventory() are programmer made; they're not part of Python. We'll learn about how to make user-defined functions in a later chapter.

In Boolean logic, truth tables are used to show the result of an operation ('and,' 'or,' or 'not'). Typically, this shows the values for two inputs called 'A' and 'B' and a result.

The truth table, shown in Table 5-2, for 'and' is as follows.

Table 5-2. *'and' Truth Table*

A	B	Result
False	False	False
False	True	False
True	False	False
True	True	True

This shows that for 'and,' the combined result of 'A' and 'B' can only be true when both 'A' and 'B' are true.

Or

Or in an 'if' statement will equate to true if either one or the other condition is true:

```
isRaining = True
isSunny = False
if isRaining or isSunny:
    print("Some kind of weather out there")
else:
    print("No weather! How unusual for this time of year")
```

The truth table for 'or' is shown in Table 5-3:

Table 5-3. *'or' Truth Table*

A	B	Result
False	False	False
False	True	True
True	False	True
True	True	True

This shows that 'or' is only false when both 'A' and 'B' are false.

Not

Not is used to negate a condition: turn it from a true to a false and vice versa. This is a unary operator and only works on a single condition:

```
isRaining = True
isSunny = False
if isRaining and not isSunny:
    print("It's raining and not sunny")
else:
    print("Sun showers")
```

The truth table (Table 5-4) for 'not' is different in that it only has one input because it is a unary operator. The truth table therefore only has the 'A' input.

Table 5-4. *'not' Truth Table*

A	Result
False	True
True	False

You can see that whatever the input is, the 'not' keyword negates it.

Nesting Ifs

When we need to make complex decisions based on a number of facts, we can do what is called "nesting." This means placing an 'if' block of code inside another 'if' block of code, for example:

```
isRaining = True
isCloudy = True
if isRaining:
    print("I will take my umbrella to work today")
elif isCloudy:
    print("It looks like it will rain. I'll take my umbrella")
else:
    print("It is sunny. I'll not bother with the brolly")
```

The truth table for this is shown in Table 5-5 to make the preceding example clearer.

Table 5-5. *'if' Block Truth Table*

IsRaining	IsCloudy	Output
True	True	I will take my umbrella to work today
True	False	I will take my umbrella to work today
False	True	It looks like it will rain, I'll take my umbrella in case
False	False	It is sunny. I'll not bother with the brolly

The format of an IF statement is therefore

```
if condition:
    Action(s)
[else:
    Action(s)]
[elif condition:
    Action(s)]
```

A Note on Switch

For users of other languages, you should note that there is no "switch" statement in Python. It was proposed for the language, but ultimately rejected. In an OO (object-oriented) language like Python, "switch" can be replaced by polymorphic (we'll get to this later!) calls. Stack Overflow (a great web site, and one you should bookmark) has a great article on how to get around "switch."

See `http://stackoverflow.com/questions/126409/ways-to-eliminate-switch-in-code` for details. The switch keyword can be easily implemented using ifs like so:

```python
character = input("Enter command (help, list): ")
if character == "help":
    print("The help screen goes here")
elif character == "list":
    print("List the items here")
else:
    print("Invalid command!")
```

Conclusion

Computers are very good at making simple decisions quickly. Using the comparison and range operators, one can determine if two values are equal, or if they are within a range (e.g., between 1 and 10).

These decisions can be combined using Boolean logic operators like And, Or, and Not and the If keyword to make branching code; run some code if true, some other code if false. We'll see in later chapters how these small building blocks can build complex systems.

## CHAPTER 6

Making the Raspberry Pi Repeat Itself

A video game repeats the action until all the players' lives have gone, or the end of the game has been reached. So far, we have only written programs that run through a sequence of commands and then terminate. With the use of certain Python keywords, we can get the computer to repeat a block of code when required, either using conditions or for a set number of times.

The for Loop

The 'for loop' in Python takes a list, and for each item in the list it performs a series of action. These actions are contained within the block of code that appears after the ':' character and are shifted to the right by one tab. The flowchart in Figure 6-1 shows what happens inside a 'for' loop.

© Sloan Kelly 2019
S. Kelly, *Python, PyGame, and Raspberry Pi Game Development*,
https://doi.org/10.1007/978-1-4842-4533-0_6

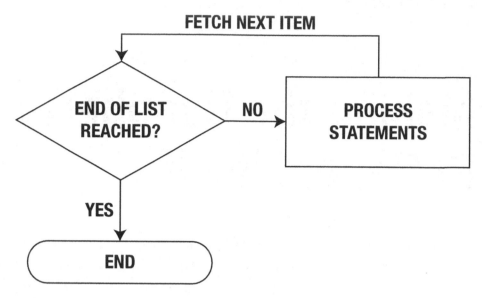

Figure 6-1. *Flowchart diagram showing a for loop*

As an example, the following program will print the numbers 1 through 5 inclusive. We'll talk about some of the quirks of the range() function in a moment.

Don't forget the hash-bang at the top of the script! Remember that you need the hash-bang to run script files from the command prompt. And you'll also need to change the file mode (chmod) and add the executable flag. See Chapter 4 ("Breaking Free from the Interpreter") if you can't quite remember how to do it.

```
for i in range(1, 6):
    print(i)
```

The 'i' variable here has a special meaning. It is acting as a control for the loop. In fact, we give any variable that controls flow the name control variable. Again, this is just a name I've given the variable. I could have called in 'n' or 'j' or 'fred.' Control variables tend to have short names. I chose this one because we're iterating through integers or whole numbers and 'i' seemed appropriate for the task.

The format of a 'for' loop is

```
for condition:
    Action(s)
```

Where 'condition' is any statement that generates a list.

The range() Function

The range() function is provided by Python and as such is referred to as an intrinsic function. It generates a list of numbers from the start value to 1-n where n is the last value in the range. The following examples are taken from statements typed into the Python interpreter:

```
>>> range(1,6)
[1, 2, 3, 4, 5]
>>> range(2,4)
[2, 3]
```

You can also specify a third parameter. This parameter indicates the count that is added to each number after each iteration of the 'for' loop. The default value is 1 (one), which is why you don't need to provide it:

```
>>> range(10, 255, 10)
[10, 20, 30, 40, 50, 60, 70, 80, 90, 100, 110, 120, 130, 140,
150, 160, 170, 180, 190, 200, 210, 220, 230, 240, 250]
>>> range (10, 0, -1)
[10, 9, 8, 7, 6, 5, 4, 3, 2, 1]
```

That's right, you can even use negative values to iterate from a larger number to a smaller number.

We'll talk about lists and dictionaries in the next chapter, but we've already established that the 'for' loop iterates through lists. So, what if we didn't have numbers? What if we had the names of characters from TV:

```
names = ['John', 'Anne', 'Fred', 'Beth']
for name in names:
    print(name)
```

The 'names' variable is assigned the value of a list of people's names. The 'for' loop iterates through each of the names and prints them on the screen. The control variable in this example is 'name.' At each iteration of the loop, the next name from the list will be pulled out and processed.

While Loops

For loops are great for iterating through a fixed list, but what if we don't know how many items we have? For example, reading the contents of a file, or getting data from a web site. This is where the 'while' keyword comes in.

Although the while loop has the same format no matter which one used, there are three types of while loop:

- Counting

- Sentinel

- Conditional

Counting

A counting while loop is pretty much just a substitute for the 'for' keyword. Sure, you can use it for a substitute for the 'for' keyword, but it doesn't look as elegant. For example:

```
#!/usr/bin/python
i = 1
while i < 6:
    print(i)
    i = i + 1
```

In this example I've kept in the hash-bang.

Whereas in the 'for' loop the control variable is contained within the 'for' statement, a 'while' loop has the control variable defined out-with the loop. The programmer also must manually update the control variable the required step each time.

> *Don't forget to update the control variable! If you don't, you'll end up in an infinite loop and will have to break out of your program using Ctrl + C!*

Notice that the format of a 'while' statement is

```
while condition:
    Action(s)
```

The 'where condition' is a statement that equates to 'True' or 'False': a Boolean. This is similar then to the 'if' keyword in that it too takes a Boolean condition as its argument. The flowchart for this 'while' loop is shown in Figure 6-2.

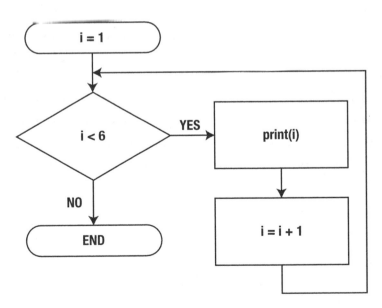

Figure 6-2. *The example 'while' loop's flowchart*

From the flowchart we can see that the statements in the 'while' block are only executed while the Boolean condition is 'True.'

This means that the 'while' loop's condition acts as a gatekeeper to the lines inside the block. If that condition is not true, don't execute the lines within. Change the initialization of 'i' to 6:

```python
#!/usr/bin/python
i = 6
while i < 6:
    print(i)
    i = i + 1
```

Run the script. What happens? Nothing. No output at all. This is because i< 6, when i = 6 returns 'False.'

Sentinel

A sentinel while loop is one that keeps looping around until a certain value is reached.

Let's return to our menu example from the previous chapter. We have three commands: list, help, and quit. When the user selects quit, the program ends.

We have no idea how many commands the user will use throughout their session with the program, and we have no idea how many times they will use the same command. This is an ideal use case for the 'while' loop because it can be used to keep a program running while a condition has not been met:

```python
cmd = input("Command: ")
while cmd != 'quit':
    if cmd == 'help':
        print("Put help here")
    elif cmd == 'list':
```

```
        print("Put list here")
    else:
        print("Invalid command!")
cmd = input("Command: ")
```

When we start getting into multiple tabs, you really have to keep the correct spacing. In your editor you should see a program like the one shown in Figure 6-3.

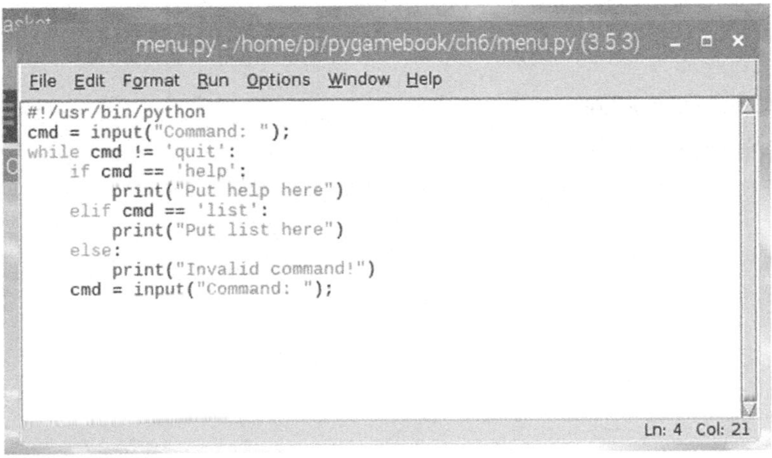

```
#!/usr/bin/python
cmd = input("Command: ");
while cmd != 'quit':
    if cmd == 'help':
        print("Put help here")
    elif cmd == 'list':
        print("Put list here")
    else:
        print("Invalid command!")
    cmd = input("Command: ");
```

Figure 6-3. *The menu program showing the indented lines of code*

If the input() function does not work for you, try raw_input() because you may be running Python 2.7

Here is a typical output from running the program:

```
Command: help
Put help here
Command: list
Put list here
Command: badcommand
Invalid command!
Command: quit
```

Conditional

These are a combination of the previous two: counting and sentinel. This is when you want to count a sequence but you don't know what sequence you are counting. Let's say you want to write a program to sum all the numbers up to a certain value. You might write something like this:

```python
#!/usr/bin/python
topNum = int(input("Sum of numbers to? "))
count = 0
while topNum > 0:
    count += topNum
    topNum = topNum - 1
print("Sum of all numbers is %d" % count)
```

To get the input as a number we have to convert to an integer (whole number) using the int() function.

The input() function always returns a string!

Conclusion

Looping is used a lot in computer programs. Based on the circumstances you will have to make a choice as to which loop to use: the for loop or the while.

If the range is known or you want to loop through a list of values (like the names example in this chapter) then the for loop is perfect for you.

There are three types of while loop: counting, sentinel, and conditional. The counting version is very rarely used and most people prefer the 'for' loop. However, sentinel and conditional are widely used to keep looping until a certain – usually at the time of writing – unknown condition is met.

CHAPTER 7

Containers

Up until now, we've mostly stored a single value in a variable like this:

```
playerName = 'Sloan'
```

Python allows you to store multiple values in the same variable. In this, you are assigning a container object a name. There are three different types of containers:

- Tuple
- List
- Dictionary

There are cases when you will use one over the other, and we'll discuss the pros and cons of each use.

Container Nomenclature

Container subparts are called elements. Each element can be indexed using the '[' and ']' characters and specifying a number between 0 and n-1 where 'n' is the number of items in the container between them. We'll see how this works in the Tuples part.

© Sloan Kelly 2019
S. Kelly, *Python, PyGame, and Raspberry Pi Game Development*,
https://doi.org/10.1007/978-1-4842-4533-0_7

Tuples

Tuples are immutable collections of objects. Neither the elements in the collection nor the container itself can be modified. This means that you can't add and remove elements from a tuple.

For video games you might want to store the position of a player – their x- and y-coordinates – in a tuple.

A tuple is a list of objects, either literals or variable names, separated by a comma and enclosed in parentheses characters '(' and ')'. For example:

```
('sloan', 'robert')
```

To access an element in the tuple, use the '[' and ']' characters and place the index value between them. Say you want the first element in the array, then you would specify '0' like so:

```
('sloan', 'robert')[0]
```

This will display

```
'sloan'
```

Removing Elements from a Tuple

If you want to remove items from a tuple (you can't) but there is a way around it. Create a new tuple! Let's say you have a tuple that contains five elements but you don't want the third element:

```
numbers = (1, 2, 3, 4, 5)
tuple(x for x in numbers if x != 3)
```

Woah! That looks needlessly complex! That's because tuples are immutable and that means they can't change. Let's break down the complexity a little. The tuple() function returns a tuple from whatever sequence it is given. For example:

```
>>> tuple('abcdef')
('a', 'b', 'c', 'd', 'e', 'f')
>>> tuple(['sloan', 'robert'])
('sloan', 'robert')
```

In the former example, the character string is split into separate characters. The latter contains a list of names and a tuple is created from that list.

The part that does all the magic is called *list comprehension*. It is used to create a list based upon existing lists.

```
x for x in range(0, 5) if x != 3
```

List comprehension takes in a list, processes each element in the list, and produces another list. As we've seen, the tuple() keyword makes a tuple out of any sequence. A string is a sequence of characters, a tuple is a (immutable) sequence of objects, and lists are also a sequence of objects.

Don't get too bogged down in the format of that statement; it is merely an example of how one would go about removing an item from a tuple.

Changing Element Values

Another 'can't do' for tuples. However, there is also a way around that. Tuples are immutable which means they cannot be changed, and so are their elements. The only alternative is to create another tuple.

In this example we have a tuple that represents the x- and y-coordinates of the player ('playPos') and another tuple that represents the speed ('speed') of the player. To get the next position of the player, we add the speed to the current position. Remember, we can't change the tuple or its elements. We must create a new tuple and assign that value to 'playPos':

```
playPos = (5, 4)
print("playPos = %d, %d" % playPos)
speed = (2, 1)
playPos = (playPos[0] + speed[0], playPos[1] + speed[1])
print("playPos = %d, %d" % playPos)
```

The line:

```
playPos = (playPos[0] + speed[0], playPos[1] + speed[1])
```

On the right-hand side of the equals sign, the new tuple is created. This is then assigned to the name 'playPos.' The tuple that 'playPos' was assigned is overwritten by this new value. This is the equivalent of the following simple assignments:

```
>>> num = 5
>>> print(num)
5
>>> num = 10
>>> print(num)
10
```

In this example, the value 'num' is initially assigned the value 5. It is then assigned the value 10. This overwrites the value initially stored in 'num.'

Tuples in Printing

We have used tuples before with respect to displaying formatted strings. For example:

```
>>> numbers = (1, 2, 3, 4, 5)
>>> print("%d %d %d %d %d" % numbers)
1 2 3 4 5
```

Deconstructing Tuples

Another common action is to deconstruct the tuple into its component parts and assign them to separate variables. This is achieved by placing the variables that are to be assigned values on the left-hand side of the equals sign and the tuple on the other. In the following example we have a vector 'vec' that contains two elements: one for the x- and another for the y-coordinate:

```
>>> vec = (2, 3)
>>> x, y = vec
>>> x
2
>>> y
3
>>>
```

Similarly, you can construct a tuple by specifying comma-separated values too. I don't recommend this; I prefer to use the explicit parenthesized syntax, but this works just as well:

```
>>> vec2 = x, y
>>> vec2
(2, 3)
>>>
```

Lists

Lists are mutable containers. This means that both the elements and the list itself can be altered. In the case of the list, this means that we can add and remove elements to the list after we create it. Items are added to the list using the append() method, and removal is through the remove() method. A method is an action that an object can perform. We will see more of methods in the object-oriented section of this text.

Lists are used a lot in video games. Your inventory is a list of items, the sprites (images) onscreen are stored as a list, and the collection of levels that make up your game could be stored in a list.

List Creation

You can create a blank list or one that is initially populated with values:

```
blankList = []
populatedList = [1, 2, 3, 4, 5]
```

The output of which, if we were to run these commands in the Python interpreter, would be

```
>>> blankList = []
>>> populatedList = [1, 2, 3, 4, 5]
>>> blankList
[]
>>> populatedList
[1, 2, 3, 4, 5]
>>>
```

Adding Values to the List

If we want to add values to the 'blankList' we simply use the append() method and place whatever we want to add within the parentheses:

```
>>> blankList.append("Python")
>>> blankList
['Python']
>>>
```

Adding another computer language name (Lua this time) would mean that our blankList would contain

```
>>> blankList.append("Lua")
>>> blankList
['Python', 'Lua']
>>>
```

Removing Values from a List

To remove an item from the list, the remove() method is used like so:

```
>>> populatedList = [1, 2, 3, 4, 5]
>>> populatedList.remove(3)
>>> populatedList
[1, 2, 4, 5]
>>>
```

You can also remove items from the list by their index value. There is no built-in method to do this in a list; instead we use the 'del' keyword. For example, to remove the first element, or index 0 (zero), we would use

```
>>> populatedList = [1, 2, 4, 5]
>>> del populatedList[0]
>>> populatedList
[2, 4, 5]
>>>
```

This means that we can remove more than one item as well; say we want to remove all the items from the list. We would do this:

```
>>> populatedList = [2, 4, 5]
>>> del populatedList[:]
>>> populatedList
[]
>>>
```

ahead and populate the list again:

```
populatedList = [1, 2, 3, 4, 5]
```

Let's say we want to delete 2 and 3 from the list. We could issue this line twice:

```
del populatedList[1]
```

Why twice? Well, index 1 of the list is the '2' element. When we delete something in a list, everything after that moves up one slot. So, the array now contains

```
[1, 3, 4, 5]
```

Which means that index 1 now contains '3.'

Typing the same command twice is a little wasteful when we can do it all at once. We can use the colon (':') to specify a range of values to remove. So now, to delete 2 and 3 at the same time we would use

```
del populatedList[1:3]
```

The number before the colon is the starting index for the deletion. The number after the column is one plus the number of elements you want to remove. If you wanted to remove everything from the first element onward, you could use

```
del populatedList[1:]
```

Doctor's Waiting Room Program

I've created a simple program to demonstrate lists using the example of a doctor's waiting room. The user has the ability to add patients, remove them from the list as they are called, and quit the program. All actions are done through a menu.

```
#!/usr/bin/python3
names = [] # an empty list of names
```

We start off with a blank list each morning.

```
cmd = ""
while cmd != '4':
```

There are four commands: 1 – list names, 2 – add name, 3 – call next patient, and 4 – quit. The user's commands will be stored in the 'cmd' variable. Note that we have a 'while' loop to keep the user inside the program until they choose to quit.

```
print("1. List names")
print("2. Add name")
print("3. Call next patient")
print("\n4. Quit")
```

The menu is displayed to let the user know the options that they can choose.

```
cmd = input("\rCommand : ")
```

The user is now prompted for a command. We'll now use a series of nested-ifs to perform the command chosen by the user.

```
if cmd == '1':
    for name in names:
        print (name)
    print ("\n")
```

If the user enters '1' then we use a 'for' loop to go through all the names in the 'names' list. In each iteration, we print the patient's name. Finally we end it with a newline character ('\n') to give us some white space onscreen.

```
elif cmd == '2':
    newName = input("Name : ")
    names.append(newName)
```

If the user enters '2' then we prompt them for the newly arrived patient's name. We then add that new name to the list of names using the append() method.

```
elif cmd == '3':
    if len(names) == 0:
        print ("There are no more patients!")
    else:
        nextPatient = names[0]
        names.remove(nextPatient)
        print ("Calling %s" % nextPatient)
```

For the third and final command, but not quite the end of our program, the user has opted to call the next patient to be seen. The practice offers a strict first-come-first-served policy. This means that the first item in the list is removed. However, if we have no items in the list, then a warning message is displayed. You can determine the length of a list of items using the 'len' keyword.

```
elif cmd != '4':
    print ("Invalid command!")
```

The final lines in the program are used to let the user know that they have typed in an invalid command: something other than 1, 2, 3, or 4.

Save the program as 'patients.py' (without the quotes) and don't forget to change the program's attributes to allow it to be executed. Remember! You only have to change this once:

```
$ chmod +x patients.py
```

To run the program:

```
$ ./patients.py
```

When you are in the same directory as the program.

Dictionaries

Dictionaries are a set of key/value pairs. This means that instead of an indexing number, you can use a user-defined key to access the information.

Dictionaries can be used in video games to look up related data. For example, if you want to look up what damage a particular sword does you could use a dictionary to store the data for each weapon in the game. You could do the same with a list, but it would take time to go through the list, one element at a time to find the data. When you want to find something quickly, use a dictionary.

As an example, we'll define a dictionary that contains telephone numbers for various people. A person's telephone number can be obtained by using their name:

```
>>> numbers = {'Sloan':'416-555-1234', 'Kevin':'212-555-4321'}
>>> numbers['Sloan']
'416-555-1234'
>>>
```

The first line defines the dictionary 'numbers' containing two entries. Each entry is a separate key/value pair. Each key/value is separated using a colon ':' and each pair is separated using a comma ','.

Iterating Through Dictionaries

We can iterate through each item using the iteritems() method for the dictionary:

```
>>> for k,v in numbers.iteritems():
...  print ("%s = %s" % (k ,v ))
...
Sloan = 416-555-1234
Kevin = 212-555-4321
>>>
```

Adding New Items to Dictionaries

Dictionaries have a simpler way of adding new items: if a key doesn't exist, that value is added to the dictionary. If a key already exists then the new value is assigned to that key.

```
>>> numbers['Frank'] = '216-555-1234'
>>> numbers
{'Sloan': '416-555-1234', 'Frank': '216-555-1234', 'Kevin': '2
>>>
```

Removing Entries from a Dictionary

To remove an entry from a dictionary, we use our old friend 'del.' To remove 'Sloan' from the dictionary 'numbers'

```
>>> del numbers['Sloan']
>>> numbers
{'Frank': '216-555-1234', 'Kevin': '212-555-4321'}
>>>
```

Conclusion

We've seen that Python offers us three different types of containers that provide options for our programs. The tuple can be used to group together like items that are immutable (cannot be changed). Use a tuple to define a structure line a point in space. The properties of a point in space are its x- and y-coordinates. These two elements don't change, and you very rarely iterate (loop) through them. The list container can be used to store a collection of items that can be added and removed. Finally, the dictionary allows items to be added and removed as well as altered.

We're going to take a break from the Python language just now to look at how to go about designing a game and taking the leap to the windowed system called LXDE that the Raspberry Pi uses. This is because we're going to start looking at PyGame in the next few chapters.

## CHAPTER 8

Putting It Together: Tic-Tac-Toe

Before we start looking at PyGame and how to create arcade-style games we should take a step back and put what we've covered in the first few chapters into a simple ASCII console game of Tic-Tac-Toe – a game for two players.

The Rules

For those of you who haven't played Tic-Tac-Toe before, here are the rules:

Draw a board on a piece of paper with nine squares, people usually do this by drawing two horizontal lines parallel to each other followed by two vertical lines parallel to each other but perpendicular to the horizontal lines like a hash symbol: # (Figure 8-1).

© Sloan Kelly 2019
S. Kelly, *Python, PyGame, and Raspberry Pi Game Development*,
https://doi.org/10.1007/978-1-4842-4533-0_8

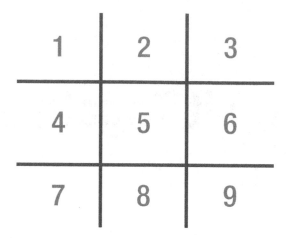

Figure 8-1. *The layout of a tic-tac-toe board*

The first player uses the token X and the second player uses the token O. Each player, starting with X, places their token on a box on the board. A slot can only take one token! The game ends when a player places a token that creates a horizontal, vertical, or diagonal three-in-a-row of their token like the examples shown in Figure 8-2.

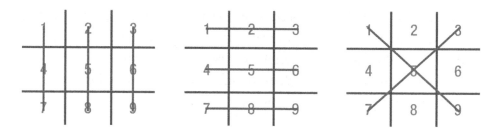

Figure 8-2. *The winning lines in a tic-tac-toe board*

Program Layout

The program will be laid out in the following general sections:

- Variable declaration and initialization – Create the variables and give them initial values

- Display a welcome message – Simple text indicating what the program does and how to play the game

- Display the board

- Get the player's input – Where do they want to position their piece on the board

- Test the validity of the input – Keep asking the player if the input is invalid

- Place the piece on the board

- Check if the player has won – If they have won, display a congratulatory message and end the game

- Jump back up to 'Display the board' if there is still a slot available to place a token

We will make use of while loop and if statements in this program. The while loops will keep the game being played while there are still slots open or no one has won. The if statements will be used to determine if we have a winner or if the player's input is valid.

Variables

We need a place to store data while the program is running and need to decide what variables we will be using. Table 8-1 shows what variables will be declared and how they will be used.

Table 8-1. *Declared Variables*

Variable	Use
board	Initially containing the characters 1 through 9, this will contain the positions of the X and O tokens on the board and will be used to draw the board onscreen
currentToken	The current token, that is, the current player and will contain either an X or an O
winningToken	One of the control variables that will be used to keep the game playing through all the player turns. When set to either X or O, the program will exit
slotsFilled	It is possible that no one will win the game – this is sometimes called a Cat's Game. In this case we need a way to exit the while loop if no other moves can be made. This second control variable will increment each time a player makes a move

The Game

Create a new folder called 'ch8' inside the 'pygamebook' folder. Create a new file called 'tictactoe.py' inside 'ch8'. Open the file in the Python IDLE and enter the following text. I will add comments as I go along to help illustrate what the code is doing.

```
#!/usr/bin/python
#
# Program:    Tic-Tac-Toe Example
# Author:     Sloan Kelly
```

The header information is useful because it can quickly identify what the purpose of this program or script is for, and who wrote it.

```
board = ['1', '2', '3', '4', '5', '6', '7', '8', '9']
```

```
currentToken = 'X'
winningToken = "
slotsFilled = 0
```

The variables used by the program are declared and initialized. The 'board' variable contains an array of strings that contain the symbols 1 – 9 inclusive. These will be used for two reasons: to show the player what number they can enter and secondly to allow the program to determine if a slot has been taken up by a token.

The 'currentToken' is set to the first player's token and the 'winningToken' and 'slotsFilled' are set to default values of an empty string ('') and 0 respectively. The latter two variables are used to control the game and ensure it keeps playing while there is no winner and there are slots to fill on the board.

```
print ("Tic-Tac-Toe by Sloan Kelly")
print ("Match three lines vertically, horizontally or
diagonally")
print ("X goes first, then O")
```

Some basic information about the program will be displayed to the player. It let's them know the name of the program, who authored it, and some basic rules of play.

```
while winningToken == " and slotsFilled < 9:
```

An example of a sentinel while loop, keeping the game running while no one has won and there are slots to be filled.

```
    print("\n")
    print("%s|%s|%s" % (board[0], board[1], board[2]))
    print("-+-+-")
    print("%s|%s|%s" % (board[3], board[4], board[5]))
    print("-+-+-")
    print("%s|%s|%s" % (board[6], board[7], board[8]))
```

Display the board to the player. Over time, the entries in the board will fill with X's and O's, but on the first turn, the board contains the symbols 1 through 9. The player will then input that number and we will have to translate it down one because in Python array indexes start at 0, not at 1.

Also – don't forget your indentations!

```python
pos = -1
while (pos == -1):
```

This while loop will keep the player inside it while they have chosen an invalid value for the slot.

```python
pos = int(input("\n%s's turn. Where to? : " %
currentToken))
if pos < 1 or pos > 9:
    pos = -1
    print ("Invalid choice! 1-9 only.")
```

Prompt the player for input and then validate it by ensuring the input is between 1 and 9 inclusive. If not, display an error message and set the 'pos' variable back to –1 (invalid entry) which keeps the player inside the while loop until they enter a correct value.

```python
pos = pos - 1
```

Move 'pos' so that it is in the 0–8 range for the 'board' array.

```python
if board[pos] == 'X' or board[pos] == 'O':
    pos = -1
    print("That spot has already been taken by %s! Try
    again" % board[pos])
```

Check to see if the value at position 'pos' on the board has been taken by a player, if so display a warning.

```python
board[pos] = currentToken
slotsFilled = slotsFilled + 1
```

Otherwise, set the board at index 'pos' to the current token and increment the 'slotsFilled' variable. Notice that these two lines are outside the while loop because the 'pos' variable has been validated at this point.

```
row1 = board[0] == currentToken and board[1] ==
currentToken and board[2] == currentToken
row2 = board[3] == currentToken and board[4] ==
currentToken and board[5] == currentToken
row3 = board[6] == currentToken and board[7] ==
currentToken and board[8] == currentToken
```

To make this program neater, I split the board, column, and diagonal checks over multiple lines of code. The first group determines the state of the rows.

```
col1 = board[0] == currentToken and board[3] ==
currentToken and board[6] == currentToken
col2 = board[1] == currentToken and board[4] ==
currentToken and board[7] == currentToken
col3 - board[2] -- currentToken and board[5] --
currentToken and board[8] == currentToken
```

The second group determines the state of the columns.

```
diag1 = board[0] == currentToken and board[4] ==
currentToken and board[8] == currentToken
diag2 = board[2] == currentToken and board[4] ==
currentToken and board[6] == currentToken
```

The final group determines the state of the diagonals.

```
row = row1 or row2 or row3
col = col1 or col2 or col3
diag = diag1 or diag2
```

The groups are combined into single variables to make the if-check easier.

```
if (row or col or diag):
```

If the player has obtained a row or a column or a diagonal, they have won and the game goes into the end game state.

```
print("\n")
print("%s|%s|%s" % (board[0], board[1], board[2]))
print("-+-+-")
print("%s|%s|%s" % (board[3], board[4], board[5]))
print("-+-+-")
print("%s|%s|%s" % (board[6], board[7], board[8]))
```

Display the board again to show the players who won.

```
print("Congratulations %s! You won!!" % currentToken)
winningToken = currentToken
```

Display a "Congratulations!" message and set the winning token. Remember – this is one of the sentinel control variables used by the main (the top) while loop. If this is set to a nonempty value, that is, we set it to the contents of 'currentToken', the main loop ends.

```
if currentToken == 'X':
    currentToken = 'O'
else:
    currentToken = 'X'
```

If the game is still playing, the current token needs to be swapped for the opposite. If the current token is X we swap for the O and vice versa.

```
if slotsFilled == 9 and winningToken == ":
    print("No one won :( Better luck next time, players!")
```

Our final if-check is outside the main loop and displays a message if neither player wins.

Save and Run

Save and run the program. If you want to run the program from the command line you will need to locate the folder in the terminal, for example:

```
$ cd ~
$ cd pygamebook
$ cd ch8
```

Then enter the chmod command to make sure that the program can execute:

```
$ chmod +x tictactoe.py
```

Finally, enter the following to run the game:

```
$ ./tictactoe.py
```

If you want to run the game from inside IDLE, press the F5 key on your keyboard or select "Run Module" from the "Run" menu.

Conclusion

It's not our first 2D graphics game, but it is our first game! A gentle introduction to writing a game with Python. We used the constructs that were talked about in the first few chapters of the book to build this game. Even though they are simple, these small building blocks – variables, loops, conditions, and containers – can help us build complex pieces of software.

CHAPTER 9

Basic Introduction to PyGame

PyGame is a free framework for Python that provides modules designed to write video games. It is built on top of the Simple DircctMedia Layer Library (SDL) that provides easy access to sound and visual elements.

In this section we will see how to set up PyGame and look at some of the elements that will be used in our future programs. The Python language does not include PyGame, and as such the framework must be imported before it can be used.

Importing the PyGame Framework

Importing a module in Python is through the 'import' keyword. To import PyGame you would add the following line to the top of the script, after the hash-bang:

```
import pygame, os, sys
from pygame.locals import *
```

The first line imports the PyGame module and its objects as well as the OS and system modules. The import keyword does not enter the names of the objects defined in pygame, os, and sys directly in the current symbol table. It only enters the module names. To access the elements of

© Sloan Kelly 2019
S. Kelly, *Python, PyGame, and Raspberry Pi Game Development*,
https://doi.org/10.1007/978-1-4842-4533-0_9

each module we have to use the module name, which is why we have to write pygame.locals. The second line says that we're going to import the constants from the PyGame framework as if they were defined locally. In this case we won't have to prefix each constant with 'pygame.' The 'from' keyword is a variant of the import keyword that allows us to import module elements as if they were defined in our (local) code base.

Initializing PyGame

Before using any of the objects in the framework, you must initialize it first. We also want to clamp the updates to 30 frames per second, so we add an fpsClock variable that we initialize to 30 frames per second.

```
pygame.init()
fpsClock = pygame.time.Clock()
surface = pygame.display.set_mode((800, 600))
```

The first line initializes PyGame. The second line creates an instance of an object and stores this value in 'fpsClock.' An object is an instance of a class. We'll cover this in detail in the object-oriented section. Everything in Python is an object, and that's part of the beauty of the language; but for now, let's just say that you can create your own data types. These user-defined data types are called 'classes.'

The third line creates a surface that we can draw our images (background and sprites) upon. The set_mode() method takes two parameters that specify the width and the height of the surface in pixels. In this example, we're creating an 800 × 600 pixel surface.

It's good practice to clear the screen before we draw on it. So, rather than plucking numbers out of thin air, we're going to create a tuple that contains the Red, Green, and Blue components of the background. A pixel onscreen is made up of combinations of red, green, and blue. These ratios determine what color is displayed. For example (0, 0, 0) is black and (255, 255, 255) is white. The tuple represents, in order, the red, green, and blue combination that makes up the color. So, (255, 0, 0) is red and (0, 0, 255) is blue.

```
background = pygame.Color(100, 149, 237) # cornflower blue
```

In this example I've chosen cornflower blue because it's not a color you see very often, so when the window appears, you'll know the program has worked.

The Main Loop

Some programs, notably those run from the command line, tend to perform a series of tasks and exit. This is not true with the majority of windowed environment programs and games. These programs stay active until the user explicitly quits. During the execution they perform what is called the main loop. This contains the series of statements that are executed over and over again until the program ends. The main loop is

```
while True:
```

This keeps the program in memory because it executes the loop while the condition is 'True.' Because the condition actually is 'True,' the loop will always execute.

```
    surface.fill(background)
```

First we clear the surface before drawing anything onscreen. This erases what was there before and allows us to start fresh.

```
    for event in pygame.event.get():
        if event.type == QUIT:
            pygame.quit()
            sys.exit()
```

PyGame provides us with events from the window manager: keypresses, button clicks, and window close requests. When we get

89

a window close request ('QUIT') we will stop PyGame and quit the application. There are a number of events that can occur during the loop, and these are held in a list that we can iterate through. So, we have to check each event to see what type it is and then act upon it. In our basic framework we're only checking for the 'QUIT' event.

```
pygame.display.update()
fpsClock.tick(30)
```

The pygame.display.update() method redraws the screen. When you place objects on the screen it is drawn to an area of memory called the back buffer. When update is called, this back buffer is made visible, and the buffer that is currently displaying data (front buffer) becomes the back buffer. This allows for smooth movement and reduces flickering.

Create a folder called 'ch9' inside the 'pygamebook' folder. Save the code in that has been presented so far in this chapter to a new file called 'firstwindow.py'. When running the program you should see a cornflower blue window appear (Figure 9-1).

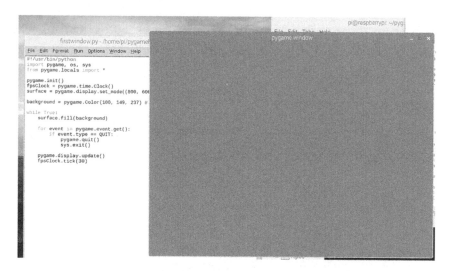

Figure 9-1. *PyGame window displaying a cornflower blue background*

Click the 'X' button on the top right to close the window.

Most modern video cards have two areas of memory; both are used to display images to the user, but only one is shown at a time. This technique is called double buffering and is shown in Figure 9-2.

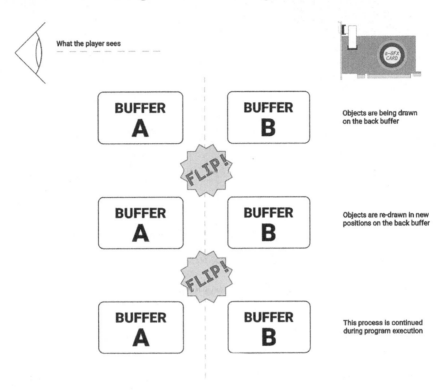

Figure 9-2. *Double buffering in a modern graphics adapter*

From the user's viewpoint, they see the items visible on the monitor. But behind the scenes, the program is drawing to the back buffer. With the flick of an electronic finger, the user is shown the images on the back buffer. Figure 9-3 shows what happens.

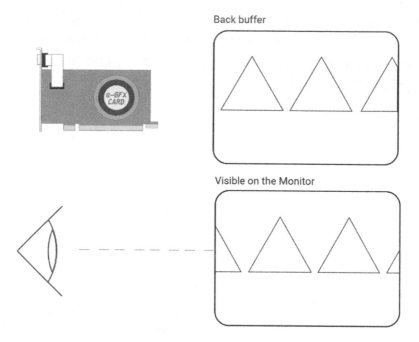

Figure 9-3. *The contents of the front and back buffers*

Theaters have used this technique to hide set changes. While the actors are out on stage, behind the curtain a new scene is being dressed. When the actor's scene is finished, the curtain opens, and the new scene is revealed.

Finally, we want to clamp the updates to 30 frames per second. To do that we call fpsClock.tick(30). This ensures that we get consistent timing in our game. This is the maximum that the clock can run at, but not the minimum. You may perform complex calculations during your game that could drop the frame rate. You will need to be aware of that when you start to write more complex games than the ones presented in this text.

Images and Surfaces

PyGame uses surfaces to draw images onto the screen. It uses the image module to load image files from disk. These are then converted to an internal format and stored in a surface object until later use. You will create at least one surface object, for your main screen. This will be the object that you will draw your sprites and other images on.

The surface that we perform the main drawing is the back buffer. We then present this back buffer to the screen by calling the update() method.

Creating Images

For the most part, you will want to create images in a third-party product, such as the Open Source GIMP (GNU Image Manipulation Program) at `www.gimp.org`. GIMP is a professional-level graphics program on par with Photoshop. If, like me, you have spent most of your professional life using Photoshop, you might find GIMP a bit frustrating to use at first – this is no fault of the application! Just relax and you'll be creating images like you did in Photoshop! Any image creation program that allows you to generate BMP, PNG, and JPG images is fine. There is a list of these in the appendices. If you are stuck with images, there are some (badly) drawn images located on this book's web site (`http://sloankelly.net`) to help you. Some of the images are part of SpriteLib through the GPL (GNU Public License); this means that the images are free to use for commercial and noncommercial works.

Loading Images

Python uses surfaces to draw images onscreen. When you load an image into memory, it is put in a special surface. For example, load an image called 'car.png':

```
image = pygame.image.load('car.png')
```

This will load the image into memory and place a reference to the newly loaded object in 'image.'

Drawing Images

Images are drawn on a PyGame Surface. Remember from our skeleton game that we created a surface that we use to draw images on the screen. To draw an image:

```
surface.blit(image, (0, 0))
```

Where 'surface' is the surface instance and 'image' is the image you want to draw onscreen. The second parameter is the location onscreen you want the image drawn.

Screen Coordinates and Resolution

The screen or monitor is the primary output device for the computer system. There are two different types of screen: Cathode Ray Tube (CRT) and Liquid Crystal Display (LCD). The latter is becoming cheaper and therefore more popular, or is that cheaper because it is popular? The computer outputs images to the monitor at a given resolution. Resolution means "How many pixels along? How many pixels down?" Physical screen resolution is measured in pixels. The word pixel is the shortened form of Picture Element. There are a variety of resolutions available on your PC from 320×240 pixels to 2560×1600 and beyond.

A graphics card inside the computer works with the CPU to produce images on the monitor. With newer graphic cards, a Graphic Processor Unit (GPU) is placed on the card to improve the 3D capabilities of the system – to make games more realistic by providing higher resolutions, special effects, and better frame rate.

Resolution defines how detailed your images will look onscreen. The number of columns (the horizontal axis) and the number of rows (the vertical axis) define the number of pixels available to the application. In the following example a 1920×1080 resolution screen map is shown. No matter what resolution your monitor is running the origin is at the top-left corner, it always has the coordinates (0,0). See Figure 9-4.

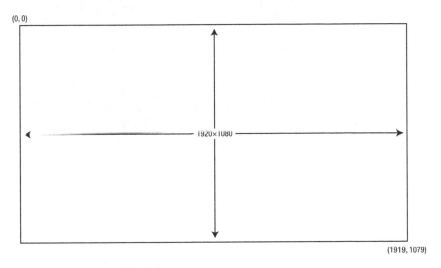

Figure 9-4. *Screen coordinates of a 1920×1080 monitor*

Sprite Sheets

Sprite sheets are commonly used to keep all frames of a character's animation on one image. The name comes from a sprite, which, in computer terms, is a small image used as an avatar in games. An example sprite sheet is shown in Figure 9-5.

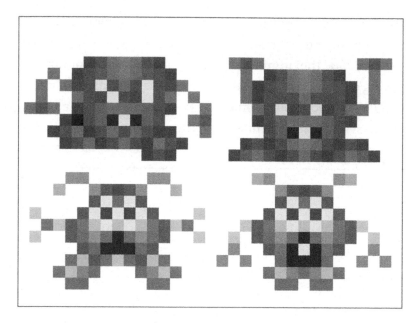

Figure 9-5. *Four-image sprite sheet*

This sprite sheet contains four images: two frames of animation for two Space Invaders characters. When we want to draw the character onscreen, we choose what cell of the sprite sheet to use. Cells are determined by the height and width of the sprite. In this case, we have 32×32 pixel sprites, so that means our sprite sheet is 64×64 pixels because we have 2×2 sprites.

PyGame allows us to display a piece of the image we want to display. So, for example, if we only wanted to show the second frame of the first invader (top right of the image) we would use a line like this:

```
surface.blit(image, (0, 0), (32, 0, 32, 32))
```

The third parameter, the tuple containing four values, is the area of the image we want to display at (0, 0). The tuple represents (x, y, width, height) of the image to display.

Full Listing

The full listing of the program in this chapter is shown as follows:

```
import pygame, os, sys
from pygame.locals import *

pygame.init()
fpsClock = pygame.time.Clock()
surface = pygame.display.set_mode((800, 600))

background = pygame.Color(100, 149, 237) # cornflower blue

while True:
    surface.fill(background)

    for event in pygame.event.get():
        if event.type == QUIT:
            pygame.quit()
            sys.exit()

    pygame.display.update()
    fpsClock.tick(30)
```

Conclusion

This chapter has introduced the basic loop that we will use for each of the games as well as how to initialize PyGame. set_mode() on the pygame. display object is called and returns a surface that will be used as a back buffer where all our images will be displayed.

Images are loaded into memory using the image.load() method and drawn on the surface using its blit() method. Images can contain multiple shapes, and these are called sprite sheets. A single frame of a sprite sheet can be drawn by specifying the rectangle of the frame to draw.

CHAPTER 10

Designing Your Game

Before we launch into programming our first game, we're going to slow things down a little. Before starting any project, whether it is home improvement, taking a trip, or programming a game, you should sit down and plan what you want to do.

This usually involves taking the following steps:

- Initial concept

- Functional specification

- Program design

- Coding

- Test

- Iteration

Coding and testing tend to go hand in hand; you will write some code and then test it. From a programming point of view this loop forms much of your time in game development.

Initial Concept

We're concerning ourselves with small projects here. In a more formal setting, this would entail going around all the people involved (stakeholders) and asking them what they want from the program. In our case, it's a video

© Sloan Kelly 2019
S. Kelly, *Python, PyGame, and Raspberry Pi Game Development*,
https://doi.org/10.1007/978-1-4842-4533-0_10

game. You'll probably be working with two or three people, and this part tends to be brainstorming ideas:

- It's gonna be a racing game

- With weapons

- And traps! You can set traps!

These ideas are all stored in a single document; Google Drive is excellent for this type of work because it allows for collaboration between developers.

Once you have all your requirements, you then move onto functional requirements. Remember though that all of these documents are "living" in that they can change. Subsequent documents/code need to be updated to reflect those changes.

The initial concept is iterated on and these documents form what is called the *game design document* or GDD for short.

Prototyping

As part of the initial phase of game design you as the programmer may be asked to do some proof of concept work called a *prototype*. This is a rough-around-the-edges sketch of what a part of the game might feel like to play. For example, in a card game it might be a discard hand animation, or a screen shake when the player dies.

Code that you generate as part of the prototyping phase is not expected to make it to production, that is, your shipped game. It does happen sometimes, so you should always try to make your code as clean as possible.

Functional Specification

Functional specification takes the requirements gathered in the first stage and removes all the "fluff" language around them. They set out a series of rules about the game that can be passed on to a coder to implement. For example, our racing game can fire weapons, so our functional requirements might have a "Weapons" section and a "Traps" section.

These sections further split down the requirements into bite-sized chunks that a programmer can take away and implement. Along with *Program Design*, this forms what is called the *technical design document* (TDD). See the following examples.

Weapon Firing

The player can fire a machine gun at another player. There should be a maximum of ten shots per second allowed per player. If the gun is held down for more than 2 seconds, it will start to heat up. This will start a 'heat' counter. After the heat counter reaches 5 seconds, the gun will no longer be fireable. It takes a further 5 seconds for the gun to cool down once the player has released the fire button.

This also gives the artist some cues as well; they will have to show the gun heating up and cooling down.

Program Design

As you can see, each step refines the previous step's information. The program design takes the functional requirements and breaks them down into modules that a programmer can take and implement. The programmer may take those modules and refine them further, making smaller modules.

The overall goal here is to take a problem and break it down until you have lots and lots of smaller, more easily solved problems. This sounds counterintuitive: take one problem and make it many. "Make a cup of tea" is a larger problem. This can be broken down into smaller problems like this:

- Boil kettle

- Place tea bag in cup

- Place boiled water in cup

- Etc., etc.

From a programming perspective, you are taking requirements (the basic idea for the game) through functional requirements (how the player interacts with the game – how the game environment works) to the program design where you take these functional requirements and figure out what needs to be done from a programming perspective.

Now, this is somewhat of a Catch-22 situation. You need to have experience to know how to take these requirements and figure out how they become program design.

Coding

Sometimes called the fun part of the process. This is where the ideas start to take form; graphics are added, and code is used to move them across the screen. The program itself, if you remember from the opening chapters, is this:

Program = Data + Algorithms

The data is called the model and is manipulated by the algorithm. Algorithms that are used to manipulate the data are called controllers and the ones that are used to render items to the display are part of the view. In object-oriented programming, this pattern is called Model View Controller.

Throughout this text, we will try and keep the model, view, and controller as separate as we can with communication going through the controller, as shown in Figure 10-1.

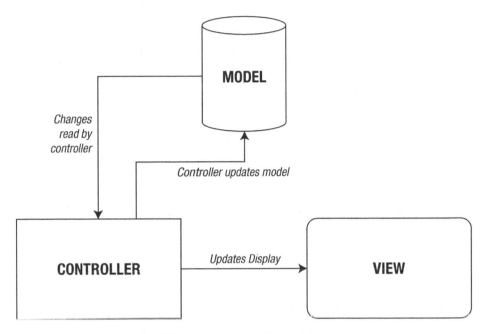

Figure 10-1. *The Model View Controller pattern*

The MVC pattern fits in nicely with our "Programs = Data + Algorithms" statement. The controller manipulates the model in code. In turn, the model's data is read by the view to render data. There can be many different views all rendering different data.

In the example shown in Figure 10-2, we see that the main view of the game displays the player and enemy sprites at full size while the smaller radar view shows the approximate positions of the player and enemies relative to the whole game world. There is a main view controller and a radar view controller. Both controllers have access to the same data: the player and enemy positions.

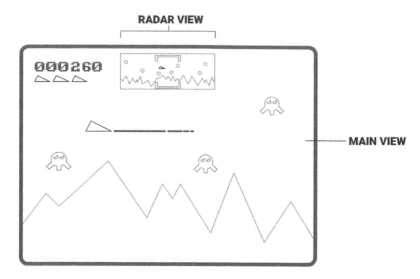

Figure 10-2. *A game displaying two views of the same objects in the game*

The code to show the aliens and the player ship in the main playing field is different to how they are displayed in the radar view. They do share one thing in common though; they use the same data. The player's model is also used to display (in yet another view) the number of lives left, the score, and the number of smart bombs at the player's disposal.

Although we won't be formally introduced to the MVC pattern until the object-oriented chapters, we will be using the spirit of this pattern in the games (Bricks and Snake) that precede that section.

Testing

During development, you will be constantly testing your code. Each time you implement (code) a new routine, you will test it to make sure that it does what you set out for it to do. How do you know that it's doing the right thing? You have documentation in the form of the "Requirements" and "Functional Specification" to ensure that what you expect to happen does happen.

From a programming perspective, there are two types of testing done at the coding level: white-box and black-box testing. The former examines each code step in turn and ensures that they perform as expected. The latter takes each separate module and treats them as a black box. Data goes in, results come out.

Iteration

As I mentioned before, the Game Design Document or GDD is a 'living' document. The people developing the game will continually play the game as it is being created. This is called *play* testing. This play testing causes a feedback loop that might change elements of the original design. You can find that the thing that made the game 'fun' becomes tiring. By iterating on the design during development you make small changes that will improve your initial concept.

Conclusion

Although you won't always create separate documents for the requirements and functional specifications, it is still a good idea to jot your thoughts down. Even if it's just a reminder as to what needs programming and what art needs creating. If you're still not keen on writing, don't forget that a drawing is worth a thousand words.

When it comes to programming, think before you put your hands on the keyboard to start typing. The biggest question you must ask yourself is, "What do I hope to achieve with the code I'm about to write?" You should have a clear idea of the goal that you're aiming for before you start typing.

Last, but certainly not least, is testing. Always, always, always test your code!

CHAPTER 11

Game Project: Bricks

In this chapter we'll review Bricks, our first game project. For those of you who haven't played this game before, you control a bat at the bottom of the screen (Figure 11-1). There is a collection of bricks above you and using the ball you must destroy all the bricks by hitting them with the ball.

Sounds simple enough, but in this project, we'll learn about

- Player movement

- Automatic (non-player) movement

- Collision detection

- Displaying images

© Sloan Kelly 2019
S. Kelly, *Python, PyGame, and Raspberry Pi Game Development*,
https://doi.org/10.1007/978-1-4842-4533-0_11

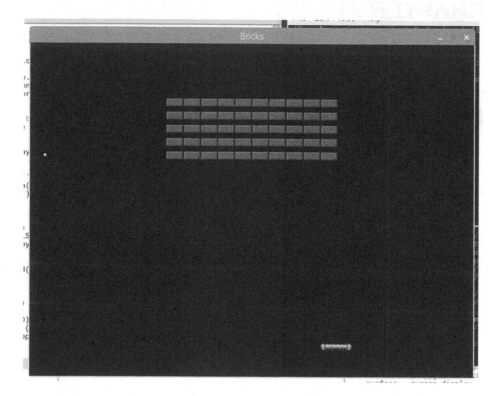

Figure 11-1. *The main brick play screen*

The Main Framework

We will lay down the main framework in this section to give you an overview of the structure of the entire game. To keep things simple for our first game, there won't be any interstitial screens such as splash screens, menus, pause screens, etc.

There will be placeholder comments through the framework indicating points where new lines will be added throughout the course of this project.

```
#!/usr/bin/python
import pygame, os, sys
from pygame.locals import *
```

```
pygame.init()
fpsClock = pygame.time.Clock()
mainSurface = pygame.display.set_mode((800, 600))
pygame.display.set_caption('Bricks')

black = pygame.Color(0, 0, 0)

# bat init
# ball init
# brick init

while True:
    mainSurface.fill(black)
    # brick draw
    # bat and ball draw
    # events
    for event in pygame.event.get():
        if event.type == QUIT:
            pygame.quit()
            sys.exit()

    # main game logic
    # collision detection

    pygame.display.update()
    fpsClock.tick(30)
```

Create a new folder inside the 'pygamebook' folder called 'bricks'. Save the file in there and call it 'bricks.py'.

Images

There are three images used in the game, all of which are downloadable from the Resources section on the book's web site (http://sloankelly.net). If you don't want to use those images, you can create your own. The game, however, assumes the following dimensions for each of the images. See Figures 11-2 to 11-4.

Figure 11-2. *Ball.png 8×8 pixels*

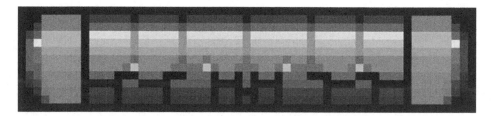

Figure 11-3. *Bat.png 55×11 pixels*

Figure 11-4. *Brick.png 31×16 pixels*

Moving the Bat

The user controls the bat using their mouse. We clamp the movement to the x-axis by ignoring the y-axis changes on the mouse. The bat is also restricted to allow movement within the confines of the screen only. The bat must remain within the play field (the screen) during the game.

Bat Initialization

Locate the following line in the framework:

```
# bat init
```

Underneath that line, add a couple of blank lines to give you some space. Type the following:

```
bat = pygame.image.load('bat.png')
```

Our bat is loaded into memory as a surface called 'bat'. It doesn't need to be called this, but it makes sense to call your variables something meaningful. You could also have called it 'batImage' or 'batSprite', for example.

```
playerY = 540
```

Our player's movement is restricted to the x-axis, so they will always be at a height of 540 pixels on the screen. This is quite near the bottom; remember that as you increase in value on the y-axis, you move further down the screen.

```
batRect = bat.get_rect()
```

The bat's rectangle will be used in our collision detection calculations later.

```
mousex, mousey = (0, playerY)
```

We give the mouse coordinates a default value. Notice that we use a tuple here? We could have also written that single line as two like this:

```
mousex = 0
mousey = playerY
```

Which would take up two lines and wouldn't imply what our values are for; they represent the coordinates of the bat in 2D space on the screen.

Drawing the Bat

Each time the main loop is executed, we clear the main surface in one line, which is already contained in the main loop:

```
mainSurface.fill(black)
```

This fills the main surface with black, fresh so that we can draw other things on top of it! Scroll down to this line:

```
# bat and ball draw
```

And add the following line after that:

```
mainSurface.blit(bat, batRect)
```

Save and run the game. What do you see? The bat should be at the top left of the screen. But why is that the case? The answer lies in 'batRect.' Take another look at the initialization of 'batRect':

```
batRect = bat.get_rect()
```

This will contain the dimensions of the bat:
(0, 0, 55, 11)
Which means that the image will be drawn at (0, 0). It's time to move the bat.

Moving the Bat

Moving the bat is achieved in two steps:

- Capturing the mouse input

- Drawing the bat image at the new location

Scroll down to the section marked

```
# events
```

Change the code underneath to read:

```
for event in pygame.event.get():
    if event.type == QUIT:
        pygame.quit()
        sys.exit()
    elif event.type == MOUSEMOTION:
        mousex, mousey = event.pos
        if (mousex < 800 - 55):
            batRect.topleft = (mousex, playerY)
        else:
            batRect.topleft = (800 - 55, playerY)
```

That's a lot of tabs! Careful with the tab placement or your code won't work.

Events

Events are generated by the Windows manager, whether that's under Microsoft Windows, Mac OS, or an X-Windows manager under a Linux operating system like the one running on your Raspberry Pi. Events that apply to the currently active window are passed to it by the system for processing. You only need to check for events that you want to perform actions for. In this game, we're only interested in checking for this:

- The user closing the window

- The user moving the mouse

- The user clicking the mouse button (later)

Quit Event

Each event is passed through as an event type with additional parameters, as required. For the QUIT event, there are no additional parameters. QUIT is just a signal to the application to shut down, which we do by exiting PyGame and the program itself.

113

Mouse Move Event

When the user moves the mouse, the information is passed from the hardware (the mouse, the physical interface, some controller chips), through some low-level OS drivers to the currently active application. In this case, our game. With it comes the position of the mouse as well as any buttons that were pressed. Like all events, this message is only passed if the event occurs (mouse is moved in this case).

The event type for mouse movement is 'MOUSEMOTION' and has a parameter called 'pos' that contains the location of the mouse. 'pos' is a tuple that contains the x- and y-coordinates of the mouse position.

The new x-coordinate is clamped within the confines of the screen and then assigned to the 'topleft' property of the 'batRect' variable.

Save and run the program. The bat will now move with the mouse movement. If it doesn't, or you get errors, check your code. It could be a stray or missing 'tab.'

Moving the Ball

Moving the ball is done entirely in code and does not require input from the user, save from the initial tap of the mouse button to get things rolling, if you pardon the pun.

Ball Initialization

Ball initialization looks very similar to the bat initialization. Locate this line in code:

```
# ball init
```

Add the following lines underneath:

```
ball = pygame.image.load('ball.png')
ballRect = ball.get_rect()
ballStartY = 200
ballSpeed = 3
ballServed = False
bx, by = (24, ballStartY)
sx, sy = (ballSpeed, ballSpeed)
ballRect.topleft = (bx, by)
```

The first two lines load the image and capture its rectangle. The next two lines set up the default values for the starting y-coordinate and speed. The 'ballServed' variable is used to determine, in the code later, if the ball has or has not been served. The remaining lines set up the initial position of the ball and its speed.

Scroll down the code to

```
# bat and ball draw
```

Add the following line to draw the ball onscreen:

```
mainSurface.blit(ball, ballRect)
```

Save and run the game. You will now see the ball in the top left of the screen. If you don't, check your code against the lines written above. Typing mistakes or typos are common, even among seasoned programmers!

Ball Movement

Ball movement is achieved by adding the speed of the ball to the current position. This is from the Physics equation:

Speed = Distance / Time

How do we do this in code? Scroll down to the line that reads

```
# main game logic
```

The formula to calculate distance is

Distance = Speed × Time

Because our rate is fixed to 30 frames per second, we will be adding our speed to the current position once every 1/30 of a second. This means that after 1 second our ball will have traveled

30 × 3 = 90 pixels

So, the actual velocity of our ball is 90 pixels per second.

Just after the 'main game logic' comment line, add the following code and run the game:

```
bx += sx
by += sy
ballRect.topleft = (bx, by)
```

A new symbol has been introduced here. The += operator is used to add the value on the left of the operator to the value on the right and place the sum in the variable on the left of the operator. It's a short form of bx = bx + sx. There are other short-form operators like −= (minus), ×= (multiply), and /= (divide) that follow the same rule we outlined for +=. The ball will now move slowly and diagonally from the top left of the screen to the bottom right. What happens if it hits the bat? What happens when it reaches the end of the screen? Nothing; the ball just passes right through the bat and sails past the edge of the screen.

Let's remedy this situation. First, we'll clamp the ball within the confines of the screen area. Our screen is 800×600 pixels in size. Our ball is 8×8 pixels in size. We'll use some Boolean logic to determine, from the ball's position, if it hits the edges. If so, we'll reverse the speed. This means that in the next loop the ball will move in the opposite direction as shown in Figure 11-5.

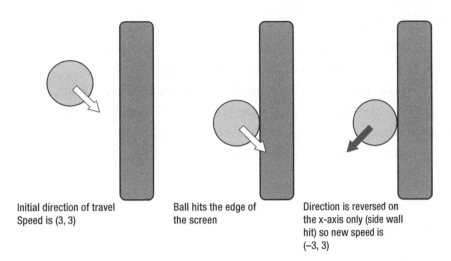

Initial direction of travel
Speed is (3, 3)

Ball hits the edge of
the screen

Direction is reversed on
the x-axis only (side wall
hit) so new speed is
(–3, 3)

Figure 11-5. *Ball hitting a side wall showing reversal of direction along the x-axis*

Figure 11-5 shows the two stages of collision: detection and response. Detection – have two objects collided and response – what are we going to do about it? In this case we are detecting whether the ball is touching the outside edge of the screen and our reaction is to reflect the ball back in the direction it came.

Detection determines if two objects have touched
Response is the action(s) that are performed when two objects collide

Add a one or two blank lines after the ball position update code and add the following:

```
if (by <= 0):
    by = 0
    sy *= -1
```

The ball's y-coordinate is checked against 0, which is the topmost row of pixels on the display. Remember that the top left of the screen is (0, 0) and the bottommost is the maximum size; in our case, that's (800, 600).

117

This code will ensure that the topmost boundary of the screen reflects the ball. The ball is only reflected on the y-axis because we have hit a vertical boundary of the screen, in this case the top edge.

Do the same for the bottom of the screen. In this case, we must subtract the size of the ball from the bottommost number. Our ball is 8×8 pixels, so that means we must subtract 8. Remember that when we draw an image onscreen, we're drawing it from the top left of the image:

```
if (by >= 600 - 8):
    by = 600 - 8
    sy *= -1
```

The sides of the screen will reflect on the x-axis instead of the y-axis:

```
if (bx <= 0):
    bx = 0
    sx *= -1
```

This will reflect the ball on the left-hand edge (when x is 0). Finally, we'll reflect when we're on the right-hand edge (when x is 800 – 8 or 792):

```
if (bx >=800 - 8):
    bx = 800 - 8
    sx *= -1
```

Save and run the game. You'll now see the ball bounces around the screen. But it still goes through the bat. We need to add more code to the game to get it to collide with the bat so that it bounces up the screen.

Bat and Ball Collision

The bat and ball collision works in a similar way to checking a collision against the bottom of the screen. We will use the colliderect method of the Rect class to determine if a collision has occurred.

Add a couple of blank lines after the last code you typed and add

```
if ballRect.colliderect(batRect):
    by = playerY - 8
    sy *= -1
```

The colliderect takes a single parameter that represents the rectangle we want to the check collision against. The colliderect method returns a Boolean 'True' or 'False' depending on whether the rectangles intersect each other. See Figure 11-6.

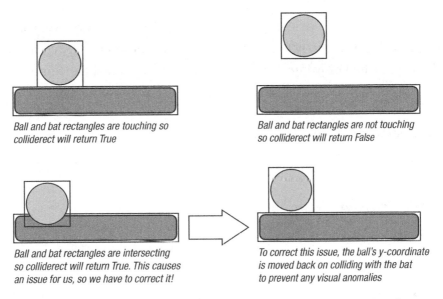

Ball and bat rectangles are touching so colliderect will return True

Ball and bat rectangles are not touching so colliderect will return False

Ball and bat rectangles are intersecting so colliderect will return True. This causes an issue for us, so we have to correct it!

To correct this issue, the ball's y-coordinate is moved back on colliding with the bat to prevent any visual anomalies

Figure 11-6. *Collision rectangles showing touching, not touching, and intersection*

The top-left image shows that when the two rectangles are touching, colliderect will return 'True.' The top-right image shows that when the two rectangles are not touching, colliderect will return 'False.'

The bottom two images show what happens when the bat and ball intersect. Colliderect will return 'True' because the two rectangles are touching, but in code, we must move the ball's position up so that they're

119

not touching. This stops any anomalies from occurring; if you hit the ball from the side it travels inside the bat! By replacing the ball to touch the top of the bat, we get around this problem, and this line:

```
by = playerY - 8
```

Is the one that solves the issue. Save and run the code and you'll be able to knock the ball back up the screen using the bat.

Serving the Ball

Up until this point we've just served the ball as the game starts. We want to restrict the ball serve to when the user clicks the left mouse button. Firstly, we'll stop the ball movement if it hasn't been served. Locate the line:

```
# main game logic
```

You should see these lines underneath:

```
bx += sx
by += sy
ballRect.topleft = (bx, by)
```

Change these lines to read

```
if ballServed:
    bx += sx
    by += sy
    ballRect.topleft = (bx, by)
```

Saving and running the game will show that the ball stays in the top left.

To get it to move, we have to change 'ballServed' to 'True.' In order to do that, we have to respond to the player clicking the left mouse button. That's in the events section of the code. Scroll up to the events section and add these lines after the last 'elif' block:

```
elif event.type == MOUSEBUTTONUP and not ballServed:
    ballServed = True
```

The MOUSEBUTTONUP tests for any button on the mouse being 'up.' So, really, right-clicking will work too. We also test for the case where ballServed is already 'True.' If the ball is already served, we don't need to serve it again.

Brick Wall

We're almost there! The last piece of this puzzle is the wall of bricks that the player must destroy. Like the screenshot at the start of this section shows, we're going to arrange the bricks in the center of the screen.

Locate the following line in the code:

```
# brick init
```

Add the following lines, column aligned with the pound sign (#) on the previous line:

```
brick = pygame.image.load('brick.png')
bricks = []
```

Once again, we load in an image that we're going to use for our bricks. We then create an empty list where we will store the positions of each of the bricks.

```
for y in range(5):
    brickY = (y * 24) + 100
    for x in range(10):
        brickX = (x * 31) + 245
        width = brick.get_width()
        height = brick.get_height()
        rect = Rect(brickX, brickY, width, height)
        bricks.append(rect)
```

Our bricks are arranged in five rows of ten bricks. We store the brick locations in the 'bricks' list. Our brick positions are stored as Rect instances because it will make collision detection easier later.

Scroll down to find this line of code:

```
# brick draw
```

Add the following lines just after:

```
for b in bricks:
    mainSurface.blit(brick, b)
```

Save and run the game. You'll now see the wall of bricks. Once again, you'll notice that the collision doesn't work, so the ball just sails through the wall. We'll fix that in our last section.

Brick and Ball Collision

Our bat and ball move and our brick wall displays. Our penultimate task in this project is to destroy the bricks as the ball hits them. This is similar to when the ball hits the bat except we will remove the brick that was hit. Luckily, PyGame provides a method on the Rect class called collidelist().

Scroll down the source code and locate

```
# collision detection
```

You will remember that our bricks are just a list of rectangles. The collidelist() method takes a list of rectangles and returns the index of the two rectangles that were hit. We will use the rectangle of the ball as the left-hand side of the test and the bricks variable as the parameter to the function:

```
brickHitIndex = ballRect.collidelist(bricks)
if brickHitIndex >= 0:
    hb = bricks[brickHitIndex]
```

Capture the index of the brick rectangle contained in bricks that intersects with the ballRect rectangle. In layman's terms, find out which brick the ball touched. If no brick was hit, this method returns a –1. So, we're only interested in values greater than or equal to zero. Remember that lists start at element zero (0), not 1 in Python.

```
mx = bx + 4
my = by + 4
if mx > hb.x + hb.width or mx < hb.x:
    sx *= -1
else:
    sy *= -1
```

We then calculate the midpoint of the ball's rectangle, which is 4 pixels in and 4 pixels down because the ball is an 8×8 image. We then test this against the width of the brick that was hit. If it is outside the width then the ball was hit from the side. Otherwise, the ball hit the brick on the top or bottom. We deflect the ball accordingly by changing its speed.

```
del (bricks[brickHitIndex])
```

Because we hit the brick, we remove it from the list.

Save and run the game. When the ball hits the bricks, they will be removed, and the ball will rebound from the hit. Now, what about hitting the bottom of the screen?

Out of Bounds

When the ball hits the bottom of the screen it should be marked as out of bounds. As it stands, we haven't done that and the ball simply bounces off the bottom.

Scroll down the source code to find the line that reads

```
# main game logic
```

You will see this block of code:

```
if (by >= 600 - 8):
    by = 600 - 8
    sy *= -1
```

Replace it with

```
if (by >= 600 - 8):
    ballServed = False
    bx, by = (24, ballStartY)
    ballSpeed = 3
    sx, sy = (ballSpeed, ballSpeed)
    ballRect.topleft = (bx, by)
```

When the ball hits the bottom of the screen, the 'ballServed' flag is reset to 'False' meaning that the ball has not been served. Because the ball hasn't been served, it will not be updated. The code also resets the ball's position and speed to the starting values.

Save and run the complete game, clicking any mouse button to serve the ball and using the mouse to move.

Conclusion

You have written your first game! This game really shows the power of Python and PyGame because a game like this contains the following:

- Mouse movement

- Automatic ball movement

- Collision

- Brick destruction

- Boundary checking

And it can all be achieved in around 120 lines of code.

Now that we have the first game under our belt, we'll spend some time learning more about the Python language.

CHAPTER 12

User-Defined Functions

A user-defined function allows you to package and name several lines of code and reuse those lines of code throughout your program. All you must do is call the name you've given your function.

What Is a Function?

A function in Python can be used to perform a simple task, and as such is just a mnemonic or special name given to a collection of lines. You can also optionally send values into a function as parameters or return a value from a function. Only one value can be returned from a function, but that value can be a tuple.

Format of a Function

The following simple function displays "Hello world" when it is called:

```
def sayHello():
    print("Hello, world!")

sayHello()
```

© Sloan Kelly 2019
S. Kelly, *Python, PyGame, and Raspberry Pi Game Development*,
https://doi.org/10.1007/978-1-4842-4533-0_12

Use the def keyword to define the function. The function consists of its name and optional parameters inside parentheses '(' and ')'.

Because it is a Python block, the first line ends in a colon and the lines that form the block are indented one tab.

Functions as a Menial Task/Mnemonic Device

At the trivial end, functions can be used as a mnemonic or replacement for multiple lines of code that you will use over and over again. For example, if you want to display a box you might want to use something like this:

```
def drawBox():
    print("+--------+")
    print("|        |")
    print("+--------+")

drawBox()
print("Between two boxes")
drawBox()
```

The output of this code is

```
+--------+
|        |
+--------+
Between two boxes
+--------+
|        |
+--------+
```

We now have consistency when we want to draw a box. Each box will look like every other box when we call drawBox().

FUNCTIONS ALLOW YOU TO REUSE CODE

This is the power of functions: they allow for something called code reuse. Code reuse means that you can use the same single block of code multiple times in your application. If you need to change that function for any reason, any code that calls it will get the changed version.

The other goal of functions is to make the place where you call it easier to read. A block of code should perform a single task rather than multiple tasks. When writing a program, consider where these breaks should occur. These should be your functions.

For example, you have been asked to read in the temperatures from the keyboard and write them to a file and calculate the average, maximum, and minimum values and store them in a separate file. You might write functions called

- getTemperatures()

- writeTemperatures()

- calcAverage()

- calcMinimum()

- calcMaximum()

- writeStats()

These would then be called from the main program in the correct sequence.

Sending Parameters

Having a block of code that you can execute repeatedly from multiple places is all well and good, but it's a bit restricting. What if you wanted to change some values each time you call it? Parameters (or arguments) can be used to provide your function with more information. For example, the width and height of the box you want to draw. Consider the following function:

```
def drawBox(width, height):
```

The drawBox() method takes two parameters: one is named width and the other height. These parameters are passed into the function from the calling line (seen later). These are just names that we use so that we can refer to the parameters in a meaningful way in the body of the function.

```
if width < 0:
    width = 3
```

The boxes are drawn on a character-based display, and as such, the minimum width that we can have is three characters; this is because we use '+' characters at each of the corners and '–' to denote the horizontal line.

```
if height < 3:
    height = 3
```

We have a similar restriction with height. Our minimum height is three because we have to have two horizontal lines and at least one line containing '|', some spaces and then '|' to represent the vertical lines of the box.

```
width = width - 2
```

Whatever our width is, it's two characters too long! This is because each row starts and ends with '|'. The number of characters is therefore width – 2 (two '|' characters).

```
print("+" + "-" * width + "+")
```

Our top line is fixed because it contains the corner pieces represented by '+'. We also use Python's handy string arithmetic to generate the string line; '+' is used to concatenate (add) two strings together, and '*' is used to multiply a string with a number to repeat a character a certain number of times.

```
for y in range(3, height + 1):
    print("|" + " " * width + "|")
```

The for loop goes through each value from '3' to the height plus one. Remember that the range goes from a starting value to one less than the number you want. Again, we use string arithmetic to generate our line.

```
print("+" + "-" * width + "+")
```

We close off the function by drawing the bottom of the box.

To call the function, you use the function's name and then pass in the parameters that we want to use:

```
drawBox(5, 4)
```

You must know what each parameter is used for, so that's why it's a good idea to name the parameters to something recognizable. In this example, if the width of the box is 5 and the height is 4, its output will be

```
+---+
|   |
|   |
+---+
```

Default Argument Values

Default values for each parameter can be specified. This means that if the user doesn't want to specify the value of an argument, they don't have to. Let's say we want to default width and height to 3. Change the function definition to

```
def drawBox(width = 3, height = 3):
```

131

If we just want a 3×3 box we can do this:

```
drawBox()
```

That will assign the default values to both width and height. Let's say we want to specify width without height. Let's create a 5×3 rectangle:

```
drawBox(5)
```

The default value must be the rightmost parameters passed to the function. The following function signatures are valid because all the parameters that follow the first parameter with a default value are also assigned default values:

```
def drawBox(width, height = 10)
def drawSprite(sprite, width = 32, height = 32, transparency = 1)
```

The following function signatures are invalid:

```
def drawBox(width = 5, height)
def drawSprite(sprite = None, width, height, transparency = 1)
```

All parameters that follow a parameter with a default value must also have default values!

Named Parameters

What about if we just want a default width, but we want to specify a height? That's easy enough; just pass in the name of the parameter you want to specify a value for:

```
drawBox(height = 10)
```

This will draw a 3×10 box. Width will default to 3 because it has not been assigned a value. This technique is called named parameters and allows you to specify the parameter by name. In other languages optional parameters – those with a default value – must be placed at the end of the parameter list. In Python, you can use named parameters to specify all or just some of the optional arguments.

Returning Values

One of the primary uses for functions is to generate a new value from the supplied arguments. Let's take a look at a trivial example first, adding two numbers together:

```
def add(first, second):
    return first + second

print(add(10, 5))
```

The function is defined as usual with the 'def' keyword and a name for the function. The function takes two parameters 'first' and 'second.'

The only line that makes up the body of the function is

```
return num1 + num2
```

The 'return' keyword takes whatever value is on the right-hand side of it and passes it back to the calling line. In our example, the calling line is this print statement:

```
print(add(10, 5))
```

'first' is assigned the value 10 and 'second' is assigned the value 5. The two are added together and returned. The 'print' keyword then displays the value returned. Because it's an integer value, this is a trivial undertaking and it just displays the result:

```
15
```

But we can add so much more than integer values:

```
print(add('sloan ', 'kelly'))
print(add(3.14, 1.61))
print(add((1,2,3), (4,5,6)))
```

Anything we can add together can use this function. We've seen that Python will return anything we want from a function, and it could depend on the arguments that are passed how that value is determined.

Returning Tuples

Tuples can be returned as whole tuples or into their separate element values. In the following example, the tuple is returned and printed to the screen:

```
def getPlayerPosition():
    return (10, 5)
print (getPlayerPosition())
```

The output is

```
(10, 5)
```

We can also explode the tuple into separate variables when we call the function for example:

```
def getPlayerPosition():
    return (10, 5)

x, y = getPlayerPosition()
print ("Player x is", x)
print ("Player y is", y)
```

Which will display

```
Player x is 10
Player y is 5
```

Accessing Global Variables

Global variables are generally thought to be bad programming practice.

They can lead to mistakes, or bugs, in code because it will take time to track down when each global variable is accessed (the value is read) and each time it is changed (a value is written to it).

Functions can read global variables with no problem, like in this example:

```
num = 5
def printNum():
    print(num)

printNum()
```

What if we change the value inside the function? What happens to it then?

```
num = 5
def changeNum():
    num = 10

print(num)
changeNum()
print(num)
```

Now, the output is

```
5
5
```

Why is this the case? Well, in order to prevent bad things from happening in your program, Python has a fail-safe technique to prevent global values being written to unless you explicitly say they can be written to. To mark the variable as being 'write-enabled' in your function, add global and the name of the global variable, like so:

```
num = 5
def changeNum():
    global num
    num = 10

print(num)
changeNum()
print(num)
```

With the addition of the global keyword and the name of the global variable, any changes to the 'num' global in printNum will be applied . The output of the program will now be

```
5
10
```

Real-World Example of a Function

Functions can contain their own variables. These variables are said to be local to the function. They cannot be seen or manipulated by anything outside of the function. This hiding of variables is called variable scope. We have seen that global variables can be accessed anywhere. With local variables they are visible only to that function and only exist if the function is executing.

We can rewrite some of the code for our Bricks game to use functions. I'll leave it as an exercise for the reader to convert other areas of the code to functions. We'll create a function to load the brick image and set up the brick positions.

Open up the Python file that contains the code for the 'Bricks' game. Right now, the code you have should have an area that looks like this:

```python
# brick init
brick = pygame.image.load('brick.png')
bricks = []
for y in range(5):
    brickY = (y * 24) + 100
    for x in range(10):
        brickX = (x * 31) + 245
        width = brick.get_width()
        height = brick.get_height()
        rect = Rect(brickX, brickY, width, height)
        bricks.append(rect)
```

Remove the line

```python
brick = pygame.image.load('brick.png')
```

And replace it with

```python
brick = None
```

Change the remaining lines to read

```python
def createBricks(pathToImg, rows, cols):
    global brick
```

The function will take in three parameters. The first is the path of the image file that we will use to draw the bricks. The second and third parameters are the number of rows and columns of bricks we want. Our brick positions are stored in a list called 'bricks' and the image is called 'brick.' We are going to create a global variable at the top of the file called brick. This holds our image of a brick.

137

```
brick = pygame.image.load(pathToImg)
bricks = []
for y in range(rows):
    brickY = (y * 24) + 100
    for x in range(cols):
        brickX = (x * 31) + 245
        width = brick.get_width()
        height = brick.get_height()
        rect = Rect(brickX, brickY, width, height)
        bricks.append(rect)
return bricks
```

Now, scroll back down to just before this line at the start of the main loop: Now add this line just above the 'while True':

```
bricks = createBricks('brick.png', 5, 10)
```

We return the list of brick data directly into our 'bricks' variable. This means that we don't need to create a variable earlier and add a global line in our function.

USE GLOBAL VARIABLES SPARINGLY!

Global variables can and should be avoided, and we'll see how throughout this book. Rather than teaching those techniques now and muddying the waters, it's best to let this infraction slip and enjoy our first game!

Save and run the game. It should work as before, but the cool thing is that now you can easily change the number of rows and columns of bricks just by changing the parameters passed to 'createBricks.'

Conclusion

In this chapter we have explored the first Python example of code reuse: functions. Functions allow us to write macro programs that perform a single task, for example, displaying sprites, saving the game, or setting up the game screen.

You can pass additional information to functions by giving values to the formal arguments (parameters) listed in parentheses after the function name. Each parameter should have a name that describes what they will be used for, for example, 'playerData,' 'width,' 'enemySprite,' etc.

Sometimes not all parameters are required for a function and you can add default values for each argument. You can also specify a named parameter when you call a function if there are multiple defaulted values and you only want to specify one or two.

CHAPTER 13

File Input and Output

Being able to save and load files from disk is an important part of game development. Assets such as levels, player sprites, etc., are loaded from files stored on disk. Progress is saved to disk to allow players to resume their game from when they last played.

In this section we will look at the basics of file input and output as well as introduce a way to store ordered data like the dictionary container we introduced in Chapter 7.

To save and load data, your script must import the 'os' (short for Operating System) module to access files on the disk.

Reading a File from Disk

This program reads the source of the program from disk and displays the contents to the screen:

```python
import os

f = open('readmyself.py', 'r')
for line in f:
    print(line)

f.close() # ALWAYS close a file that you open
```

© Sloan Kelly 2019
S. Kelly, *Python, PyGame, and Raspberry Pi Game Development*,
https://doi.org/10.1007/978-1-4842-4533-0_13

The open keyword's first argument is the file that we want to access. The second argument is the mode that we want to access the file:

- 'r' – Read the contents of the file

- 'w' – Write data to the file

- 'a' – Append (add on to the end of an existing file) data to the file

The default is 'r' for read, so we could omit this argument in this instance. Finally, this is for text mode only. This means that if we pass a '\n' it will be converted to the platform-specific line ending. On UNIX and Raspbian this is '\n' but on Windows it's '\r\n'.

You can add 'b' to the access mode parameter (e.g., 'rb' or 'wb') to specify binary mode. This mode is commonly used for things like images or complex save data.

The open keyword returns a File object. We can use this to read information from the file, or write out data, depending on what we want to do.

DON'T FORGET TO CALL close() ON ANY FILE YOU OPEN!

Save the program as 'readmyself.py' inside a folder called 'ch13' inside the 'pygamebook' folder and run it. The program will display the content, but it adds blank lines between each line of the code:

```
import os

f = open('readmyself.py', 'r')

for line in f:

    print(line)

f.close()
```

They are not there in the file, so where do they come from? Well, on disk, each line is terminated with a '\n' which is a newline, and the print keyword adds its own newline making those empty lines.

To get around this, you can add .rstrip('\n') to each print, like so:

```
print(line.rstrip('\n'))
```

The rstrip() function returns a copy of the string where all the specified characters have been removed (stripped) from the end of the string. By default, this is all whitespace characters, but in this case we only want to strip out the 'newline' character.

Writing Data to a File

Writing text to a file uses the write method of the file object. This next program takes a list of high scores and writes it out to a text file.

```
players = ['Anna,10000', 'Barney,9000', 'Jane,8000', 'Fred,7000']
```

The list contains the names of the players and their scores separated by a comma.

```
f = open('highscores.txt', 'w')
```

The file is opened in 'write' mode because we are sending data to the file. The file's name can be whatever you want it to be, but it should be something that makes sense. It doesn't even have to end in .txt.

```
for p in players:
    f.write(p + '\n')
```

All the values in the list are cycled through and the write method of the File object is called with the list item followed by a '\n'. If we didn't include that, the file would have all the names and scores mashed together on a single line.

```
f.close()
```

You must always remember to close the file when you're finished with it. When I'm writing a file read/write, I always write the open and close lines first, then code what I want to do with the file. This means that I never forget to close the file.

Locate the 'highscores.txt' file on disk and enter the following command:

```
$ more highscores.txt
```

You should see the following output:

```
Anna,10000
Barney,9000
Jane,8000
Fred,7000
```

While this is what we want, the internal structure of the data is wrong. We typically do not store the player name and their score as a single string. Instead, we use a container of some kind.

Reading and Writing Containers to a File

There are two methods for reading and writing complex data to a file. The first method that will be illustrated is the manual write-your-own format. The second will be using the JSON format to organize our data so that the structure is maintained in the file.

Writing data in memory to a file is called serialization and reading the data back from a file into memory is called deserialization. Code the writes data to disk is called a serializer and code that reads data from a disk is called a deserializer. We will look at writing our own serializer and deserializer and then using Python's provided JSON library to make reading and writing complex data to and from a disk easier.

WRITING DATA FROM MEMORY TO A FILE IS CALLED SERIALIZATION

READING DATA FROM A FILE TO MEMORY IS CALLED DESERIALIZATION

Typically, you will write your own serialization methods when you have a proprietary data structure or format or if you want to obfuscate (scramble and muddle) what you are storing to disguise what you are doing from potential hackers of your game.

Writing Your Own Serializer

The player and their score are related but should not be stored together in a single string. Instead, the high score table will be a dictionary containing the player's names (the key) and their scores (the value):

```
players = { 'Anna': 10000, 'Barney': 9000, 'Jane': 8000,
'Fred': 7000 }
```

We can iterate through the values in the dictionary using the 'for' keyword and obtaining the key for each element in turn. With the key, we can unlock the value like so:

```
for p in players:
    print(p, players[p])
```

This will display the following (almost familiar) output:

```
Anna 10000
Barney 9000
Jane 8000
Fred 7000
```

Create a new program called 'serializer.py' and enter the following code:

```python
def serialize(fileName, players):
    f = open(fileName, 'w')

    for p in players:
        f.write(p + ',' + str(players[p]) + '\n')

    f.close()
```

The serialization method takes two parameters. The first is the name of the file the high score table will be written to and the second is the dictionary containing the player names and scores. Wrapping the score inside the str() function converts the value to a string so that we can use string concatenation (adding two or more strings together).

```python
players = { 'Anna': 10000, 'Barney': 9000, 'Jane': 8000,
'Fred': 7000 }
serialize('highscores.txt', players)
```

The 'players' dictionary is created just above the call to the serialize function – no need to add 'global' inside the function either because the code does not change the 'players' dictionary and we are passing it as a parameter.

This gives us the format that we had before because the same information is written to the file:

```
Anna,10000
Barney,9000
Jane,8000
Fred,7000
```

Now, how do we read the data back from the file and into memory?

Writing Your Own Deserializer

The deserialization has a twist because the data is in a string format – we are writing to a string file after all – and the name and score are separated by a comma (,). Comma separated values are quite common and there is a function called 'split()' that will make separating string values easier. Splitting a string returns an array of strings:

'my, string, here' will split to become *['my', 'string', 'here']*

To ensure that our score is stored in the correct data type the 'int()' function is used. Putting this all together our deserialization function looks like this:

```
def deserialize(fileName, players):
    f = open(fileName, 'r')

    for entry in f:
        split = entry.split(',')
        name = split[0]
        score = int(split[1])

        players[name] = score
```

The function takes two parameters; the first is the name of the file that contains the high score data and the second is the player's dictionary.

Each line is read in from the file and the split() function is called using the comma (,) as the separator. This will split the values into the player name and score. An entry to the dictionary is added where the name is the key and the integer version of the score is the value.

```
players = { }
deserialize('highscores.txt', players)
print(players)
```

147

The 'players' variable is set to be a blank dictionary. Calling the function and displaying the contents:

```
{'Anna': 10000, 'Barney': 9000, 'Jane': 8000, 'Fred': 7000}
```

JSON

JSON stands for JavaScript Object Notation and is a common way for systems to serialize and deserialize data for storage or transmission across a network. The format of a JSON object is very similar to the way that a Python dictionary looks. In fact, they are almost identical. This is the high score table formatted as a JSON string:

```
{"Anna": 10000, "Barney": 9000, "Jane": 8000, "Fred": 7000}
```

Spooky, right!?

Python provides the 'json' module to make reading and writing JSON objects easier through the 'json' object's 'dump()' and 'load()' methods.

To use JSON you must add the following line to the top of your program with the rest of the imports:

```
import json
```

JSON Serialization

JSON serialization is done in one line. Revisiting the high score serializer from earlier, we can rewrite the 'serialize()' function:

```
import json

def serialize(fileName, players):
    f = open(fileName, 'w')
    json.dump(players, f)
    f.close()
```

Instead of having to write out our own format, we let the 'json' object do the heavy lifting. The 'dump()' method writes out the object, no matter what it is, as a JSON formatted string to the file 'f'.

```
players = { 'Anna': 10000, 'Barney': 9000, 'Jane': 8000,
'Fred': 7000 }
serialize('jsonhiscore.txt', players)
```

The part the calls the 'serialize()' method doesn't change; it still passes in two values, but this time I changed the location of the file. Handy things functions!

To view the contents of the file:

```
$ more jsonhiscore.txt
```

This will display the following:

```
{"Anna": 10000, "Barney": 9000, "Jane": 8000, "Fred": 7000}
```

JSON Deserializer

The 'deserialize()' function will change slightly because we will be returning the 'player' dictionary and so we do not need to pass that in as an argument. The 'deserialize()' method program looks like this:

```
import json

def deserialize(fileName):
    f = open(fileName, 'r')
    players = json.load(f)
    f.close()

    return players
```

The 'load()' method on the 'json' object is called passing in the file handle. This function takes the string contents of the file and builds the appropriate Python data structure. The output of this function is stored in the variable 'players' and that is returned to the caller.

```
players = deserialize('jsonhiscore.txt')
print (players)
```

At the function call site, we can see that the 'deserialize()' method has lost a parameter but gained a return value. The return value is a dictionary and that is demonstrated by the output of the 'print()':

```
{'Anna': 10000, 'Barney': 9000, 'Jane': 8000, 'Fred': 7000}
```

Handling Errors

File access can sometimes be a tricky action because files can become locked by the system (virus checkers) or the file you expect to be there might not exist. To handle this, you can use structured error handling (SEH for short). Your program won't crash, but you should handle the event gracefully.

Create a new program in the 'ch13' folder called 'filenotfound.py'. It demonstrates a function that can be used to determine if a file exists or not. The function tries to read the file. If it succeeds, the function returns True, otherwise it returns False:

```
import os

def fileExists(fileName):
    try:
        f = open(fileName, 'r')
        f.close()
        return True
    except IOError:
        return False
```

The code that we want to 'try' to execute is placed inside the 'try' block. If a problem happens, the code inside the 'except' is run. Code inside the 'try' block will stop as soon as it encounters a problem, so if you have a lot of processing in there, some of that code might not execute so it's best to keep the 'try' block as short as possible.

```
print (fileExists('filenotfound.py'))
print (fileExists('this-does-not-exist.txt'))
```

The output of this program is

```
True
False
```

Conclusion

You should now understand how to read from and write to a file. Remember to close the file when you are done. Don't keep the file open for longer than you must; just open it, do what you need to do, and close it as quickly as possible.

Serialization is the process of writing the contents of a variable in memory to a file on disk. The code that writes to disk is called a *serializer*. Deserialization is the process of reading the contents of a file on disk and constructing an in-memory object from it. The code that reads data from disk is called a *deserializer*.

You can write your own serialization/deserialization methods, but it is often easier to use a predetermined format like JSON to perform these operations.

Disk access is sometimes error prone because you are calling the operating system. Occasionally the file may be in use and you will not have access to it. Be sure to use *structured error handling* or SEH for short to safely access files.

CHAPTER 14

Introducing Object-Oriented Programming

Until now we have been using Python as a structured language. Each line is executed one after the other. If we want to reuse code, we create functions. There is another way to program called *object-oriented programming*. In object-oriented programming we create little objects that not only hold our data but group the operations – the things we want to do with that data – with the data itself. The main features of object-oriented programming, or OOP for short, are

- Encapsulation
- Abstraction
- Inheritance
- Polymorphism

The next two chapters will cover the basics of OOP and how it can be used for your games. We will be using a lot of new terms in this chapter. It is a whistle-stop overview of the topic, so don't feel you have to run through this quickly, please take your time.

© Sloan Kelly 2019
S. Kelly, *Python, PyGame, and Raspberry Pi Game Development*,
https://doi.org/10.1007/978-1-4842-4533-0_14

Classes and Objects

A 'class' is a definition of an abstract thing. The 'class' defines methods (actions) that can be taken on the data (attributes) of the 'instance.' Class definitions can be written in the same file as the rest of your Python game. It is, however, more common to place classes in a file of their own.

Function and class definitions stored in a file are called *modules*. We've used modules before to import additional functionality into our games, for example, pygame, os, and sys.

An 'instance' of a class is called an 'object.' An 'instance' of a user-defined class is much like '5' is an instance of an integer, or "Hello, World" is an instance of a string. Both 'integer' and 'string' are abstractions, and '5' and "Hello, World" are instances of each respectively.

OOP allows you to chop your program into discrete bundles, like we did with functions, but where all the data and the code associated with a class are stored together.

Encapsulation

Encapsulation is all about data privacy. The contents of a class – it's state – is kept private and is only accessible to the code inside the class.

The data contained inside a class is called a *private field*. Fields are variables and can be changed and read directly by only the class that owns them.

Fields can be exposed too, although in languages like Java, C#, and C++ this is generally frowned upon. Instead, the internal fields are hidden behind methods called *getters* (for getting data) and *setters* for giving a value to a field. In either case fields are also known as *attributes*.

The functions that are exposed to others are called *public methods*. These allow the outside code to interact with the class.

Abstraction

Along with encapsulation you want to make your class as simple as possible. You don't want people using it to have to do some complex series of steps, or to know too much about the internal workings of your class to use it.

This is where abstraction comes in. To turn on a games console and start playing a game, you press the power button. This is a simple interface – the button – that does a number of steps: performs a self-check called a POST (power on self-test), loads code from the BIOS which in turn launches the Operating System. All you had to do was push a button.

Inheritance

Sometimes you will start writing a class and realize that it copies quite a bit of code from another class. In fact, most of the code is the same as the other class. If only there was a way to share that code. There is! It's called *inheritance* and it allows one class to *derive* from another. This way you only have to write the specific code that changed from your base class. Talking of which, a parent class is called a *base class* and a class that uses another as a basis is called a *subclass* or *derived class*.

Polymorphism

Polymorphism is from Greek and means *many shapes*. In OOP it is sometimes necessary to alter subclasses. Polymorphism can go hand in hand with inheritance. For example, we might have a Shape class that Circle, Square, and Triangle are derived from. The Shape class has a *draw()* method that the other classes implement drawing different shapes onscreen.

Why Should You Use OOP?

OOP allows us to create code that is

- Data hiding

- Reusable

- Easier to code and test separately

Data Hiding

Rather than passing data around the program, or worse of all having global data, the information is stored inside the classes. The data held in these classes can only be accessed through methods exposed by the class. These methods make up the *interface*, that is, how the class is accessed by the other code in your game.

Reusable

Much like functions, classes can be reused by multiple games. You can build up quite a big library of classes over your years programming. Each one of these classes can be used in subsequent projects.

Easier to Code and Test Separately

On a larger project the workload can be divided between developers. With the workload divided the programmers can write the classes and test them in isolation from the rest of the game. By writing and testing the classes separately you increase the chance of reusability because the classes do not rely on each other and can work independently.

The Ball Class

Let's take an example of an object we've seen before: a ball. A ball can be described by its size, shape, and color. These are its attributes. In a game world, we can't do much with a ball, but what we can do is update its position, check for collisions, and draw it onscreen. These actions are called methods.

Create a new folder inside 'pygamebook' called 'ch14.' Copy the 'ball. png' image from the 'Bricks' project to this folder. Inside the folder create a new file called 'BallClass.py.' Add the following lines to the top of the file to tell the shell where to find the Python executable and what modules we will require:

```
#!/usr/bin/python
import pygame, os, sys
from pygame.locals import *
```

In Python we would describe the ball class like this:

```
class Ball:
```

A class is defined using the class keyword. You must give your class a name. Something short and meaningful is perfect, but avoid plurals. If you have a collection of items (like balls) use BallCollection rather than Balls for the name of the class.

```
x = 0
y = 200
speed = (4, 4)
img = pygame.image.load('ball.png')
```

These variables are called 'member fields' and they are stored on a per-object basis. This means that each object gets a separate bit of memory for each field. In our Ball class, we have four such member fields: one each for the coordinates on the x- and y-planes, the ball speed, and one for the ball's image.

```
def update(self, gameTime):
    pass
```

Methods are defined as you would a function with the def keyword, the method/function name, and the parameter list. The major difference is the use of the 'self' keyword as the first entry of the parameter list.

Earlier I mentioned that the member fields are per object. The 'self' keyword is used because Python passes in a reference to the object being used for that operation. Whereas the data is different for each object, the code is not. It is shared between all instances of the class. This means that the same piece of code that updates a ball is used by all instances of the Ball class.

You must always put a 'self' keyword as the first argument in your method's parameter list, even if you have no other parameters.

THE FIRST ARGUMENT IN A CLASS METHOD'S PARAMETER LIST IS ALWAYS 'self'

There's a new keyword in there, and this isn't part of OOP but it's vital in this example. We've produced what is effectively a stub. This means that our class doesn't do much. None of the methods perform any reasonable operation either, but because Python can't have an empty block, we must use the 'pass' keyword instead. This would be the equivalent in a C-style language of doing '{ }'.

```
def hasHitBrick(self, bricks):
    return False
```

This method will return true if the ball has hit a brick. In our stub-code, we always return False.

```
def hasHitBat(self, bat):
    return False
```

Our stub method for testing whether the ball has hit the bat:

```
def draw(self, gameTime, surface):
    surface.blit(self.img, (self.x, self. y))
```

This isn't a stub because we know exactly how this will be achieved. We use the main surface to blit our image to the screen at the correct x- and y-coordinates. To access the object's member field, we must use the 'self' keyword. Attributes and methods belonging to the current object are accessed through 'self' followed by a dot ('.') followed by the attribute or method. When calling the method, you don't pass in 'self,' Python will handle that for you. 'self' is only placed in the parameter list at the method declaration.

```
if __name__ -- '__main__':
```

Python knows the name of each module – remember that a Python file that contains functions and/or class definitions is a *module* – that it is running because it is the name of the file without the '.py' extension.

When you execute a Python script using one of the following methods:

```
$ ./myprogram.py
$ python3 myprogram.py
```

The entry file is given a special name, so instead of 'myprogram,' the name of the entry point file is '__main__.' We can use this to our advantage because it means that we can put our classes in separate files; import them as required; and more importantly, test them in isolation.

This is the beauty of OOP: the fact that you can take small objects, test them in isolation, and then combine them into a much larger program.

In simplest terms, this 'if' statement checks to see if this is the main entry point into our program, and if it is it will run the code block underneath. If it is not, the code block underneath will be ignored. We don't have to remove this code when we use the 'Ball' class in other programs because it will be ignored.

```
pygame.init()
fpsClock = pygame.time.Clock()
surface = pygame.display.set_mode((800, 600))
```

Creating an Instance of the Class

This is our almost-standard initialization code for PyGame. We initialize PyGame and create a clock to clamp our game to 30 frames per second. We create a surface that is 800×600 pixels.

```
ball = Ball()
```

To create an instance of a class, this is all that is required: you assign a new instance of the class to a name, just as you would when you assign a number to a name. The major difference is the parentheses at the end of the assignment. This allows for parameters to be passed to a special method called a constructor. We'll see what a constructor in Python looks like later.

```
while True:
    for event in pygame.event.get():
        if event.type == QUIT:
            pygame.quit()
            sys.exit()
```

We've employed the same code as in the Bricks program to ensure that we listen for system events, especially when those events tell us to close the window.

The ball's position is updated by calling the 'update()' method of the ball object. The implementation of this method will be coded as follows; remember it just contains 'pass' for now:

```
ball.update(fpsClock)
```

Our display update starts with this line:

```
surface.fill((0, 0, 0))
```

Clear the screen for drawing. We don't bother with creating colors here, just passing in a tuple representing the Red, Green, and Blue components (all zero is black) is good enough for our test code.

```
ball.draw(fpsClock, surface)
```

In this line we call the draw() method on the ball object we created a few lines earlier. Although the method signature has three arguments (self, gameTime, and surface) we don't explicitly pass in 'self.' This is passed in my Python itself as the 'ball' instance of the Ball class.

```
pygame.display.update()
fpsClock.tick(30)
```

Finally, we update the display to flip the back buffer to the front buffer and vice versa. We also tick the clock to ensure a steady 30 frames per second.

The Ball update() Method

When we run the program it won't do much; it will in fact just draw the ball in the top left-hand corner of the playing screen. Go back up to the ball's update() method and change it to look like this:

```
def update(self, gameTime):
    sx = self.speed[0]
    sy = self.speed[1]
```

We can't assign values directly to tuples so we'll copy the values into local variables; it saves us typing as well. We can reassign the tuple later.

```
self.x += sx
self.y += sy

if (self.y <= 0):
    self.y = 0
    sy = sy * -1
if (self.y >= 600 - 8):
    self.y = 600 - 8
    sy = sy * -1
if (self.x <= 0):
    self.x = 0
    sx = sx * -1
if (self.x >=800 - 8):
    self.x = 800 - 8
    sx = sx * -1

self.speed = (sx, sy)
```

Any changes to 'sx' and 'sy' will be reassigned to the 'speed' member field.

Save and run the program. You should see the ball bouncing around the screen.

Constructors

A constructor is a special method that is called when an object is instantiated. The method isn't called using the conventional calling method with the object, a dot, and the method name. You've actually been calling the constructor when you created the ball:

```
ball = Ball()
```

Although you didn't explicitly create a constructor, Python creates one for you. It doesn't contain any code and it would look something like this (don't ever do this, it's not worth it; just let Python create one for you behind the scenes):

```
def __init__(self):
    pass
```

The double underscores before and after a name, like __init__, are special method names used by Python. When you want to do something different from the default behavior you will override the default method with your own. Python describes these names as 'magic' and as such you should never invent your own and only use them as documented. Like when we want to create our own constructors.

In Python the constructor method is called init. It takes at least one parameter, the 'self' keyword. In our Ball class, we'll create our own constructor. Remove all these lines from the class:

```
x = 0
y = 24
speed = (4, 4)
img = pygame.image.load('ball.png')
```

Replace them with

```
def __init__(self, x, y, speed, imgPath):
    self.x = x
    self.y = y
    self.speed = speed
    self.img = pygame.image.load(imgPath)
```

Notice that we have to add 'self.' to the name of the member field when we read or write values to it. This is the same when we're in the constructor. Scroll down the source code to the ball initialization line and change that to

```
ball = Ball(0, 200, (4, 4), 'ball.png')
```

This will pass in the start coordinates, speed, and image file used for the ball graphic to the Ball instance that is created. As with functions, the ability to pass values to a constructor is very powerful and allows your objects to be used in many situations.

SOLID

What does all this mean? Well, in an OOP language we have created a class to represent our Ball. We don't care what happens inside that class so long as it does what we expect it to do. Although we will be writing the classes in this book ourselves, we could farm out the work to other developers and give them a specification or interface to code to. So for example, all action objects must have an update() method that takes in an FPS clock.

Classes describe attributes and methods that describe and perform actions, respectively, of an abstract data structure. There is an acronym that describes five principles of object design. For our games, we will try to adhere to these principles:

- Single responsibility

- Open-closed principle

- Liskov substitution

- Interface segregation

- Dependency inversion

The initials of these spell out SOLID. While it is not important to use these techniques in all your games, you should strive to make your classes in such a way that they try to adhere to the principles laid out in the following sections. You may skip this and move onto the conclusion if you wish.

Single Responsibility

Each class should have a single responsibility and that responsibility should be contained within the class. In other words, you have a ball class and its functionality should be wrapped within that class. You should not implement additional functionality, like a Bat inside that same class. Create a separate class for each item. If you have lots of space invaders, you only need to create one Invader class, but you can create an InvaderCollection class to contain all your invaders.

Open-Closed Principle

Your class should be thoroughly tested (hint: name ==' main ') and should be closed from further expansion. It's OK to go in and fix bugs, but your existing classes shouldn't have additional functionality added to them because that will introduce new bugs. You can achieve this in one of two ways: extension or composition.

With extension, you are extending the base class and changing the existing functionality of a method. With composition, you encapsulate the old class inside a new class and use the same interface to change how the caller interacts with the internal class. A class interface is just the list of methods (the actions) that can be performed on the class.

Liskov Substitution

This is by far the trickiest of all the SOLID principles. The idea behind this principle is that when extending a class the subclass should act no different than the class it extends. This is also known as the substitutability of a class.

Interface Segregation

Interface segregation means that you should code to the interface, rather than the implementation. There are other ways to achieve this in other OOP languages, but Python uses something called Duck Typing.

In certain programming languages like Java, C#, and C++, an object's type is used to determine if it is suitable. In Python, however, suitability is determined by the presence of the method or property rather than the type of the object.

If it walks like a duck and it quacks like a duck, it's a duck

Python will try and call a method on an object with the same name and parameters even if they're not the same object. Take this example program. We create two classes: Duck and Person. Each class has a method called Quack(). Watch what happens in the makeItQuack() function. The parameter that is passed gets its Quack() method called

```
class Duck:
    def Quack(self):
        print ("Duck quack!")

class Person:
    def Quack(self):
        print ("Person quack!")
```

```
def makeItQuack(duck):
    duck.Quack()

duck = Duck()
person = Person()

makeItQuack(duck)
makeItQuack(person)
```

We have sort of seen Duck Typing before when we created the add()
function to add two things together; integers, real numbers, strings, and
tuples all worked because they can all be added together using the plus
('+') operator.

Dependency Inversion

Last is dependency inversion. Dependency inversion is a form of decoupling
where higher-level modules (classes) should not depend on lower-level
modules (classes). They should instead both depend on abstractions.
Second, abstractions should not depend on details. Details should depend
on abstractions. Let's create an example to better illustrate this.

```
class Alien(object):
    def __init__(self):
        self.x = 0
        self.y = 0

    def update(self):
        self.x = self.x + 5

    def draw(self):
        print("%d, %d" % (self.x, self.y))
alien1 = Alien()
alien1.update()
alien1.draw()
```

The Alien class breaks the Open/Closed principle because it is closed for extension; we'd have to create a new class if we wanted to have an alien that moved diagonally. What we need is another class to calculate the new position of the alien, like this:

```
class Strafe(object):
    def update(self, obj):
        obj.x = obj.x + 5
```

We have a separate class to represent how each alien in our game moves across the screen. These classes can be passed into the Alien object when it is created. Let's say we want to move an alien diagonally:

```
class Diagonal(object):
    def update(self, alien):
        obj.x = obj.x + 5
        obj.y = obj.y + 5
```

The movement classes Strafe and Diagonal don't need to know what they are moving, so long as they have fields called 'x' and 'y.' Similarly, the Alien class does not need to know what the Strafe and Diagonal classes do so long as they have an update() method.

```
class Alien(object):
    def __init__(self, movement):
        self.x = 0
        self.y = 0
        self.movement = movement

    def update(self):
        self.movement.update(self)
```

```python
    def draw(self):
        print("%d, %d" % (self.x, self.y))

class Strafe(object):
    def update(self, obj):
        obj.x = obj.x + 5

class Diagonal(object):
    def update(self, obj):
        obj.x = obj.x + 5
        obj.y = obj.y + 5

alien1 = Alien(Strafe())
alien2 = Alien(Diagonal())

alien1.update()
alien1.update()

alien2.update()
alien2.update()

alien1.draw()
alien2.draw()
```

It seems a little over the top to create separate classes for each movement method, but it does mean that in this example you wouldn't have to create a new alien class for each movement method. For example if you wanted to add a vertical movement it's a simple matter of adding a few lines of code. In fact, the movement class could take input from another player from the other side of the world, the Alien class would never need to know.

Conclusion

This has been a short introduction to OOP. By this point you should understand the following:

- Attributes are member fields and contain data that describes the class.

- Methods are functions that belong to a class that perform actions on the class.

- Self is used to reference.

- A constructor can be used to initialize member fields when the object instance is created.

- Python uses Duck Typing; when you see a bird that walks like a duck, swims like a duck, and quacks like a duck ... it's a duck.

As an exercise, create a new blank file called BatClass and implement a class called 'Bat.' You can use the code from the Brick game as a starting point.

CHAPTER 15

Inheritance, Composition, and Aggregation

When most people learn about object-oriented programming, they learn three things:

- Objects have attributes (data) that contain the object's state.

- Methods that control access (change or view) the object's state.

- Objects can be extended using a technique called inheritance.

There are others, but those are the three main things that people remember about their first introduction to object-oriented programming.

Most people fixate on that last one: object extension by inheritance. That's true in a lot of cases, but there are ways that objects can be extended using techniques called composition and aggregation. This section will introduce the three methods of object extension.

© Sloan Kelly 2019
S. Kelly, *Python, PyGame, and Raspberry Pi Game Development*,
https://doi.org/10.1007/978-1-4842-4533-0_15

Inheritance

Inheritance occurs at the very base level of the Python language. When you create a new class, you are extending a base class called 'object.' This simple object

```
class Foo:
    def bar(self):
        print("bar")

foo = Foo()
foo.bar()
```

can be rewritten explicitly as

```
class Foo(object):
    def bar(self):
        print("bar")

foo = Foo()
foo.bar()
```

Indeed, if you are using the newer Python syntax you are encouraged to use this syntax. You will see it used in the 'Invaders' game later in this very text. For more information regarding the old way vs. the new way, please visit https://wiki.python.org/moin/NewClassVsClassicClass.

USE THE NEWER MyClass(object) SYNTAX WHEN DEFINING CLASSES.

Taking this a step further, let's create two classes. The first is a base class.

A base class contains the basic level of functionality that is required to perform a given set of actions. It can contain methods that are placeholders for actions that will be implemented by a child class.

A child class is any class that derives from another class. In actuality, every class you create is a child class of the Python base 'object' class.

Base and Child Classes

Create a new folder inside 'pygamebook' called 'ch15' and inside this new folder, create a file called 'baseclass.py' and enter the following code:

```
class MyBaseClass(object):
    def methodOne(self):
        print ("MyBaseClass::methodOne()")
```

When a class derives from another class, remember to put the base class' name in parentheses after your new class' name:

```
class MyChildClass(MyBaseClass):
    def methodOne(self):
        print ("MyChildClass::methodOne()")
```

We'll create a function to call the methodOne() method of each class:

```
def callMethodOne(obj):
    obj.methodOne()
```

This method takes in a single parameter 'obj' and calls the methodOne() method of that object.

```
instanceOne = MyBaseClass()
instanceTwo = MyChildClass()
```

It then creates an instance of the 'MyBaseClass' and 'MyChildClass' classes.

```
callMethodOne(instanceOne)
callMethodOne(instanceTwo)
```

Using the function, we pass in our instances of the base and child classes. Save and run the program. You should see

```
MyBaseClass::methodOne()
MyChildClass::methodOne()
```

The function is called and it, in turn, takes the parameter and calls the methodOne() method of the object that it receives. Add another line after the last callMethodOne() line:

```
callMethodOne(5)
```

Run the program. You should see output similar to

```
MyBaseClass::methodOne()MyChildClass::methodOne()
Traceback (most recent call last):
File "baseclass.py", line 26, in <module>
callMethodOne(5)
File "baseclass.py", line 17, in callMethodOne
obj.methodOne()
AttributeError: 'int' object has no attribute 'methodOne'
```

This is because the 'int' object that is built into Python does not contain a method called 'methodOne.'

Python uses a technique called duck typing.

> *When I see a bird that walks like a duck and swims like a duck and quacks like a duck, I call that bird a duck.*

This means that when Python sees a method call on an object, it assumes that that message can be passed to it. The benefit of this technique is that inheritance has been almost superseded by a technique called programming to the interface.

Programming to the interface means that you don't need to worry about the internal workings of the object; you just need to know what methods are available.

There is still an applicable use for inheritance though. For example, you may have a base class that provides much of the functionality required. Subclasses would then implement their specific methods.

Programming to the Interface

Let's take a look at another example. Rather than using inheritance, we'll use the same method for two different objects:

```
class Dog(object):
    def makeNoise(self):
        print ("Bark!")

class Duck(object):
    def makeNoise(self):
        print ("Quack!")

animals = [ Dog(), Duck() ]

for a in animals:
    a.makeNoise()
```

Our two classes – Dog and Duck – both contain a method called makeNoise(). A list of animals is created that contains an instance of Dog and Duck classes. Iteration through the list is then used to call the makeNoise() method for each object.

A Note About Constructors and Base Classes

To round off inheritance, we need to mention the recommended steps in calling the base class of an object's constructor. Take the following two classes as an example:

```
class Foo(object):
    x = 0

    def __init__(self):
        print ("Foo constructor")
        self.x = 10
```

175

```
    def printNumber(self):
        print (self.x)

class Bar(Foo):
    def __init__(self):
        print ("Bar constructor")

b = Bar()
b.printNumber()
```

When you run this code you will get the following output:

```
Bar constructor
0
```

Even though 'Bar' extends 'Foo', it hasn't initialized the 'x' field because the init () method of the parent class was not called. To properly do that, change the constructor of 'Bar' to

```
    def __init__(self):
        super(Bar, self).__init__()
        print ("Bar constructor")
```

What is going here? The super() method allows us to reference the base class; however, the base class needs to know two things: the derived class type and the instance. We achieve this by passing in the type of our derived class – 'Bar' in this case and 'self.' We can then call the method __init__() to set up our fields correctly. When you run the program, you should see

```
Foo constructor
Bar constructor
10
```

You must always call your base class's constructor before you write any other code in your derived class's constructor. This is especially true if you are creating a base class with lots of functionality and inheriting from it. Make sure you call the base class's constructor!

176

Composition

Composition is the containment of one or more objects inside another. With composition, the contained objects' creation and destruction are controlled by the container object. The container object generally acts as a controller for the contained objects. For example:

```
class Alien:
    def __init__(self, x, y):
        self.x = x
        self.y = y

    def draw(self):
        pass
```

The 'Alien' class contains just the x- and y-coordinates that would be used to display an alien at a particular point onscreen. Other attributes that you might want to add would be the type of alien or its shield strength.

```
class AlienSwarm:
    def __init__(self, numAliens):
        self.swarm = []
        y = 0
        x = 24
        for n in range(numAliens):
            alien = Alien(x, y)
            self.swarm.append(alien)
            x += 24
            if x > 640:
                x = 0
                y += 24
```

The __init__() method takes a single parameter that represents the number of aliens in the swarm. The logic in the method ensures that the swarm is evenly distributed across the screen. Each alien is separated by 24 pixels across and 24 pixels down.

177

```python
    def debugPrint(self):
        for a in self.swarm:
            print ("x=%d, y=%d" % (a.x, a.y))

    def isHit(self, x, y):
        alienToRemove = None
        for a in self.swarm:
            print ("Checking Alien at (%d, %d)" % (a.x, a.y))
            if x>=a.x and x <= a.x + 24 and y >= a.y and
            y <= a.y + 24:
                print ("  It's a hit! Alien is going down!")
                alienToRemove = a
                break
        if alienToRemove != None:
            self.swarm.remove(alienToRemove)
            return True

        return False

swarm = AlienSwarm(5)
swarm.debugPrint()
```

The 'break' keyword is used to exit from the enclosed loop. When the 'break' keyword is executed the control of the program jumps to the line immediately after the loop statements. A related keyword is 'continue.' Continue stops processing the remaining statements in the current iteration of the loop and moves control back to the top of the loop. Both 'break' and 'continue' work with any loop structure.

The Alien class is never called outside the AlienSwarm. It is created by the AlienSwarm class, and any interaction with the outside world is also done through this class.

Aggregation

Aggregation is, conceptually, much like composition. A container object has a link to other objects and it manipulates them in some form, through a method or methods. However, the big difference is that the creation and destruction of the objects are handled elsewhere outside of the class. With aggregation, the container class must not delete objects that it uses.

Say we have a Collision class and we want to check if any of the player's bullets have hit an alien, we could implement something like this – assuming Alien and AlienSwarm remain unchanged:

```
class Bullet:
    dcf __init__(self, x, y):
        self.x = x
        self.y = y

class Player:
    def __init__(self):
        self.bullets = [Bullet(24, 8)]
        self.score = 0

    def getBullets(self):
        return self.bullets

    def removeBullet(self, bullet):
        self.bullets.remove(bullet)

class Collision:
    def __init__(self, player, swarm):
        self.player = player
        self.swarm = swarm

    def checkCollisions(self):
        bulletKill = []
```

```
        for b in player.getBullets():
            if swarm.isHit(b.x, b.y):
                bulletKill.append(b)
                continue

    for b in bulletKill:
        self.player.score += 10
        print ("Score: %d" % self.player.score)
        self.player.removeBullet(b)

swarm = AlienSwarm(5)
player = Player()
collision = Collision(player, swarm)
collision.checkCollisions()
```

The Collision class is an aggregation, that is, it contains a reference to two other classes: Player and AlienSwarm. It does not control the creation and deletion of those classes.

This ties in with our SOLID principal; each class should have a single purpose and should be independent of each other. In this case, our Player class does not need to know about aliens, and likewise the AlienSwarm class doesn't need to know about players. We can use our interfaces to create a class that sits in between the two to allow us (the programmer) to determine if a collision has occurred.

Conclusion

Python allows for standard OOP techniques but offers its own unique twist: duck typing. By programming to the interface, we can ensure that our classes can be written independently of each other.

PROGRAM TO THE INTERFACE TO KEEP YOUR CLASSES SMALL AND NIMBLE

CHAPTER 16

Game Project: Snake

For our second game we are going to re-create the classic Snake game. Snake has been with us since the late 1970s and, if you had a Nokia phone, you probably had a version of the game on it. You control a snake, and you move around the screen using the cursor keys. You must eat fruit to grow. You are not allowed to touch the outside walls or yourself. Did I mention that you are growing? See Figure 16-1.

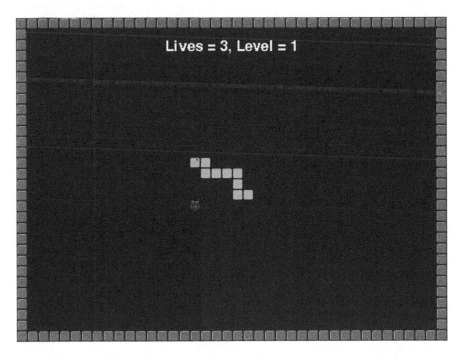

Figure 16-1. *Snake game running*

© Sloan Kelly 2019
S. Kelly, *Python, PyGame, and Raspberry Pi Game Development*,
https://doi.org/10.1007/978-1-4842-4533-0_16

In this game we are going to introduce the following:

- Class declarations and instances (objects)

- File input

- Cell-based collision detection

- Functions

- Text fonts

Snake will use more functions than object-oriented techniques. For the most part, our objects in this game will be for organizational purposes only. There will be very little OOP involved.

Functions

The following functions are defined:

- drawData

- drawGameOver

- drawSnake

- drawWalls

- headHitBody

- headHitWall

- loadImages

- loadMapFile

- loseLife

- positionBerry

- updateGame

We can create a structured diagram in Figure 16-2 showing how these functions all work together.

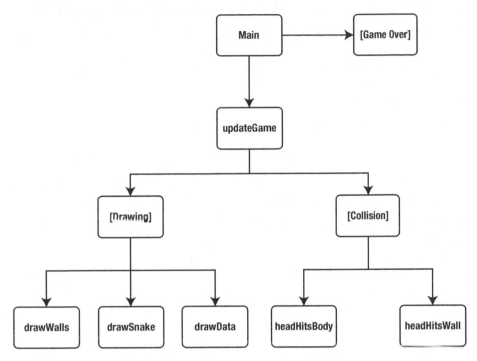

Figure 16-2. *Structured diagram for the Snake game*

The structured diagram shows how each function interacts with each other. The functions enclosed in parentheses don't exist. They are used to group together like functions. For example, drawing the game calls three separate functions. We could create another function – I will leave that to the reader's discretion.

Snake Framework

The basic outline for the Snake game is shown in the following. Create a new file in your working folder and call it snake.py. Type the code in exactly as follows. Don't forget to read the comments as you go to help you understand what's going on and what the intent of the author (me) was. We'll replace some of the comments with code later on in this section. You should include the comments in your own listings as you type the code. This will act as placeholders for the later code.

```
#!/usr/bin/python
import pygame, os, sys
import random
from pygame.locals import *
```

By now you should recognize the familiar start to our programs! The hash-bang and the import of the Python modules we need: PyGame, OS, and System. We're also importing a new one for this game: Random. This module will allow us to generate a random starting position for the berry.

```
pygame.init()
fpsClock = pygame.time.Clock()
surface = pygame.display.set_mode((640, 480))
font = pygame.font.Font(None, 32)
```

To keep the map size down, the game will run in a 640×480 window. We'll see in a second how to create the map. Our PyGame initialization and clock to keep everything at 30 frames per second are also initialized here. Our last bit of initialization is to create a font object using the default font with a size of 32 pixels.

```
class Position:
    def __init__(self, x, y):
        self.x = x
        self.y = y
```

Our first class is a simple one: Position. This holds the position of a map block. We use the constructor (in Python, that's the init () method) to pass in the x- and y-coordinates.

```
class GameData:
    def __init__(self):
        self.lives = 3
        self.isDead = False
        self.blocks = []
        self.tick = 250
        self.speed = 250
        self.level = 1
        self.berrycount = 0
        self.segments = 1
        self.frame = 0

        bx = random.randint(1, 38)
        by = random.randint(1, 28)

        self.berry = Position(bx, by)
        self.blocks.append(Position(20,15))
        self.blocks.append(Position(19,15))
        self.direction = 0
```

The GameData holds just about everything we need to store about the game. The majority of this data is for the player's snake.

- lives – The number of lives the player has left.

- isDead – Is set to true when the snake's head touches a piece of the tail or a wall.

- blocks – The list of blocks that make up the tail of the snake.

- tick – The running total used to count down to the next animation frame. In milliseconds.

- speed – The default tick speed. Also in milliseconds.

- level – The current level of difficulty.

185

- berrycount – The number of berries consumed by the snake in this level.

- segments – The number of segments added when a berry is consumed. This value changes each level.

- frame – The current animation frame used to draw the snake's head. The snake has two frames of animation, not unlike Pacman.

- direction – The current traveling direction of the snake. 0 is right, 1 is left, 2 is up, and 3 is down. The snake can only move in one of those four directions. They also cannot reverse direction. For example, if the snake is traveling right, the player cannot move to the left. They can move either up or down, or continue going right.

The snake starts out with two blocks that are represented by two instances of the 'Position' class; that means that it has one head segment and one tail segment. The number of segments grows every time a berry is consumed.

Berry positions, bx and by, are used to position a berry at a location on the game screen. These are stored in the 'berry' attribute of the GameData class.

```
def loseLife(gamedata):
    pass

def positionBerry(gamedata):
    pass

def loadMapFile(fileName):
    return None

def headHitBody(gamedata):
    return False
```

```
def headHitWall(map, gamedata):
    return False

def drawData(surface, gamedata):
    pass

def drawGameOver(surface):
    pass

def drawWalls(surface, img, map):
    pass

def drawSnake(surface, img, gamedata):
    pass

def updateGame(gamedata, gameTime):
    pass

def loadImages():
    return {}
```

These are all the functions that were drawn on the structured diagram.

They will be discussed in detail when we start implementing the functionality for the game.

```
images = loadImages()
images['berry'].set_colorkey((255, 0, 255))
```

Our images are loaded in using the loadImages() function. The images are stored in a dictionary. The key is a string value, and the example given shows that we are setting the color key of the 'berry' image to purple (Red = 255, Green = 0, and Blue = 255). PyGame will not draw any pixel of that image that matches the supplied color. This means that you can have transparent pixels in your image. This is handy for windows or complex shapes like a berry.

```
snakemap = loadMapFile('map.txt')
data = GameData()
quitGame = False
isPlaying = False
```

These local (to the main game loop) variables are used to store the
map, create an instance of the GameData class, a control variable to
determine if the user quits the game, and finally one to determine if the
user is playing the game. The default value is 'False' because we want to
start the game in "Game Over" mode to allow the user to choose whether
to play the game or exit the application.

```
while not quitGame:
    for event in pygame.event.get():
        if event.type == QUIT:
            pygame.quit()
            sys.exit()
```

In a real game you probably wouldn't want to quit the game if the user
closed the window. Or, at the very least you would want to prompt them to
confirm the action. In this simple game, however, we just close the game
and quit to the desktop.

```
    if isPlaying:
        x = random.randint(1, 38)
        y = random.randint(1, 28)
```

Our screen size is 40 blocks along by 30 blocks down. For a 640×480
screen that means that we have a block size of 16×16 pixels. The random
value that is generated here will be used to place the berry that will be
consumed by the player-controlled snake.

Our random values are between 1 and 38 because we want to produce
a value in the range 1 to 38 inclusive. Our map is going to be a solid block
that makes up the border of the playing area. We'll discuss this in detail in
a following section.

```
rrect = images['berry'].get_rect()
rrect.left = data.berry.x * 16
rrect.top = data.berry.y * 16
```

Now that we have our random values for the x- and y-coordinates we will assign them to the left and top fields of the berry image rectangle.

The coordinates are multiplied by 16 because each cell is 16×16 in size.

```
# Do update stuff here
```

Our update routines will go here. This is just a placeholder comment. This type of comment will be used throughout the book. If you see comments as part of the 'type in' code, please include it with your own source code. We will return to this point later on in the text, and if you don't have it, it could lead to confusion.

```
isPlaying = (data.lives > 0)
```

This is a nice short form way to set the isPlaying variable to false if the player has no lives left. You could easily rewrite this as an 'if' statement. How would you go about that?

```
if (isPlaying):
```

The value to isPlaying could have changed after the previous line. This is why we do another if-check of this variable here.

```
        surface.fill((0, 0, 0))
        # Do drawing stuff here
    else:
```

If the game is *not* playing then it's in the "Game Over" mode. Be careful with this 'else' because it is paired with the *previous* 'if' statement. The "Game Over" mode displays a message to the user. If they want to play the game again, the user must press 'space' on the keyboard.

```
keys = pygame.key.get_pressed()

if (keys[K_SPACE]):
    isPlaying = True
    data = None
    data = GameData()
```

If the user presses the spacebar, we set the isPlaying flag to true and reset the data to a new instance of GameData. It is good practice when you have finished with an object to set the variable that points to it to 'None.'

```
drawGameOver(surface)
```

The "Game Over" screen is drawn by calling the drawGameOver() function.

```
pygame.display.update()
fpsClock.tick(30)
```

Our last lines flip the screen (double-buffered display) and clamp the frame rate to a maximum of 30 frames per second. Save the program. The program won't run just now; we need to load the images and the map data first before we can see anything onscreen.

Images

The game needs the following images:

- berry.png – The berry that the snake eats

- snake.png – A multiframe image that contains all the images used by the snake

- wall.png – A block that the snake cannot travel through

Our images are 16×16 except for snake.png, which is 144×16 pixels. The reason for this is that all the images that we want for the snake are included in the same file. See Figure 16-3.

Figure 16-3. *The frames of the snake*

These images, as with all the examples in this book, can be downloaded from http://sloankelly.net.

Loading the Images

Copy or make the images and put them in the same directory as the snake. py file. Locate the loadImages() function and change it to look like this:

```
def loadImages():
    wall = pygame.image.load('wall.png')
    raspberry = pygame.image.load('berry.png')
    snake = pygame.image.load('snake.png')
```

The images are loaded in separately, but we're going to put them in a dictionary to keep all the images together.

```
    return {'wall':wall, 'berry':raspberry, 'snake':snake}
```

The next step is to create and load the map that makes up the game screen.

The Game Map

The map for the game is held in a text file called map.txt. Create a new file called 'map.txt' in the same folder as 'snake.py'. In this file enter the following text:

```
1111111111111111111111111111111111111111
1000000000000000000000000000000000000001
1000000000000000000000000000000000000001
1000000000000000000000000000000000000001
1000000000000000000000000000000000000001
1000000000000000000000000000000000000001
1000000000000000000000000000000000000001
1000000000000000000000000000000000000001
1000000000000000000000000000000000000001
1000000000000000000000000000000000000001
1000000000000000000000000000000000000001
1000000000000000000000000000000000000001
1000000000000000000000000000000000000001
1000000000000000000000000000000000000001
1000000000000000000000000000000000000001
1000000000000000000000000000000000000001
1000000000000000000000000000000000000001
1000000000000000000000000000000000000001
1000000000000000000000000000000000000001
1000000000000000000000000000000000000001
1000000000000000000000000000000000000001
1000000000000000000000000000000000000001
1000000000000000000000000000000000000001
1000000000000000000000000000000000000001
1000000000000000000000000000000000000001
1000000000000000000000000000000000000001
1000000000000000000000000000000000000001
1000000000000000000000000000000000000001
```

```
100000000000000000000000000000000000000001
100000000000000000000000000000000000000001
111111111111111111111111111111111111111111
```

That's 30 lines of text. The top and bottom lines are

```
111111111111111111111111111111111111111111
```

And the rest of the lines are

```
100000000000000000000000000000000000000001
```

You can experiment with different patterns of 0s and 1s if you like. Each '0' represents an open space that the snake can travel through. Each '1' represents a wall block that will kill the snake if it is touched. Save this file and open snake.py. Locate the loadMapFile() function and change it to

```
def loadMapFile(fileName):
    f = open(fileName, 'r')
    content = f.readlines()
    f.close()
    return content
```

The readlines() method reads each line of text in a file into a list. Save the 'snake.py' file.

Drawing the 'Game Over' Screen

If we run the game now, we will see nothing because we have not implemented any of the drawing methods. Let's start by showing the "Game Over" screen. Locate the drawGameOver() function and change it to

```
def drawGameOver(surface):
    text1 = font.render("Game Over", 1, (255, 255, 255))
    text2 = font.render("Space to play or close the window", 1,
    (255, 255, 255))
```

Font's render() method creates a PyGame surface that will fit the text exactly. The parameters that the render() method takes are the string that is to be displayed, the anti-aliasing level, and the color.

Anti-aliasing means that the text won't appear with jaggy edges. In Figure 16-4 you can see the effects of anti-aliasing vs. having no aliasing.

Figure 16-4. *The anti-aliased version of the font is shown in the bottom half of the image*

The image has been split down the middle and shows the anti-aliased text to the left of the red line and the aliased version to the right.

```
cx = surface.get_width() / 2
cy = surface.get_height() / 2
textpos1 = text1.get_rect(centerx=cx, top=cy - 48)
textpos2 = text2.get_rect(centerx=cx, top=cy)
```

We're using named arguments here because we don't need to specify all the values for the text positions. These two lines create the rectangles that are used to place the text in the middle of the screen.

```
surface.blit(text1, textpos1)
surface.blit(text2, textpos2)
```

The blit() method of the surface instance passed to the function is used to draw the text on the surface. Save and run the game. You should now see the following screen (as shown in Figure 16-5) appear when you run the game:

Game Over

Space to play or close the window

Figure 16-5. *The "Game Over" screen, as it appears when the game starts*

Close the window when you've finished. If you press 'space' the screen will go blank and nothing will happen because we haven't added the functions to update or draw the screen. Let's add the drawing functions now.

Drawing the Game

The drawing of the snake, the playing area, and the game data (player's lives, score, and level text) are performed by three functions:

- drawWalls

- DrawSnake

- drawData

In 'snake.py', scroll down in the source code to the line that reads

```
# Do drawing stuff here
```

Add the following lines just underneath that comment. Be sure that you get the right number of tabs per line. The left column of each line should start directly under the '#' of the comment:

```
drawWalls(surface, images['wall'], snakemap)
surface.blit(images['berry'], rrect)
drawSnake(surface, images['snake'], data)
drawData(surface, data)
```

There isn't a specific routine for drawing the berry, so we just call the main surface's blit() method directly. There is an order to how we draw things onscreen. Images drawn on the screen after other images will appear on top. So, the walls appear behind the snake, and the snake appears behind the lives/score display.

Drawing the Walls

The walls are drawn in the drawWalls() function. Locate this function in the source code and change it to read

```
def drawWalls(surface, img, map):
```

The function takes three parameters. The first argument is the main surface that we will draw our wall blocks on. The second is the image we will use to represent a brick in the wall, and finally the third argument is the map data. This is the data we loaded from the file earlier on.

```
row = 0

for line in map:
    col = 0
    for char in line:
        if ( char == '1'):
```

For each character in the line we examine it. If the character is '1' we put down a block. Because we are keeping count of the row (variable 'row') and column (variable 'col'), calculating the onscreen position is just a matter of multiplying each by 16. Why? Because our block image is 16×16 pixels and our file is not mapped per pixel. Instead, each character in the map file represents a 16×16 block.

It is an array of characters arranged from zero to the maximum row and column we have given. In this game's case, that maximum is 40 blocks by 30 blocks. For a 640×480 screen, that's 16×16 pixels per block.

```
imgRect = img.get_rect()
imgRect.left = col * 16
imgRect.top = row * 16
surface.blit(img, imgRect)
```

The image rectangle's left and top values are changed each time a block is drawn to ensure the image is drawn to the surface at the right position.

```
        col += 1
    row += 1
```

Save and run the game. When you press the spacebar to start the game, you will see the wall around the playing field and the berry. Close the game when you are ready and let's start adding the lives, level, and score display. See Figure 16-6.

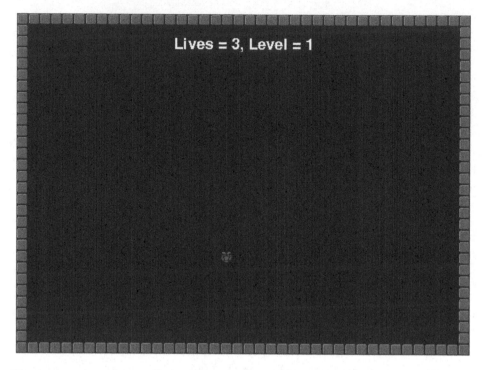

Figure 16-6. *The wall and berry displayed when the game is run with the code up to this point*

Drawing the Player Data

The player needs some feedback on how well they are doing. This is usually an indicator of their score, the number of lives left, and usually the current level. We will add code to the drawData() function to give our player's feedback. Locate the drawData() function in code and change it to this:

```
def drawData(surface, gamedata):
```

The function takes in two parameters. The first is the surface we will draw the data on. The second is the actual game data itself. A new string function is introduced called format. It's similar to the one used for the print() method, but the result can be stored in a variable. Instead of %d and %s for numbers and strings, placeholders are used. The first variable is {0}, the second is {1}, and so on:

```
text = "Lives = {0}, Level = {1}"
info = text.format(gamedata.lives, gamedata.level)
text = font.render(info, 0, (255, 255, 255))
textpos = text.get_rect(centerx=surface.get_width()/2, top=32)
surface.blit(text, textpos)
```

The data is rendered as text using a tuple to inject the data into a string. This is called string formatting and we saw this kind of code when we looked at tuples in the previous sections.

Save the program at this point. You can run it if you wish. This time, when the game starts you will see the player's lives and current level at the top of the screen.

Drawing the Snake

Drawing the snake is a little more complex than our previous drawing functions – that's why I left it for last! Our snake image (the actual .png file) is 144 pixels by 16, which means that it contains nine 16×16 images. We need to somehow slice them up into individual images.

Locate the drawSnake() function in the code and change it to read

```
def drawSnake(surface, img, gamedata):
```

The function takes in three parameters. The first is the surface that the snake is to be drawn on. The second is the snake image, and last the third parameter is the GameData instance. This holds all the information about our snake. Specifically, the blocks attribute of the GameData class contains a list of coordinates in the range 0..39 for the column and 0..29 for the row. The coordinates are stored as instances of the 'Position' class.

199

These coordinates are instances of the Position class. The blocks attribute is a list and as the snake grows, the number of items in this list grows.

```
first = True
```

This is set to true because the first block drawn is special. It is the head of the snake. The image that we draw here depends on

- The direction the snake is facing

- Whether its mouth is open or not

Look at the snake image again in Figure 16-7.

Figure 16-7. *The snake image contains coded data for the snake's head and its tail section*

There is actually a pattern to the sub-images. The last cell is the normal tail block. The remaining eight blocks represent the head of the snake. Their position in the array corresponds to the direction of the snake:

- 0 – Right

- 1 – Left

- 2 – Up

- 3 – Down

If we multiply the direction number – which is stored in GameData's direction attribute – by two we get the starting cell number for the image we want. The snake's head is animated, too – it opens and closes. All we have to do is add the current frame (GameData's frame attribute) to get the required image.

```
for b in gamedata.blocks:
    dest = (b.x * 16, b.y * 16, 16, 16)
```

We cycle through all the blocks (positions) of the snake in the list. The destination is a simple calculation: the position multiplied by the dimensions of a single cell (16×16 pixels) to give the screen coordinate.

```
if first:
    first = False
    src = (((gamedata.direction * 2) + gamedata.frame)
    * 16, 0, 16, 16)
```

If we are at the head of the list, we draw the head of the snake. Remember that we can draw a part of an image by specifying a tuple that represents the starting x- and y-pixels of the sub-image and its width and height.

For our snake, our sub-image's x-coordinate is calculated using this formula:

((direction * 2) + animation_frame) * 16

Our image is taken from the top of the sprite sheet, the top is where the y-coordinate is 0 (zero). Our dimensions of width and height are also fixed at 16×16 pixels.

```
else:
    src = (8 * 16, 0, 16, 16)
```

For normal blocks, we just want to draw the last image in the snake.png file. This is the rightmost 16×16 square, which happens to be the eighth frame of the image. We could have hard-wired the value, but 8 * 16 makes for a little more descriptive code in this case.

```
surface.blit(img, dest, src)
```

Save and run the game and you will see the snake, the wall, and the player data, as shown in Figure 16-8.

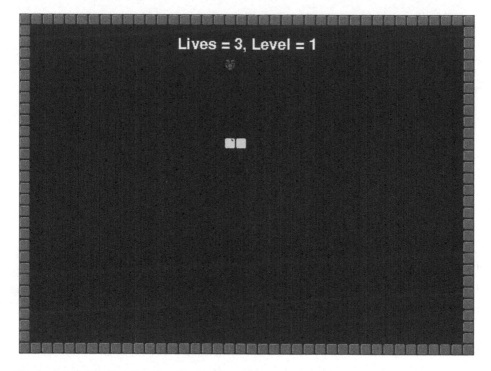

Figure 16-8. *Snake, berry, and walls*

Updating the Game

Static screens, as fun as they are, are no substitute for actually playing the game! However, we haven't implemented any routines to get player input, check for collisions, or update the player's data. Locate the following line:

```
# Do update stuff here
```

Just after the line, add the following code:

```
updateGame(data, fpsClock.get_time())
```

The majority of the update code resides in the updateGame() function. We'll examine that in detail in a moment.

```
crashed = headHitWall(snakemap, data) or headHitBody(data)
if (crashed):
    loseLife(data)
    positionBerry(data)
```

We now test to see if the snake's head has hit a wall (headHitWall() function) or its own body (headHitBody() function). If that's the case, the player loses a life and the berry is repositioned.

The updateGame() Method

This is the largest method in the game and it does the most work. Its purpose is to

- Update the snake's head and tail

- Get input from the player

- Check to see if the snake's head hit the berry

Browse to the part of the code that looks like this:

```
def updateGame(gamedata, gameTime):
    pass
```

Change this function to

```
def updateGame(gamedata, gameTime):
    gamedata.tick -= gameTime
    head = gamedata.blocks[0]
```

Each part of your game can update at a different rate. For example, you may only want to update certain parts of your game once per second, and others you might want to update 30 times a second. This can be achieved by reading the system clock and determining the number of milliseconds since the code was last called. In this method, we are passing in the difference (in milliseconds) since the last call as 'gameTime.'

203

The gamedata's tick is decremented by the current game time. When this counter hits zero, we update the snake's head to show it closed (if it's currently open) or open if it's currently closed. We also take note of the current position of the head of the snake. This is always the zeroth element of the blocks attribute of the 'gamedata.'

```python
if (gamedata.tick < 0):
    gamedata.tick += gamedata.speed
    gamedata.frame += 1
    gamedata.frame %= 2
```

If the tick attribute is less than zero, we add the speed to it to start the timer all over again. We then add one to the current frame count. We use the modulo calculation to clamp the value to 0 or 1 because we only have two frames of animation. In other languages there is a 'switch' or 'case' statement. This isn't the case (sorry) in Python, but it's easily achievable using nested if/elif statements.

```python
if (gamedata.direction == 0):
    move = (1, 0)
elif (gamedata.direction == 1):
    move = (-1, 0)
elif (gamedata.direction == 2):
    move = (0, -1)
else:
    move = (0, 1)
```

In the game of Snake, the snake is always moving; the player only controls direction. Based upon the direction the player wants the snake to move, the appropriate tuple is created.

```python
newpos = Position(head.x + move[0], head.y + move[1])
```

This tuple is then used to generate and store the new position for the head of the snake.

```
first = True
for b in gamedata.blocks:
    temp = Position(b.x, b.y)
    b.x = newpos.x
    b.y = newpos.y
    newpos = Position(temp.x, temp.y)
```

The tail of the snake moves up to follow the head. This of course is just an illusion; what we actually do is move the segments of the snake to the previous segment's position.

Snake Movement

Keeping with the updateGame() function; snake movement is clamped to one of four directions: left, right, up, and down. The player can only really suggest the movement: the snake itself moves under its own steam. The snake's direction is chosen by the player by pressing one of the arrow keys on the keyboard.

To get the keyboard input we fetch the list of keys that are currently pressed:

```
keys = pygame.key.get_pressed()
```

The get_pressed() method returns a dictionary of Boolean values. Now that we have the keys pressed, we can test each of the arrow keys to see if the player has depressed it. We also must make sure that they are not trying to go in the opposite direction. The player can't turn right if they are already heading left, they can't turn up if they are already heading down, etc.

```
if (keys[K_RIGHT] and gamedata.direction != 1):
    gamedata.direction = 0
elif (keys[K_LEFT] and gamedata.direction != 0):
    gamedata.direction = 1
elif(keys[K_UP] and gamedata.direction != 3):
    gamedata.direction = 2
elif(keys[K_DOWN] and gamedata.direction != 2):
    gamedata.direction = 3
```

We store the current direction in the direction field of the 'gamedata' instance.

Touching a Berry

The last part of the updateGame() function is to handle our reaction to the snake head touching a berry. To progress through the game, the player must get the snake to 'eat' the berries that appear on the playing field. To 'eat' the berries, the player has to steer the head of the snake over the cell that the berry appears. Once the berry has been 'devoured,' a new berry is positioned at another random position onscreen and the snake grows by a certain number of segments. The number of segments depends on what level the player is on. The higher the level, the more segments are added to the snake.

```
if (head.x == gamedata.berry.x and head.y == gamedata.berry.y):
    lastIdx = len(gamedata.blocks) - 1
    for i in range(gamedata.segments):
        blockX = gamedata.blocks[lastIdx].x
        blockY = gamedata.blocks[lastIdx].y
        gamedata.blocks.append(Position(blockX, blockY))
```

If the head of the snake is in the same cell as the berry, then we append the appropriate number of segments to the end of the snake. The number of segments we add to the end depends on the level in the game. The higher the level, the more segments are added. This makes that game more difficult in later levels because the snake will have more segments for each berry that is consumed.

```
bx = random.randint(1, 38)
by = random.randint(1, 28)
gamedata.berry = Position(bx, by)
gamedata.berrycount += 1
```

Next, we generate a new position and set that as the location of the berry. We also increment a counter holding the number of berries that our snake has consumed.

If our snake has consumed ten berries, we move up to the next level. This has the added effect of increasing the speed of the snake (adding a little extra excitement!), and the number of segments added to the player each time the snake eats a berry.

We clamp the number of segments to 64 and the update speed (In milliseconds) to 100:

```
if (gamedata.berrycount == 10):
    gamedata.berrycount = 0
    gamedata.speed -= 25
    gamedata.level += 1
    gamedata.segments *= 2
    if (gamedata.segments > 64):
        gamedata.segments = 64

    if (gamedata.speed < 100):
        gamedata.speed = 100
```

Collision Detection

As we have seen, collision detection in this game is done on a per-cell basis rather than per pixel. In some ways, this makes our job easier because all we need to do is determine when one block overlaps another, in other words, they occupy the same cell.

Helper Functions

There are four functions that we haven't filled in, but without them we won't be able to detect whether the player has hit a wall or whether the snake has touched itself. Our missing implementations are for

- loseLife()

- positionBerry()

- headHitBody()

- headHitWall()

Losing a Life

When the snake's head hits its own tail or a wall, the player loses a life. When this happens, we removed all the current blocks that make up the tail of the snake and subtract one from the number of lives. We then add two blocks to the snake to start the player off again. Find 'loseLife' in the code and change it to look like this:

```
def loseLife(gamedata):
    gamedata.lives -= 1
    gamedata.direction = 0
```

Mark the number of lives down by one and reset the direction to the right.

```
gamedata.blocks[:] = []
```

This line removes all the items in the list.

```
gamedata.blocks.append(Position(20,15))
gamedata.blocks.append(Position(19,15))
```

Add two new blocks to the snake in the default position.

Repositioning the Berry

When the player dies, we have to find a new position for the berry. Find the 'positionBerry' function in the code and change it to look like this:

```
def positionBerry(gamedata):
    bx = random.randint(1, 38)
    by = random.randint(1, 28)
    found = True
```

First, we generate a random number in our playing field. We then cycle through all the game blocks to make sure that we don't randomly generate a position within the snake itself:

```
while (found):
    found = False
    for b in gamedata.blocks:
        if (b.x == bx and b.y == by):
            found = True
```

Checking to see if the berry occupies the same position as a snake block is easy. We just have to check two values for equality: the x- and y-coordinates of the berry and each of the blocks.

```
if (found):
    bx = random.randint(1, 38)
    by = random.randint(1, 28)
```

If the berry is on a cell that contains a block, 'found' is set to True. If this happens, we assign new values to our 'bx' and 'by' variables and try again.

```
gamedata.berry = Position(bx, by)
```

Once we find a block that doesn't contain a piece of snake, we assign the position to the berry field of the game data.

Testing Snake Body Hits

The snake's head cannot 'touch' its body. Each time we update the snake, we must also check to see if the head has touched the body. Our cell-based collision detection makes this easy. We only have to check the x- and y-coordinates of the snake's head against the x- and y-coordinates of the rest of the blocks that make up the body of the snake. Locate the 'headHitBody' function and change it to look like this:

```
def headHitBody(gamedata):
    head = gamedata.blocks[0]
```

Create a variable to hold a reference to the first block in the list of blocks that make up the snake. This is the head of the snake.

```
    for b in gamedata.blocks:
```

Go through each of the blocks one at a time.

```
        if (b != head):
```

If the block is not the head, check to see if the head is in the same cell as the current block.

```
            if(b.x == head.x and b.y == head.y):
                return True
```

If the head is in the same position as a block in the snake's body, return True to the function's caller.

```
return False
```

Otherwise, return False indicating to the caller that there has been no collision.

Testing Wall Hits

The final function we need to fill in is to test whether the snake's head hits the wall. Locate the 'headHitWall' function and change it to this:

```
def headHitWall(map, gamedata):
    row = 0
    for line in map:
        col = 0
        for char in line:
            if ( char == '1'):
```

For each character in the line we check to see if it is a wall character. Our map file contains 0's and 1's; any '1' represents a wall in the play field. Our control variables 'col' and 'row' are checked against the current position of the zeroth element of the blocks. This is the head of the snake.

```
                if (gamedata.blocks[0].x == col and gamedata.
                blocks[0].y == row):
                    return True
            col += 1
        row += 1
    return False
```

Conclusion

Save the game and run it. You should be able to start playing Snake. If you get any errors, check the code against the text in the book and make sure you haven't transposed any letters. Remember that whitespace is important: those 'tab' characters need to be in the right place! As a final alternative, download the code from `http://sloankelly.net` and check yours against the code there.

As an exercise, alter the Lives/Level indicator to show the number of berries collected. What if each berry was worth five points and moving to another level gave the player an additional 100 points? What variables would you need to add to GameData?

CHAPTER 17

Model View Controller

Model View Controller was mentioned before in the "Designing Your Game" section to describe how the interactions between different objects can be used to simplify the problem: breaking down a bigger problem into smaller easier-to-manage chunks. See Figure 17-1.

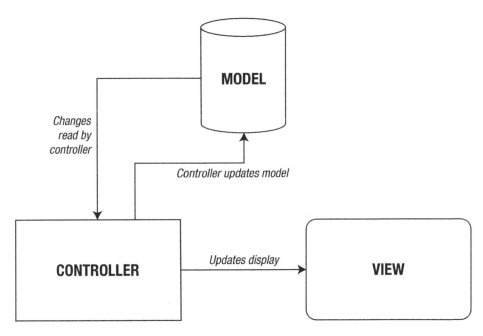

Figure 17-1. *Model View Controller design pattern*

© Sloan Kelly 2019

S. Kelly, *Python, PyGame, and Raspberry Pi Game Development*,
https://doi.org/10.1007/978-1-4842-4533-0_17

Model

The model represents the data or attributes associated with the object. For example, a player has a position in space, lives, shield strength, and score. The model usually has very few methods, possibly to do with saving or serializing data out to cheap storage like a disk drive. This would be used to save game data. However, it is more likely that you would have a save controller that would read the data from the models and store them.

View

The view is the visual representation of each of the models in the game. Some models don't have a direct visual representation in the game. For example, the data associated with an NPC (non-player character) in an RPG (role-playing game)

Controller

The controller is the glue that links the model to the view. The player interacts with the view (clicking a button, moving a player), and this calls a method on the controller. In turn, the controller updates the model to represent the new state.

In computing terms, state is the current value for an object or value. For example, in one state a player might be jumping, in another they could be running. In each state the internal variables (the object's fields) are set to particular values.

Why Use MVC?

MVC allows you, the programmer, to split the functionality of the object from its visual representation and data. With each responsibility handled by different classes, it's very easy to swap out different controllers and views.

As an illustrative example of MVC, let's create a little game that moves a robot around the screen using the cursor keys. We'll add a second view that contains a little blip in a radar view. We'll start by separating out the classes into separate files and then combine them into one game using another file as the 'glue code', the main game loop. See Figure 17-2.

Figure 17-2. *The robot 'game' showing the robot in the middle. Radar in the top left*

The Classes

The classes we are going to create are

- RadarView

- RobotController

- RobotGenerator

- RobotModel

- RobotView

You don't need to add 'Model,' 'View,' and 'Controller' to each class that you create, but it shows us clearly in this example what class performs what purpose.

RadarView

The radar view displays a small blip that represents the robot in a smaller version of the screen in the top-left corner of the window.

RobotController

The robot controller alters the state of the model based upon the player's input.

RobotGenerator

The robot generator generates a robot in a random position on the screen after a specified period. The maximum number of robots can also be set.

RobotModel

The robot model holds the state of the robot. It has no methods at all, just data.

RobotView

The robot view displays the robot on the screen. It does not alter the robot model; it just reads the data from the model and decides what to display based upon the state of the model.

Folder

Create a new directory inside the 'pygamebook' folder called 'ch17.' We will create all the files inside this directory.

The Robot Model

The model class, called RobotModel, contains just the data for the robot. The updating of each instance of this class will be done using the RobotController, a class that will be defined subsequently.

Create a new file called 'robotmodel.py' and type in the following code:

```
class RobotModel(object):
```

Classes are defined with just a name. In our example, we're going to post-fix each class with its intended purpose. You might not want to do that, or it might not make sense to do so. Use your judgment on your own class names.

```
    def __init__(self, x, y, frame, speed):
```

The __init__ method (functions inside a class definition are called methods) is a special method called a constructor. It takes four parameters for the start position of the robot, the current animation frame, and its update speed. The first parameter 'self' is required by Python and refers to the object being created.

```
        self.x = x
        self.y = y
        self.frame = frame
        self.speed = speed
        self.timer = 0
```

We'll use the 'timer' member field to control the current frame of the robot; it has a 'walking' animation. The rest of the RobotModel class are methods to access and change the data of the model:

```
    def setPosition(self, newPosition):
        self.x, self.y = newPosition

    def getPosition(self):
        return (self.x, self.y)

    def getFrame(self):
        return self.frame

    def nextFrame(self):
        self.timer = 0
        self.frame += 1
        self.frame %= 4
```

The nextFrame() method is called by the RobotController to move the robot onto the next frame. It adds one to the frame count then uses the modulo operator (%) to clamp the self.frame field to between 0 and 3.

```
    def getTimer(self):
        return self.timer

    def getSpeed(self):
        return self.speed

    def setSpeed(self, speed):
        self.speed = speed
```

These getter and setter methods will be used by the RobotGenerator and RobotController classes.

Getters and Setters are so called because they start with either 'get' or 'set' and are used to access data contained in a class instance

The Robot View

The RobotView class displays the large graphic of the robot at the position in the robot's model. The graphic used by the robot contains four frames and each frame is 32×32 pixels. See Figure 17-3.

Figure 17-3. *The robot, a 128×32 pixel image with four 32×32 frames*

The current frame is calculated in the RobotController class, which we'll see in just a moment. In the meantime, create a new file called robotview.py and enter the following text:

```
import pygame
from pygame.locals import *
```

We need this import for the Rect class.

```
from robotmodel import RobotModel
```

219

Our RobotView class uses RobotModel, so we need to import that file.

```
class RobotView(object):
    def __init__(self, imgPath):
        self.img = pygame.image.load(imgPath)

    def draw(self, surface, models):
        for model in models:
            rect = Rect(model.getFrame() * 32, 0, 32, 32)
            surface.blit(self.img, model.getPosition(), rect)
```

The draw() method takes in the surface that the robots are to be drawn on and also the list of models. The for loop iterates through each robot instance in 'models' and draws them on the surface.

Because we only want to show a small 32×32 portion of our image. The source area to copy to the screen is calculated using the model's frame. The model has four frames: 0, 1, 2, and 3. If this value is multiplied by 32, the possible rectangles are (0, 0, 32, 32), (32, 0, 32, 32), (64, 0, 32, 32), and (96, 0, 32, 32), as shown in Figure 17-4.

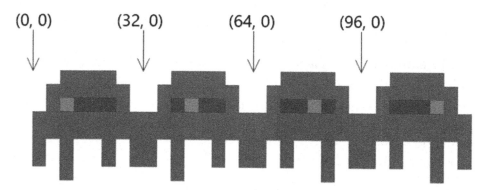

Figure 17-4. *The start coordinates of each frame of the robot's animation*

The Radar View

The radar view shows a tiny blip (3×3 pixels, white) on a radar screen. The radar screen is a 66×50 pixels image with a 1-pixel border. See Figure 17-5.

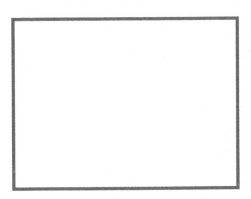

Figure 17-5. *The 66×50 radar image*

The area of the radar is 64×48 pixels, but the graphic is slightly larger to accommodate the 1-pixel border around the outside. The scale of the radar is 1:10 of the main playing area which is 640×480 pixels. This is also why the blips are 3×3 pixels because it is a close approximation to the robot's 32×32 pixel actual size.

Create a new file called radarview.py and enter the following text:

```
import pygame
from robotmodel import RobotModel

class RadarView(object):

    def __init__(self, blipImagePath, borderImagePath):
        self.blipImage = pygame.image.load(blipImagePath)
        self.borderImage = pygame.image.load(borderImagePath)
```

The constructor takes two arguments: one for the blip image path and the second is the border image path. The images are loaded and placed into fields for later use by the draw() method.

```
def draw(self, surface, robots):
    for robot in robots:
```

The draw method takes in the surface the robots will be drawn onto and the list of robots.

```
        x, y = robot.getPosition()
        x /= 10
        y /= 10

        x += 1
        y += 1

        surface.blit(self.blipImage, (x, y))
```

The 'blip' representing the robot requires us to do some math. We need to convert the coordinate that is a value between 0..639 on the x-axis and 0..479 on the y-axis to a value between 0..63 on the radar's x-axis and 0..47 on the radar's y-axis. This means that we have to divide the robot's position by 10 and add 1 because remember that our 1 pixel radar border doesn't count.

```
        surface.blit(self.borderImage, (0, 0))
```

Finally, the border is drawn completing the radar view.

The Robot Controller

The robot controller is the glue that binds the model and the view together; it uses the clock to update the current frame and it polls the keyboard to read the input from the player. It uses this input to update the player's position based upon the speed (in pixels per second) of the robot.

Create a new file called robotcontroller.py and type in the following code:

```
from robotmodel import RobotModel
```

The robot's model RobotModel is imported from the robotmodel.py file because the controller class reads and writes values to the robot models.

This means that the controller changes the state of each robot in the game.

```
class RobotController(object):
    def __init__(self, robots):
        self.robots = robots
```

The RobotController's constructor take in a list of robots that it will update once per frame. Rather than calling an update on each object, a single update method – the RobotController's update() method is called once and it updates each model. This is a really efficient way to process a number of like items.

```
    def update(self, deltaTime):
        for robot in self.robots:
            robot.timer += deltaTime
            if robot.getTimer() >= 0.125:
                robot.nextFrame()
```

Each robot is processed in a loop. Using the data stored for each robot, the code determines whether to update the next frame or to move the object by changing its position (see the following text).

The time difference from the last time this method was called, and this time is added to the 'timer' field of the model. If the 'timer' is greater than or equal to 0.125 seconds, we tell the model to move to the next frame.

```
speed = self.multiply(robot.getSpeed(), deltaTime)
pos = robot.getPosition()

x, y = self.add(pos, speed)

sx, sy = robot.getSpeed()
```

The model's position is incremented by the pixels per second multiplied by the time difference from when the method was last called. This is explained in detail as follows:

```
if x < 0:
    x = 0
    sx *= -1
elif x > 607:
    x = 607
    sx *= -1

if y < 0:
    y = 0
    sy *= -1
elif y > 447:
    y = 447
    sy *= -1

robot.setPosition((x, y))
robot.setSpeed((sx, sy))
```

The values on the x- and y-axes are clamped to the screen in this series of if statements. The new position and speed are then set on the current robot model.

```
def multiply(self, speed, deltaTime):
    x = speed[0] * deltaTime
    y = speed[1] * deltaTime

    return (x, y)
```

```
def add(self, position, speed):
    x = position[0] + speed[0]
    y = position[1] + speed[1]

    return (x, y)
```

Two helper functions to make working with tuples easier. Tuples are immutable, which means we cannot change the value of any of the elements. We can make new tuples, we just can't change the ones we have. The two helper methods make multiplying and adding tuples a little easier.

The Robot Generator

The last class is not part of the MVC pattern, but I needed a way to generate the robots at random positions and speeds. To achieve this, I created the RobotGenerator class. Create a new file called 'robotgenerator.py' and enter the following code:

```
import random
from robotmodel import RobotModel

class RobotGenerator(object):
    def __init__(self, generationTime = 1, maxRobots = 10):
        self.robots = []
        self.generationTime = generationTime
        self.maxRobots = maxRobots
        self.counter = 0
```

The RobotGenerator's constructor allows the caller – the part of the code that creates the instance of the class – to specify the number of seconds between creation of the robots and the maximum number of robots. The 'self.counter' field stores the current time in seconds. If the 'self.counter' is greater than or equal to 'self.generationTime,' a robot is created (see following update).

```
def getRobots(self):
    return self.robots
```

Get the list of robots. This method is accessed in two ways; it is passed as an argument to the RobotController constructor and as a parameter to the RadarView and RobotView draw() methods.

```
def update(self, deltaTime):
    self.counter += deltaTime
```

The timer is incremented by deltaTime which itself is a fraction of a second.

```
if self.counter >= self.generationTime and len(self.
robots) < self.maxRobots:
    self.counter = 0
    x = random.randint(36, 600)
    y = random.randint(36, 440)
    frame = random.randint(0, 3)
    sx = -50 + random.random() * 100
    sy = -50 + random.random() * 100

    newRobot = RobotModel(x, y, frame, (sx, sy))
    self.robots.append(newRobot)
```

If the counter reaches a certain time (generationTime) and the number of robots is less than the maximum number of robots, we add a new robot to the scene. The position and speed of the generated robot are randomized.

Ensuring Constant Speed

We want to ensure that we have a constant speed when our objects are moving. Sometimes other routines take longer to run, and we can't ensure this. For example, if we decide that our robot should move at 200 pixels per second. If we assume that our routine will get called 30 frames per second, then we should just increment the speed by 6.25 each frame. Right? Wrong!

Our robot's position should change by 200 pixels per second. If the player holds down the right cursor key, the robot should move to the right 200 pixels after 1 second. What happens if the update method only gets called 15 times per second? This means that our robot will only move 15 × 6.25 = 93.75 pixels in 1 second.

Remember in "Snake" we used the clock's tick of milliseconds to update parts of the code when we wanted them to be updated. We can use this delta time to calculate the distance we need to travel in a single 'tick' of the game. A tick is each time the game loops around.

This means that even with a variable frame rate, you will still have a constant speed because the delta time will ensure that your speed remains constant over time.

With delta time, your 15 times per second update will still result in a displacement of 200 pixels after 1 second of holding down the right cursor key. Why? Because with each update, we multiply the desired speed by the fraction of a second since the last call. For a 15th of a second, that's 66 milliseconds.

0.066 × 200 = 13.2 pixels each update

13.2 pixels × 15 updates = 198 pixels per second

Which is roughly the speed we want. If our frame rate increases to 60 frames per second:

60 frames per second is 16.67 milliseconds

0.01667 × 200 = 3.333 pixels each update

3.333 pixels × 60 updates = 200.00 pixels per second

You can see that with 60 frames per second, we get a much more accurate speed than at 15 frames per second. For our purposes, though, 30 frames per second is more than adequate for our needs.

The Main Robot Program

The main robot program takes all these individual classes and combines them into a single 'game' example. Create a new file called robot.py. In this new file, add the following code:

```
import pygame, sys
from pygame.locals import *
```

Our more-than-familiar imports to access the PyGame library of routines and classes as well as the OS and System libraries supplied with Python.

```
from robotview import RobotView
from robotcontroller import RobotController
from robotgenerator import RobotGenerator
from radarview import RadarView
```

These import the RobotModel, RobotView, RadarView, RobotGenerator, and RobotController from the respective files. We use the 'from' keyword to minimize the amount of typing required. With 'from,' we need only type the class name rather than 'robotview.RobotView'.

```
pygame.init()
fpsClock = pygame.time.Clock()
surface = pygame.display.set_mode((640, 480))
```

Next, we initialize PyGame and set up a clock, so we can clamp our frame rate to a maximum of 30 frames per second. Our test game will be 640×480 pixels in size.

```
lastMillis = 0
```

The 'lastMillis' keeps the last number of milliseconds between frames. This value is returned by 'fpsClock.tick()'.

```
generator = RobotGenerator()
view = RobotView('robot.png')
radar = RadarView('blip.png', 'radarview.png')
controller = RobotController(generator.getRobots())
```

This is where we create instances of our classes. The constructor arguments are passed through. We're just using hard-coded values in this example, but you could easily read in this data from a text file if you so desired.

```
while True:
    for event in pygame.event.get():
        if event.type == QUIT:
            pygame.quit()
            sys.exit()
```

Our main loop has the get-out-of-jail escape we've seen before; when the user closes the window, we quit PyGame and signal to the operating system that we're exiting the application.

```
deltaTime = lastMillis / 1000

generator.update(deltaTime)
controller.update(deltaTime)
```

Generally, you want to update your classes before you draw their visual representations. Both the generator and controller need an update call so that new robots get generated and the ones that have been generated are updated. Remember, all the controller code is in one class, if we change anything in that controller class, ALL our robots are affected. This is really powerful!

```
surface.fill((0, 0, 0))

view.draw(surface, generator.getRobots())
radar.draw(surface, generator.getRobots())
```

Next, the screen is cleared with black, the tuple for the fill() method is for the red, green, and blue components of a color, and black is the absence of all color so all the values are zero. The main view is drawn first, so this draws all the robots at their positions with their current animation frame. Next the radar is drawn on top.

This is called draw order. The images that are drawn to the screen first are drawn behind images drawn later. Think of it as photographs being placed on a table. Those placed first will get obscured by those placed on top.

```
pygame.display.update()
lastMillis = fpsClock.tick(30)
```

Our last actions in the main game loop are to flip the front buffer to the back and vice versa and clamp the frame rate to 30 frames per second. The 'lastMillis' is stored and this will give us an approximate time of how long it took to generate the last frame. That will be used to determine the position and animation frame of each robot.

Save and run the game. After about a second a robot will appear, then another and another until there are ten onscreen. Notice that the 'radar' view updates with the relative position of each of the robots.

Conclusion

The Model View Controller design pattern can be used to functionally split up an object into three separate classes. This enables you, the programmer, to decide how to combine those classes later. For example, if you only want to provide keyboard support at the start of development, a new controller that allows for joystick support can be easily added at a later stage. This new addition will not impact the view or model classes.

MVC is ideal if you have many NPCs onscreen at any one time. You can use one class to store their positional/frame data (model), one class to perform the update (the controller), and another to display them (view). In fact, you can have different views depending on what type of NPC it is, for example a BlacksmithView only draws blacksmiths, ChefView only draws chefs. This reduces the amount of data in memory because only one class (BlacksmithView) has an instance of the image for the blacksmith, and only one class (ChefView) has an instance of the image for the chef. In a more traditional OOP setting you might have the position and shape data together meaning you could have potentially thousands of images in memory.

CHAPTER 18

Audio

Audio is an important part of making a game. You can have the best visuals in the world, the best mechanics, but something is missing – it's audio! In this chapter we take a look at playing one-off sounds such as explosions or effects as well as music.

Sounds are played using PyGame's built-in mixer object. Like, PyGame, you must first initialize the sound mixer before using it.

```
pygame.mixer.init()
```

Likewise, when you stop using the sound mixer, you should shut it down gracefully by calling the quit method:

```
pygame.mixer.quit()
```

You can check to see if the mixer is playing sounds by calling the 'get_busy()' method:

```
pygame.mixer.get_busy()
```

This will return a Boolean True or False to indicate that the mixer is still doing something. We will use this in the two example programs to keep the program running.

The Sound class' init() method takes a single parameter, which is usually just the path to the sound file on disk. You can also pass in buffers and other things, but we'll only be passing in the path to the sound file.

```
shootSound = pygame.mixer.Sound('playershoot.wav')
```

© Sloan Kelly 2019
S. Kelly, *Python, PyGame, and Raspberry Pi Game Development*,
https://doi.org/10.1007/978-1-4842-4533-0_18

Like every other class, calling the constructor – the init() method – passes back an instance of the class. The Sound class can load Ogg Vorbis or WAV files only. Ogg files are compressed and are therefore more suited to machines that have a tight space requirement.

Playing a Sound

Create a new folder inside 'pygamebook' called 'ch18.' Inside that folder create a new Python script file called 'testsound.py.' Enter the following code and run it to play the sound. The file playershoot.wav is available on the web site (http://sloankelly.net) in the Resources section. If you don't want to download that file, you can supply your own.

```
import pygame, os, sys
from pygame.locals import *
```

Import the usual modules.

```
pygame.mixer.init()
```

Initialize the sound mixer.

```
shootSound = pygame.mixer.Sound('playershoot.wav')
```

Load in the playershoot.wav sound file and name it shootSound.

```
shootSound.play()
```

Play the sound by calling the play() method.

```
while pygame.mixer.get_busy():
    pass
```

This is a dummy while statement to keep the program busy while the sound is playing. Remember the pass keyword? It's like a blank statement that does nothing in Python. You can use it to create stub code for functions or, as in this case, to create blank while loops.

```
pygame.mixer.quit()
```

Always quit the mixer when you are finished with audio. Save and run the program and you will hear a 'pew!' noise before it closes. This is an example of a one-off sound effect. That's one part of the audio story for games. The second is music and we will cover that next.

Playing, Pausing, and Changing Volume

The sound object allows you to change the volume that the music is being played back. The mixer can also perform a nice fade out. The following program will start playing a piece of music and allow the player to control the volume and can play/pause the music as well. When finished, the music will fade out and the program will stop.

In this section we will introduce

- pygame.mixer.fadeout()

- pygame.mixer.pause()

- pygame.mixer.unpause()

- Sound.set_volume()

Create a new Python script inside 'ch18' called 'playsong.py' and add the following code. As usual, I will explain as we go:

```
import pygame
from pygame.locals import *
```

Required imports for PyGame to run.

```
class Print:
    def __init__(self):
        self.font = pygame.font.Font(None, 32)

    def draw(self, surface, msg, position):
        obj = self.font.render(msg, True, (255, 255, 255))
        surface.blit(obj, position)
```

This is a small helper class that will make printing text easier in the main code. It creates a Font instance and the 'draw()' method renders the given text to a surface and that in turn is blitted onto the given surface.

```
pygame.init()
pygame.mixer.init()
```

Initialization of both PyGame and the sound mixer.

```
fpsClock = pygame.time.Clock()
surface = pygame.display.set_mode((640, 480))
out = Print()
```

Creating the clock, the main drawing surface, and the instance of the 'Print' object. The display is 640×480 pixels because we don't need to display much information for this project.

```
song = pygame.mixer.Sound('bensound-theelevatorbossanova.ogg')
song.play(-1)
```

Load the song into memory and immediately play it. Note that the 'play()' method is passed a parameter of –1 which means that it will keep repeating until it is told to stop.

```
running = True
paused = False
fading = False
volume = 1
```

These control variables are, from the top:

- To keep the program running while the music is playing

- Is the music paused

- Is the music fading out

- The music volume

Entering the main loop:

```
while running:
    for event in pygame.event.get():
        if event.type == QUIT:
            pygame.mixer.fadeout(1000)
```

The main loop is kept running by checking the 'running' variable. If that variable contains 'True,' the program will keep looping back and executing the body of the loop. The first part of which is the 'for' loop that determines what state the game should be in. The first check (above) is to see if the player has quit the game (i.e., they clicked the X button on the window). If so, we instruct the mixer to fade out the music for 1000 milliseconds or 1 second.

```
        elif event.type == KEYDOWN:
```

The next check is to see if the player has pressed a key. If they have, we want to react to it, the space key is used to pause/unpause the music, the [and] keys are used to decrease and increase the volume, respectively, and the escape key (ESC) is used to quit the game.

```
            if event.key == pygame.K_SPACE:
                paused = not paused
                if paused:
                    pygame.mixer.pause()
                else:
                    pygame.mixer.unpause()
```

If the player presses the space bar, the 'paused' variable is set to be the opposite of the value that it currently holds. This means that if it is 'True,' it will be set to 'False' and vice versa. The appropriate method is called on the mixer object to pause/unpause the music.

```
elif event.key == pygame.K_ESCAPE and not fading:
    fading = True
    pygame.mixer.fadeout(1000)
```

If the player pressed the escape key and the game is not fading the music, set 'fading' to True so that the player can't keep fading the music and inform the PyGame mixer that the music should fade from full volume to zero over 1 second (1000 milliseconds). The fadeout() method takes a numeric value in milliseconds.

```
elif event.key == pygame.K_LEFTBRACKET:
    volume = volume - 0.1
    if volume < 0:
        volume = 0
    song.set_volume(volume)
```

Sound volume is between 0 and 1 inclusive. 0 is off (muted) and 1 is full volume. If the player presses the left [bracket, the volume of the sound should decrease. To do this we subtract 0.1 from the current volume. There is then a check to make sure that it stays in the range 0..1 and then 'set_volume()' is called on the 'song' object to apply this new volume. The 'song' object is the .ogg file that we loaded in earlier.

```
elif event.key == pygame.K_RIGHTBRACKET:
    volume = volume + 0.1
    if volume > 1:
        volume = 1
    song.set_volume(volume)
```

If the player presses the right] bracket, the volume of the sound should increase. To do this we add 0.1 to the current volume. There is then a check to make sure that it stays in the range 0..1 and then 'set_volume()' is called on the 'song' object to apply this new volume.

Now that the events have been taken care of, the final update step is to check to see if we are still playing audio, if not we should quit the loop:

```
if not pygame.mixer.get_busy():
    running = False
```

If 'running' is False, the game quits.

```
surface.fill((0, 0, 0))
```

```
out.draw(surface, "Press <SPACE> to pause / unpause the music",
(4, 4))
out.draw(surface, "Press <ESC> to fade out and close program",
(4, 36))
out.draw(surface, "Press [ and ] to alter the volume", (4, 68))
out.draw(surface, "Current volume: {0:1.2f}".format(volume),
(4, 100))
```

```
pygame.display.update()
fpsClock.tick(30)
```

Draw the text onscreen to let the player know the keys to press.

```
pygame.mixer.quit()
pygame.quit()
```

When the game is over, make sure to quit both the mixer and PyGame.

Save and run the program; you should see something like the output shown in Figure 18-1. You will also hear the song being played.

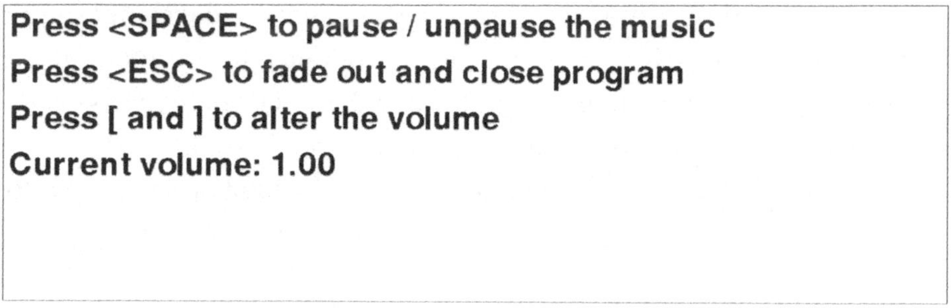

Press <SPACE> to pause / unpause the music
Press <ESC> to fade out and close program
Press [and] to alter the volume
Current volume: 1.00

Figure 18-1. *The output from the 'playsong.py' script*

Conclusion

This has been a small introduction to what you can achieve with the PyGame sound mixer. Adding audio to your game is very important because it can enhance the sense of fun and really help convey (for example) the weight of objects or how much damage has been taken.

Remember to always quit the mixer when your game ends!

CHAPTER 19

Finite State Machines

A state can be described as a condition of a program or entity. Finite defines that there is only a set number of states that the program or entity can be defined by. The entity is controlled by a series of rules that determine what the next state of the program or entity is to be placed in.

Finite State Machines are used in video games for Artificial Intelligence (AI) as well as menu systems and the overall game state as well.

Game State

A game is a computer program that has unique, discrete, compartmentalized states, for example, splash screen, playing the game, game over, the main menu, and the options menu. Each part can be viewed as a separate state.

Menu System

Menu systems used to control various aspects of the game can also be compartmentalized into separate states, for example, the main menu, display options, control options, and sound options. These are all separate states.

© Sloan Kelly 2019
S. Kelly, *Python, PyGame, and Raspberry Pi Game Development*,
https://doi.org/10.1007/978-1-4842-4533-0_19

Non-player Artificial Intelligence

This is the most common use of Finite State Machines (FSMs) and the one that most people associate with FSMs. At a basic level, each enemy that the player encounters has a Finite State Machine attached to them. By attached, I mean that it has a reference to a Finite State Machine in the form of a member variable, like 'self.fsm', for example.

Enemy FSMs can run independently of each other, or there can be an overarching 'pack AI' that controls a whole series of enemies. For example, you might have ten enemies but the 'pack AI' will control how many enemies are used to attack the player, how many will 'run away,' etc.

In a specific case, let's take an example of a guard. He might have two states: patrol and attack. The guard stays in the patrol state until an enemy (the player) comes within range, say 50 units, and they then move to the attack state.

FSMs are usually described using a diagram. Each block represents the state and each arrow shows the rule and the direction of transition. That is, if that rule is met, the arrow points to the state that the entity should use. See Figure 19-1.

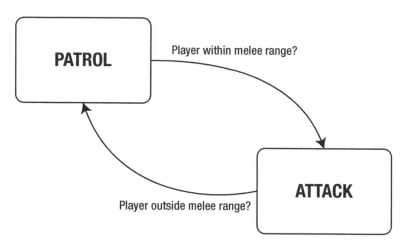

Figure 19-1. *Finite State Machine showing a simple two-state patrol/attack for an enemy AI*

If the guard is in the patrol state and the player enters the melee range, the guard will move to the attack state. This no doubt will contain code that attacks the player. Similarly, if the guard is in attack state and the player moves outside the melee range, it will transition back to the patrol state.

A Finite State Machine Example

This example shows a three-state FSM. Each state has the following methods:

- enter()
- exit()
- update()

There is a FSM manager that controls the current state of the program. This manager has two methods:

- changeState()
- update()

The changeState() method transitions the entity from one state to another, and the update() method calls the update() method of the current state.

In the following section we will create an example Finite State Machine (FSM). Create a new folder inside 'pygamebook' called 'ch19.' Inside the 'ch19' folder, create a new Python file called 'fsm.py.' When it is completed you will see the following output:

```
Entering State One
Hello from StateOne!
Hello from StateOne!
Hello from StateOne!
Hello from StateOne!
Hello from StateOne!
```

```
Exiting State One
Entering State Two
Hello from StateTwo!
Hello from StateTwo!
Hello from StateTwo!
Hello from StateTwo!
Hello from StateTwo!
Exiting State Two
Entering Quit
Quitting...
```

If you don't, recheck your code.

Finite State Machine Manager

The finite machine manager class is defined below. Remember to type it (and the rest of the code!) explicitly. You can change whatever you want later, but first type in the code exactly as seen.

The FSM manager controls the current state of the entity. In our example, we're going to have three states. The first two states display "hello" messages, the latter quits the application. The transition rule is diagrammed below in Figure 19-2.

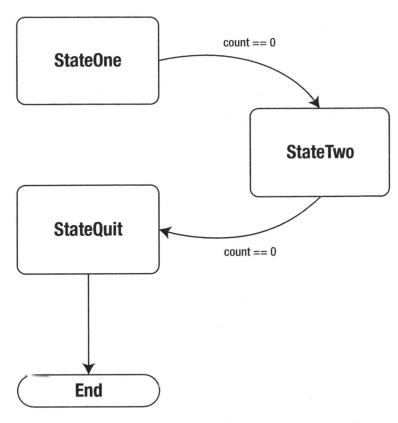

Figure 19-2. *FSM example state machine showing transitions*

StateOne transitions to StateTwo when the count reaches zero. StateTwo transitions to StateQuit when the count reaches zero. StateQuit calls Python's exit() method to quit the application.

```
class FsmManager:
    def __init__(self):
        self.currentState = None
```

The current state is set to None. We will call the changeState() method explicitly in the main part of the program below.

```
def update(self):
    if (self.currentState != None):
        self.currentState.update()
```

The update() method checks to see if we have a current state, and if so, we call the update() method of it. Notice that we're using Python's duck typing here.

```
def changeState(self, newState):
    if (self.currentState != None):
        self.currentState.exit()
```

When we change state, we want to give the current state the chance to 'shutdown' or 'clean up' before we transition to the new state. The exit() method does just that, or at least it's up to the developer who implements the state to put the code they want in the exit() method.

```
self.currentState = newState
self.currentState.enter()
```

Similarly, when we enter a new state, we need to let the state know that this event has occurred. The developer of each state will place code in the enter() method if they want to act upon that event.

```
class StateOne:
```

In general, there is very little difference between StateOne and StateTwo apart from the text messages that appear onscreen.

```
class StateOne:
    def __init__(self, fsm):
        self.count = 5
        self.fsm = fsm
        self.nextState = None
```

246

We will set the nextState field in the main part of the program. This is the next state that this current state will transition to. There are far more complex FSM systems that apply rules to the various states and make for an even more flexible system. This, being a simple example, bakes the rules inside each of the states.

```
def enter(self):
    print("Entering State One")
```

The enter() method is used to set up various values for the current state. In this example, we just write a message to the screen.

```
def exit(self):
    print("Exiting Slate One")
```

The exit() method could be used to clean up the current state before it transitions to the new state. In this example, we show a simple message.

```
def update(self):
    print("Hello from StateOne!")
    self.count -= 1
    if (self.count == 0):
        fsm.changeState(self.nextState)
```

The update() method is called by the FSM manager. In our example, we count down until we reach zero and then transition to the next state.

```
class StateTwo:
    def __init__(self, fsm):
        self.count = 5
        self.fsm = fsm
        self.nextState = None

    def enter(self):
        print("Entering State Two")
```

```
    def exit(self):
        print("Exiting State Two")

    def update(self):
        print("Hello from StateTwo!")
        self.count -= 1
        if (self.count == 0):
            fsm.changeState(self.nextState)
```

There isn't much difference in StateOne and StateTwo. The quit state is also very simple; it just exits the application.

```
class StateQuit:
    def __init__(self, fsm):
        self.fsm = fsm

    def enter(self):
        print("Entering Quit")

    def exit(self):
        print("Exiting Quit")

    def update(self):
        print("Quitting...")
        exit()
```

We don't need to update any variables; we're just quitting the application at this point.

```
fsm = FsmManager()
stateOne = StateOne(fsm)
stateTwo = StateTwo(fsm)
stateQuit = StateQuit(fsm)
```

Here we create our FSM manager and the states. Each state takes the FSM manager as an argument in the constructor.

```
stateOne.nextState = stateTwo
stateTwo.nextState = stateQuit
```

The next state for stateOne and stateTwo are assigned. StateOne's next state is stateTwo and stateTwo's next state is stateQuit.

```
fsm.changeState(stateOne)
```

We set the initial state for the FSM manager to be the StateOne.

```
while True:
    fsm.update()
```

Our while loop is very simple; just call the FSM manager's update() method. That's it. Our states handle the program flow from there.

Save and run the file and you should see the output we showed at the start of this chapter.

Conclusion

The goal of any object-oriented pattern is to make classes and main programs as small as possible. This reduces the amount of code that you have to read for a particular class, making it easier to understand. Each class should have a single purpose. Our FSM manager class has a single purpose: run the currently selected state. Each state has a single purpose too: perform certain actions until the rule changes then transition to a new state.

FSMs are perfect for Artificial Intelligence (AI) because you can design quite complex interactions based upon known criteria: Is the user within weapons range? Am I able to fire my weapon? Can the player see me? Etc., etc.

You can also use FSMs to control program state. Let's take an example of the flow of a typical game application. See Figure 19-3.

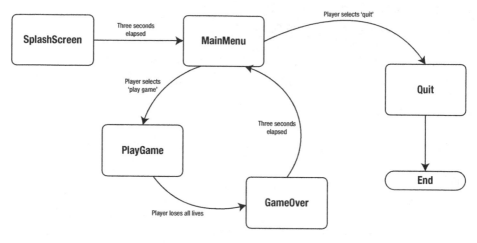

Figure 19-3. *FSM for a game*

The entry state is SplashScreen and this screen transitions after 3 seconds to the main menu. The main menu gives the user two choices: play the game or quit to the OS. If the user is playing the game and they die, the game transitions to the GameOver state. It remains in this state for 3 seconds, and after that, the game transitions to the MainMenu state.

Our next project "Invaders" ties our Model-View-Controller (MVC) and Finite State Machine (FSM) knowledge together.

CHAPTER 20

Game Project: Invaders

Our final arcade-style game project is Invaders and it brings together everything that we've done up until this point. We've got sounds, animation, MVC, and FSM all wrapped in one game. See Figure 20-1.

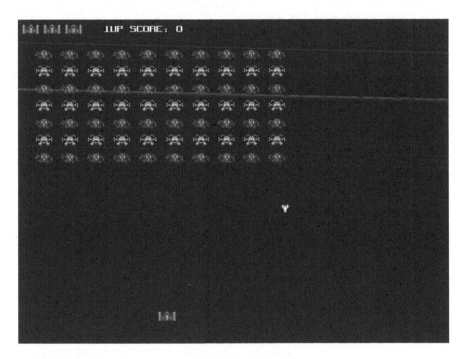

Figure 20-1. *The Invaders game in action*

© Sloan Kelly 2019
S. Kelly, *Python, PyGame, and Raspberry Pi Game Development*,
https://doi.org/10.1007/978-1-4842-4533-0_20

Before we get started, create a new folder inside 'pygamebook' called 'projects,' if there isn't one there already. Inside 'projects,' create another folder called 'invaders.' This is where all the files that we create will be stored for this project. We're going to be using several files for this project, and they are

- bitmapfont.py – Contains a sprite sheet for a bitmap font

- bullet.py – Bullet classes

- collision.py – Collision classes

- interstitial.py – Interstitial screens, that is, the "Get Ready" and "Game Over" screens

- invaders.py – The actual runnable game; this is the 'main' program, which creates the framework and instantiates all the objects

- invadersgame.py – The actual 'play game' state class

- menu.py – Menu classes

- player.py – Player classes

- raspigame.py – Base classes that you can use to extend for your own games

- swarm.py – Alien swarm classes

There are three WAV files for our sound effects:

- aliendie.wav

- playerdie.wav

- playershoot.wav

We also have several PNG files that contain the animation frames for all the invaders, the player, the display font (we're using a bitmap font), and the bullets:

- alienbullet.png

- bullet.png

- explosion.png

- fasttracker2-style_12×12.png

- invaders.png

- ship.png

The entire source and all the resources (the images and the sound files) can all be downloaded from sloankelly.net in the Resources section.

The Classes

The following classes will be defined as part of this project:

- BitmapFont – Permits the drawing of a bitmap font on a PyGame surface.

- BulletController, BulletModel, BulletView – The MVC classes for the 'bullet' entities. Bullets can be 'owned' by a swarm of aliens or by the player.

- CollisionController – Handles the collision detection for the game. This includes player/bullet and alien/bullet as well as player/alien collision detection.

- ExplosionController, ExplosionModel, ExplosionModelList, ExplosionView – The MVC classes for the 'explosion' entities. When an alien invader or the player dies, an explosion is shown in their place.

- GameState – The base class for all of the game's states.

- InterstitialState – Interstitial screens are used in video games to display "Game Over" or "Get Ready" messages. This is a 'state of being' for the program; therefore InterstitialState is derived from a state base class called 'GameState.'

- InvaderModel, SwarmController, InvaderView – The alien invader swarm's MVC classes. There is no individual controller for each alien; instead the 'SwarmController' updates the position of each alien and determines which one is firing on the player.

- PlayGameState – Play game state.

- MainMenuState – Main menu state.

- PlayerController, PlayerLivesView, PlayerModel, PlayerView – The 'player' entity's MVC classes.

- RaspberryPiGame – Contains the main update loop that we've seen in our previous programs. This is effectively the Finite State Manager.

The Finite State Machine

The game is controlled using a finite state machine (FSM). The diagram in Figure 20-2 shows the distinct states and how the game transitions between them.

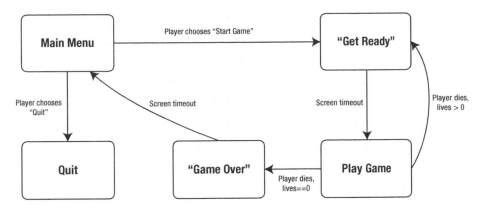

Figure 20-2. *The 'Invaders' game Finite State Machine*

The game starts with the main menu state and ends with the 'quit' game state. The 'quit' game state isn't really a state, as you will see; it's actually the absence of state; we set the current state of the game to 'None' and the code handles this by neatly quitting the program. In our implementation, the base class for each state is defined as 'GameState.'

MVC and 'Invaders'

Each entity (the player, alien swarm, alien) has a corresponding model, view, and controller class. For the alien invaders, the controller handles more than one alien entity.

The Framework

The basic state class and state machine manager are defined in a file called 'raspigame.py'. Create this file and type in the following code:

```
import pygame, os, sys
from pygame.locals import *

class GameState(object):
```

The game state class defines an interface that is used by the RaspberryPiGame class. Each state manages a particular function of the game. For example: main menu, the actual game play, and interstitial screens. The GameState class uses the new format for class definition. Each class that uses the new format must extend from the object. In Python, extending a class means that you place the name of the base class in parentheses after the class name.

```
def __init__(self, game):
    self.game = game
```

Initialize the Game state class. Each subtype must call this method. Take one parameter, which is the game instance.

```
def onEnter(self, previousState):
    pass
```

The base class 'GameState' does not contain any code for onEnter(). Classes that extend 'GameState' are expected to provide their own definition. This method is called by the game when entering the state for the first time.

```
def onExit(self):
    pass
```

The base class 'GameState' does not contain any code for onExit(). Classes that extend 'GameState' are expected to provide their own definition. This method is called by the game when leaving the state.

```
def update(self, gameTime):
    pass
```

The base class 'GameState' does not contain any code for update(). Classes that extend 'GameState' are expected to provide their own definition. This method is called by the game allowing the state to update itself. The game time (in milliseconds) is the time since the last call to this method.

```python
def draw(self, surface):
    pass
```

The base class 'GameState' does not contain any code for draw(). Classes that extend 'GameState' are expected to provide their own definition. This method is called by the game, allowing the state to draw itself. The surface that is passed is the current drawing surface.

```python
class RaspberryPiGame(object):
```

Basic game object-oriented framework for the Raspberry Pi. Users create 'states' that alter what is being displayed onscreen/updated at any particular time. This is really just a glorified state manager.

```python
def __init__(self, gameName, width, height):
    pygame.init()
    pygame.display.set_caption(gameName);

    self.fpsClock = pygame.time.Clock()
    self.mainwindow = pygame.display.set_mode((width, height))
    self.background = pygame.Color(0, 0, 0)
    self.currentState = None
```

The class constructor takes in the name of the game which will be used to change the window's title bar. The constructor creates the main window, the FPS clock, and the default background color for the game. The current state is initially set to 'None.'

```python
def changeState(self, newState):
    if self.currentState != None:
        self.currentState.onExit()
```

```
    if newState == None:
        pygame.quit()
        sys.exit()

    oldState = self.currentState
    self.currentState = newState
    newState.onEnter(oldState)
```

This method transitions from one state to another. If there is an existing state, the state's onExit() method is called. This will clean up the current state and perform any tasks that the state needs to do when exiting. The new state's onEnter method is called unless newState is 'None.' If the newState is 'None' then the game will terminate.

```
def run(self, initialState):
    self.changeState( initialState )

    while True:
        for event in pygame.event.get():
            if event.type == QUIT:
                pygame.quit()
                sys.exit()

        gameTime = self.fpsClock.get_time()

        if ( self.currentState != None ):
            self.currentState.update( gameTime )

        self.mainwindow.fill(self.background)
        if ( self.currentState != None ):
            self.currentState.draw ( self.mainwindow )

        pygame.display.update()
        self.fpsClock.tick(30)
```

Our main game loop, which we've seen several times before, has been moved to the run() method. This handles all the event management, state update, and display.

Save the file.

Bitmap Font

Before we can test the player's tank and bullets, we must first define the bitmap font class. A normal font contains a mathematical representation of each of the characters. A bitmap font provides a sprite sheet that contains all the individual characters that make up the font. We then use PyGame's built-in functionality to 'cut up' the sprite sheet into those individual characters. See Figure 20-3.

Figure 20-3. *Example of a bitmap font taken from* https:// opengameart.org/content/8x8-ascii-bitmap-font-with-c-source

Thanks to user 'darkrose' on OpenGameArt (a great resource!) for the sample bitmap font used in this example. As you can see from the preceding image, each letter of the alphabet and the symbols are displayed in a grid. They are arranged in the order that they appear in the ASCII (American Standard Code for Information Interchange) character set. The first printable character is space, which ironically prints a blank space. Space is the 33rd character in the ASCII character set, and because we start numbering at zero, this makes space ASCII 32.

Cutting Up the Image

To access the exclamation mark beside the space, ASCII 33, we use some modulo and division trickery to calculate the row and column of the character.

The row is calculated by taking the ASCII value of the character (in this case 33) and dividing it by the number of columns:

33 / 16 = 2

The column is calculated by taking the ASCII value of the character and modding it with the number of columns:

33 mod 16 = 1

So, our character (!) is located at row 2, column 1. We then multiply those values by the number of pixels in each cell. Our characters are generated from an 8×8 grid, so we multiply each value by 8:

*2 * 8 = 16*
*1 * 8 = 8*

The starting x- and y-coordinates of the start of the 8×8 grid that makes up the exclamation character are (8, 16) as shown in Figure 20-4.

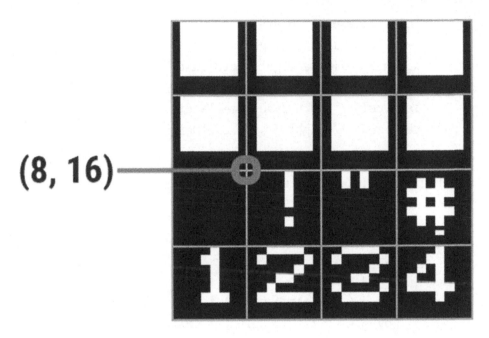

Figure 20-4. *Close-up of a bitmap font showing the pixel start position of the 8×8 grid for the exclamation mark character*

In the 'Invaders' game, bitmap font display is handled by the BitmapFont class. We'll define that class now. Create a new file and call it 'bitmapfont.py'. Enter the code below and save the file.

There is a little twist to this though. The font included with the 'Invaders' project doesn't have the first non-printable 32 characters. It starts with the space character. This is not really an issue, but it adds an extra step to move the characters down 32 positions. Take note of the toIndex() method.

```
import pygame, os, sys
from pygame.locals import *

class BitmapFont(object):
    def __init__(self, fontFile, width, height):
        self.image = pygame.image.load(fontFile)
```

```
self.cellWidth = width
self.cellHeight = height
width = self.image.get_rect().width
height = self.image.get_rect().height
self.cols = width / self.cellWidth
self.rows = height / self.cellHeight
```

The constructor loads the file and based upon the width and height of each character, it calculates the number of columns and rows for the character table.

```
def draw(self, surface, msg, x, y):
    for c in msg:
        ch = self.toIndex(c)
        ox = ( ch % self.cols ) * self.cellWidth
        oy = ( ch / self.cols ) * self.cellHeight
```

This is the part of the code that calculates the x- and y-offset into the bitmap for the current character in the message.

```
cw = self.cellWidth
ch = self.cellHeight
sourceRect = (ox, oy, cw, ch)
surface.blit(self.image, (x, y, cw, ch), sourceRect)
x += self.cellWidth
```

Finally, the partial image is blitted to the surface.

```
def centre(self, surface, msg, y):
    width = len(msg) * self.cellWidth
    halfWidth = surface.get_rect().width
    x = (halfWidth - width) / 2
    self.draw(surface, msg, x, y)
```

The centre() method calculates the overall width of the message and centres it on the line.

```
def toIndex(self, char):
    return ord(char) - ord(' ')
```

The bitmap font that we use for 'Invaders' starts at space (ASCII 32). We use the ord() function that Python provides to get the ASCII value of the character. Subtracting the ASCII value for space gives us our index value into the bitmap font.

Interstitial Screens

Interstitial screens are the images that are displayed in between levels ("Get Ready!") when the pause screen is shown or when the player dies, that is, the "Game Over" screen appears. Create a new file called 'interstitial.py' and type in the following code:

```
import pygame, os, sys
from pygame.locals import *
from bitmapfont import *
from raspigame import *
class InterstitialState(GameState):
```

Our InterstitialState class extends GameState. Remember: if we extend from a class, we place that parent (or base) class' name in parentheses after the name of the class.

```
def __init__(self, game, msg, waitTimeMs, nextState):
    super(InterstitialState, self).__init__(game)
```

The base class' constructor must be called. Under Python, the child class name and the child class instance 'self' must be passed to the super() method. Python 3.0 'fixes' this by way of 'syntactic sugar' and just allowing you to call super(). Not so with the version of Python that ships with the Raspberry Pi.

263

We must also call the constructor directly; that's why the call is to the __init__() method. The base class' constructor expects an instance of RaspiGame, so this is duly passed to the base class' constructor.

```
self.nextState = nextState
self.font = BitmapFont('fasttracker2-style_12x12.png',
12, 12)
self.message = msg
self.waitTimer = waitTimeMs
```

The fields for the interstitial state are initialized.

```
def update(self, gameTime):
    self.waitTimer -= gameTime
    if ( self.waitTimer < 0 ):
        self.game.changeState(self.nextState)
```

The update method waits until the timer runs down. When the timer reaches zero, the game is told to move to the next state.

```
def draw(self, surface):
    self.font.centre(surface, self.message, surface.get_
    rect().height / 2)
```

Save the file.

The Main Menu

The main menu contains two items:

- Start game

- Quit

Like the interstitial screen, the main menu is a subclass of GameState. Create a new file called 'menu.py' and enter the following code:

```
import pygame, os, sys
from pygame.locals import *
from raspigame import *
from bitmapfont import *
```

Our main menu state uses the bitmap font class to draw the text on screen and the raspigame file is imported because MainMenuState is a subclass of GameState. GameState is defined in the raspigame.py file.

```
class MainMenuState(GameState):
    def __init__(self, game):
        super(MainMenuState, self).__init__(game)
        self.playGameState = None
        self.font = BitmapFont('fasttracker2-style_12x12.png',
        12, 12)
        self.index = 0
        self.inputTick = 0
        self.menuItems = ['Start Game', 'Quit']
```

The currently selected item is stored in 'index,' and the menu items are contained in the 'menuItems' list.

```
    def setPlayState(self, state):
        self.playGameState = state
```

The current play state is set to 'state.'

```
    def update(self, gameTime):
        keys = pygame.key.get_pressed()
        if ( (keys[K_UP] or keys[K_DOWN]) and self.inputTick == 0):
            self.inputTick = 250
            if ( keys[K_UP] ):
                self.index -= 1
                if (self.index < 0):
                    self.index = len(self.menuItems) -1
```

```
        elif ( keys[K_DOWN] ):
            self.index += 1
            if (self.index == len(self.menuItems)):
                self.index = 0
```

The user presses the up and down arrow keys to select a menu item. To prevent the menu selection from spinning out of control, the updates are clamped to four per second (250 milliseconds).

```
        elif ( self.inputTick >0 ):
            self.inputTick -= gameTime
        if ( self.inputTick < 0 ):
            self.inputTick = 0
```

The selection is prevented from spinning by updating the inputTick control variable. Once it reaches zero, input is allowed again.

```
        if ( keys[K_SPACE] ):
            if (self.index == 1):
                self.game.changeState(None) # exit the game
            elif (self.index == 0):
                self.game.changeState(self.playGameState)
```

When the user presses the spacebar, the current selected index is tested. If the user chose the zeroth element, the game changes to the playGameState. If the user chooses the first element, the game exits.

```
    def draw(self, surface):
        self.font.centre(surface, "Invaders! From Space!", 48)

        count = 0
        y = surface.get_rect().height - len(self.menuItems) * 160
        for item in self.menuItems:
            itemText = "   "
```

```
if ( count == self.index ):
    itemText = "> "

itemText += item
self.font.draw(surface, itemText, 25, y)
y += 24
count += 1
```

Each menu item is drawn onscreen. The selected menu item is prefixed with a '>' character to indicate to the player that the item has been selected.

Save the file.

Player and Bullets

The bullet classes deal with the position and collection of bullets that have been fired. Like all the entities in this game, the bullets are split into separate model, view, and controller classes. MVC plays a big part in this game!

The Bullet Classes

Create a new Python file in the Invaders folder and call it 'bullet.py'. Enter the following text:

```
import pygame, os, sys
from pygame.locals import *
class BulletModel(object):
```

Our bullet model is super simple. It is a class that contains an x- and y-coordinate representing the bullet's position in 2D space. It has one method, and only one method called update() that takes a single delta value. This is added to the y-coordinate of the bullet's position.

```
def __init__(self, x, y):
    self.x = x
    self.y = y
```

sets the bullet's position to (x, y) on the screen.

```
def update(self, delta):
    self.y = self.y + delta
```

updates the bullet's y-coordinate.

```
class BulletController(object):
```

The bullet controller contains a list of bullets. Each bullet is updated each time the update() method is called.

```
def __init__(self, speed):
    self.countdown = 0
    self.bullets = []
    self.speed = speed
```

The constructor creates a blank array of bullet objects and sets the speed of each bullet to 'speed.' The countdown variable is used as a cooldown for the player. They can only fire a bullet every 1000 milliseconds.

```
def clear(self):
    self.bullets[:] = []
```

Clear the bullet list.

```
def canFire(self):
    return self.countdown == 0 and len(self.bullets) < 3
```

The player can only fire if the countdown has expired and there are less than three active bullets.

```
def addBullet(self, x, y):
    self.bullets.append(BulletModel(x, y))
    self.countdown = 1000
```

A bullet is added to the system and the countdown is reset to 1 second (1000 milliseconds). When the countdown reaches zero, the player can fire again. The countdown field is updated in the update() method.

```
def removeBullet(self, bullet):
    self.bullets.remove(bullet)
```

Bullets are removed from the list when they have either killed an alien or they pop off the top of the screen.

```
def update(self, gameTime):
    killList = []
```

The killList holds bullets that will be removed in this update. Bullets that pop off the top of the screen are removed from the list.

```
    if (self.countdown > 0):
        self.countdown = self.countdown - gameTime
    else:
        self.countdown = 0
```

The gameTime (in milliseconds) is subtracted from the countdown field.

When the countdown field reaches zero, the player can fire again.

```
    for b in self.bullets:
        b.update( self.speed * ( gameTime / 1000.0 ) )
        if (b.y < 0):
            killList.append(b)
```

Each bullet is updated. If their y-coordinate is less than zero (the bullet has popped off the top of the screen), then it is marked for removal.

```
    for b in killList:
        self.removeBullet(b)
```

Our final bullet class is the view. This takes all the data from the bullet controller and displays each bullet onscreen.

```
class BulletView(object):
    def __init__(self, bulletController, imgpath):
        self.BulletController = bulletController
        self.image = pygame.image.load(imgpath)
```

Initialize the bullet view with the bullet controller and the path to the bullet image.

```
    def render(self, surface):
        for b in self.BulletController.bullets:
            surface.blit(self.image, (b.x, b.y, 8, 8))
```

Save the file.

The Player Classes

Create a new file called 'player.py' and enter the following code. The MVC components of the player entity are contained in this one file.

```
import pygame, os, sys
from pygame.locals import *
from bullet import *
from bitmapfont import *

class PlayerModel(object):
    def __init__(self, x, y):
        self.x = x
        self.y = y
        self.lives = 3
        self.score = 0
        self.speed = 100 # pixels per second
```

The player model contains all the data for the player entity: its position onscreen in the form of x- and y-coordinates, the number of lives, the player's score, and their movement speed in pixels per second. Remember: by using pixels per second we can ensure that no matter the speed of the machine, we get a consistent movement speed.

```python
class PlayerController(object):
    def __init__(self, x, y):
        self.model = PlayerModel(x, y)
        self.isPaused = False
        self.bullets = BulletController(-200) # pixels per sec
        self.shootSound = pygame.mixer.Sound('playershoot.wav')
```

The constructor creates an instance of the player model and a BulletController. The bullet controller takes in a single parameter representing the movement speed in pixels per second. It is a negative value because we are going 'up' the screen, which is tending to zero. Why? Well, remember that in computing, the top left of the screen is position (0, 0) and the bottom-right corner is the maximum value on the x- and y-axes.

```python
    def pause(self, isPaused):
        self.isPaused = isPaused
```

Prevent the player from moving the tank.

```python
    def update(self, gameTime):
        self.bullets.update(gameTime)

        if ( self.isPaused ):
            return

        keys = pygame.key.get_pressed()

        if (keys[K_RIGHT] and self.model.x < 800 - 32):
                self.model.x += ( gameTime/1000.0 ) * self.
                model.speed
```

271

```
elif (keys[K_LEFT] and self.model.x > 0):
        self.model.x -= ( gameTime/1000.0 ) * self.
        model.speed
```

The player can move left and right using the cursor (arrow) keys on the keyboard. The position is updated by a percentage of the movement speed based upon the game time. This allows us to have smooth movement no matter the speed of the CPU or our frame rate.

```
if (keys[K_SPACE] and self.bullets.canFire()):
    x = self.model.x + 9 # bullet is 8 pixels
    y = self.model.y - 16
    self.bullets.addBullet(x, y)
    self.shootSound.play()
```

When the player hits the space bar, a bullet is added to the current list of bullets and we play the bullet shooting sound. The firing is restricted by the canFire() method of the 'BulletController' class.

```
def hit(self, x, y, width, height):
    return (x >= self.model.x and y >= self.model.y and x
    + width <= self.model.x + 32 and y + height <= self.
    model.y + 32)
```

This method allows us to test collisions against any other object by boiling the object down to its purest form: its position in space and its width and height.

There are two view classes for the player: PlayerView displays the player's tank at the bottom of the screen, and PlayerLivesView displays the number of lives the player has left.

```
class PlayerView(object):
    def __init__(self, player, imgpath):
        self.player = player
        self.image = pygame.image.load(imgpath)
```

```
def render(self, surface):
    surface.blit(self.image, (self.player.model.x, self.
    player.model.y, 32, 32))
```

The PlayerView class has one main method called 'render.' This displays the tank at the player's position. The player model is passed into the view.

```
class PlayerLivesView(object):
    def __init__(self, player, imgpath):
        self.player = player
        self.image = pygame.image.load(imgpath)
        self.font = BitmapFont('fasttracker2-style_12x12.png',
        12, 12)
```

The constructor takes two arguments: the player model and a string that represents the image path to a bitmap font.

```
def render(self, surface):
    x = 8

    for life in range(0, self.player.model.lives):
        surface.blit(self.image, (x, 8, 32, 32))
        x += 40

    self.font.draw(surface, '1UP SCORE: ' + str(self.
    player.model.score), 160, 12)
```

The render method draws the ship image 'lives' number of times and then displays the player's score as '1UP SCORE: 00000.'

Testing Player

We can test the Player classes by adding the following code to the player. py file. This part is optional, but it gives a clear example that classes can be

273

tested in isolation from the main program. If you don't want to add this, you can just save the file and move to the next section.

```
if ( __name__ == '__main__'):
```

Each Python file is given a name at runtime. If this is the main file, that is, this is the file that is run, it is given the special name 'main.' If that is the case we will initialize PyGame and create our code to test our classes.

```
pygame.init()
fpsClock = pygame.time.Clock()

surface = pygame.display.set_mode((800, 600))
pygame.display.set_caption('Player Test')
black = pygame.Color(0, 0, 0)

player = PlayerController(0, 400)
playerView = PlayerView(player, 'ship.png')
playerLivesView = PlayerLivesView(player, 'ship.png')
```

Create one each of controller, view, and lives view for our Player.

```
while True:

    for event in pygame.event.get():
        if event.type == QUIT:
            pygame.quit()
            sys.exit()

    player.update(fpsClock.get_time())

    surface.fill(black)
    playerView.render(surface)
    playerLivesView.render(surface)

    pygame.display.update()
    fpsClock.tick(30)
```

Our main loop checks to see if 'QUIT' has been selected by the user (i.e., they closed the window), if not then the update() method is called and each display is rendered. Save the 'player.py' file.

The Alien Swarm Classes

Create a new Python file called 'swarm.py'. We will implement the following classes in this file:

- InvaderModel

- SwarmController

- InvaderView

```
import pygame, os, sys
from pygame.locals import *
from bullet import *
```

The PyGame libraries need to be referenced for image manipulation. The alien swarm also uses bullets, so we need to import the 'bullet.py' file too. Our InvaderModel contains minimal code; it is mostly just data that is used to describe the alien to the AlienView.

There are two frames of animation for each type of alien, and there are also two alien types.

```
class InvaderModel(object):
    def __init__(self, x, y, alientype):
        self.x = x
        self.y = y
        self.alientype = alientype
        self.animframe = 0
```

The constructor takes three arguments, not including 'self'. The first two are the starting coordinates of the alien, and the last one is the alien type.

There are two alien types: one red and one green. They score differently when hit which is why we need to store what type of alien this model represents.

```
def flipframe(self):
        if self.animframe == 0:
                self.animframe = 1
        else:
                self.animframe = 0
```

The flipframe() method toggles the current frame of animation from 0 to 1 back to zero again. The aliens only have two frames of animation.

```
def hit(self, x, y, width, height):
        return (x >= self.x and y >= self.y and x + width
        <= self.x + 32 and y + height <= self.y + 32)
```

The last line in the hit() method is all on one line. The hit() method is used by the Collision class to determine if a hit has occurred.

The SwarmController class is actually the controller for the multiple aliens. It uses composition because each individual alien is created and destroyed by the Swarm class.

```
class SwarmController(object):
        def __init__(self, scrwidth, offsety, initialframeticks):
                self.currentframecount = initialframeticks
                self.framecount = initialframeticks
```

The current animation frame is controlled from here. This ensures that each alien 'marches' in time with the other aliens.

```
                self.invaders = []
                self.sx = -8
                self.movedown = False
                self.alienslanded = False
```

The current alien direction is set to a negative (left) direction. The 'movedown' flag is set when the aliens have to move down the screen when they hit a side. The final flag 'alienslanded' means that it's game over for the player when this is True.

```
self.bullets = BulletController(200) # pixels per sec
```

The BulletController class is also part of the SwarmController. The pixels per second value for bullet speed is positive because we are going down the screen. Remember that for the player, it was negative because the player's bullets go up screen.

```
self.alienShooter = 3 # each 3rd alien (to start
with) fires
self.bulletDropTime = 2500
self.shootTimer = self.bulletDropTime # each bullet
is fired in this ms interval
self.currentShooter = 0 # current shooting alien

for y in range(7):
        for x in range(10):
                invader = InvaderModel(160 + (x * 48) +
                8, (y * 32) + offsety, y % 2)
                self.invaders.append(invader)
```

The nested for-loop is used to generate the alien swarm. Each swarm member is an instance of the InvaderModel class.

```
def reset(self, offsety, ticks):
        self.currentframecount = ticks
        self.framecount = ticks

        for y in range(7):
                for x in range(10):
```

```
            invader = InvaderModel(160 + (x * 48) +
            8, (y * 32) + offsety, y % 2)
            self.invaders.append(invader)
```

The 'reset' method is used reset the alien swarm for the next attack, speeding up their descent.

```
def update(self, gameTime):
        self.bullets.update(gameTime)
        self.framecount -= gameTime
        movesideways = True
```

The 'framecount' member field is used as a timer. The gameTime is subtracted from the current time in 'framecount,' and when it reaches zero, we 'tick' the swarm. This is how we control the update speed of our objects. We can specify different 'tick' times. The smaller the 'framecount,' the quicker the update occurs because we must subtract less time.

```
        if self.framecount < 0:
            if self.movedown:
                self.movedown = False
                movesideways = False
                self.sx *= -1
                self.bulletDropTime -= 250
                if ( self.bulletDropTime < 1000 ):
                    self.bulletDropTime = 1000
                self.currentframecount -= 100
                if self.currentframecount < 200: #clamp
                the speed of the aliens to 200ms
                    self.currentframecount = 200

                for i in self.invaders:
                    i.y += 32
```

If we have to move down, the section of code under 'if self.movedown' provides the steps required to move the alien swarm down the screen. When the swarm moves down screen, the 'currentframecount' is updated. This is because the aliens speed up each time they drop further toward the player.

```python
self.framecount = self.currentframecount +
self.framecount
for i in self.invaders:
        i.flipframe()

if movesideways:
        for i in self.invaders:
                i.x += self.sx

x, y, width, height = self.getarea()

if ( x <= 0 and self.sx < 0) or ( x + width
>= 800 and self.sx > 0 ):
        self.movedown = True
```

The getarea() method determines the area used by all the aliens left on the playing field. We then use this information to determine if that area has 'hit' the sides. If the area hit the sides, we mark the swarm to move down the next tick.

```python
self.shootTimer -= gameTime
if ( self.shootTimer <= 0):
        self.shootTimer += self.bulletDropTime
        # reset the timer
        self.currentShooter += self.alienShooter

        self.currentShooter = self.
        currentShooter % len(self.invaders)
```

```
shooter = self.invaders[self.
currentShooter]
x = shooter.x + 9 # bullet is 8 pixels
y = shooter.y + 16
self.bullets.addBullet(x, y)
```

The shooting timer works on a different 'tick' than the frame update. When the timer reaches zero, the current shooter is incremented by 'alienShooter'; therefore it's not part of the main swarm tick.

The 'currentShooter' field is clamped to the number of aliens we have left. This ensures that we don't ever try and access an alien outside our list. The current shooter is then referenced, and we add a bullet at the shooter's position. I chose 3 (three) as the incrementor because it gave a pseudo-random feel to the shooting.

```
def getarea(self):
        leftmost = 2000
        rightmost = -2000
        topmost = -2000
        bottommost = 2000
```

Setting up the maximum and minimum boundaries.

```
        for i in self.invaders:
            if i.x < leftmost:
                    leftmost = i.x

            if i.x > rightmost:
                    rightmost = i.x

            if i.y < bottommost:
                    bottommost = i.y

            if i.y > topmost:
                    topmost = i.y
```

Using some simple range checking, we calculate the leftmost, rightmost, topmost, and bottommost points from all the aliens.

```
width = ( rightmost - leftmost ) + 32
height = ( topmost - bottommost ) + 32

return (leftmost, bottommost, width, height)
```

Our final Invader class is the view class. It uses aggregation because it references the SwarmController class.

```
class InvaderView:
    def __init__(self, swarm, imgpath):
        self.image = pygame.image.load(imgpath)
        self.swarm = swarm
```

The constructor takes in two arguments. The first is the SwarmController instance, and the second is the path to the image file that represents our alien sprites.

```
def render(self, surface):
    for i in self.swarm.invaders:
        surface.blit(self.image, (i.x, i.y, 32, 32),
        (i.animframe * 32, 32 * i.alientype, 32, 32))
```

The 'render' method loops through all the invaders in SwarmController's 'swarm' field and displays it onscreen. The 'animframe' field of the Invader model is used to control how far to the left the slice is taken of the sprite sheet. The 'alientype' field is how far up the slice is.

Save the file. We're going to need this and the other files for collision detection.

Collision Detection

Our collision detection classes are stored in the 'collision.py' file. Create a new blank file and call it 'collision.py'. This will hold the following classes:

- ExplosionModel

- ExplosionModelList

- ExplosionView

- ExplosionController

- CollisionController

We will examine each in the order that they appear in the file.

Explosions

Action games require loud noises and explosions. Our game is no different! The four explosion classes – ExplosionModel, ExplosionModelList, ExplosionView, and ExplosionController – are used by the CollisionController to create and update the various explosions that occur throughout the game. Each explosion is drawn onscreen using a sprite sheet that consists of a series of animation frames.

Our file starts in the familiar way with a series of imports:

```
import pygame, os, sys
from pygame.locals import *
from player import *
from bullet import *
from swarm import *
from interstitial import *
```

Our own classes from player, bullet, swarm, and interstitial are required.

```python
class ExplosionModel(object):
    def __init__(self, x, y, maxFrames, speed, nextState = None):
        self.x = x
        self.y = y
        self.maxFrames = maxFrames
        self.speed = speed
        self.initialSpeed = speed
        self.frame = 0
        self.nextState = nextState
```

The 'ExplosionModel' class contains no methods, much like all our other models. It only contains fields that describe an explosion; it's position, the number of frames, the update speed, the current frame, and the next state.

```python
class ExplosionModelList(object):
    def __init__(self, game):
        self.explosions = []
        self.game - game

    def add(self, explosion, nextState = None):
        x, y, frames, speed = explosion
        exp = ExplosionModel(x, y, frames, speed, nextState)
        self.explosions.append(exp)

    def cleanUp(self):

        killList = []

        for e in self.explosions:
            if ( e.frame == e.maxFrames ):
                killList.append(e)

        nextState = None
```

```
        for e in killList:
            if (nextState == None and e.nextState != None):
                nextState = e.nextState

            self.explosions.remove(e)

        if (nextState != None):
            self.game.changeState(nextState)
```

The cleanUp() method needs a little explanation. With this mechanism, we can encode in our explosion the ability to move the game to another state. For example, when the player dies and they have no more lives, we can change the state of the game to 'Game Over.'

```
class ExplosionView(object):
    def __init__(self, explosions, explosionImg, width, height):
        self.image = pygame.image.load(explosionImg)
        self.image.set_colorkey((255, 0, 255))
        self.explosions = explosions
        self.width = width
        self.height = height

    def render(self, surface):
        for e in self.explosions:
            surface.blit(self.image, ( e.x, e.y, self.width,
            self.height ), (e.frame * self.width, 0, self.
            width, self.height) )
```

The 'ExplosionView' loops through all the explosions and displays each one of them in turn.

```
class ExplosionController(object):
    def __init__(self, game):
        self.list = ExplosionModelList(game)
```

```
def update(self, gameTime):
    for e in self.list.explosions:
        e.speed -= gameTime
        if ( e.speed < 0 ):
            e.speed += e.initialSpeed
            e.frame += 1
    self.list.cleanUp()
```

The 'ExplosionController' is the simplest controller we've encountered. It has an initialization method that creates an 'ExplosionModelList' (an example of composition) and an update() method. The update() method only needs to increment the frame count. When the count reaches the maximum frame count, it is automatically removed in the cleanUp() method of the 'ExplosionModelList' class.

Collision Controller

The 'CollisionController' class doesn't need a corresponding model or view because it does not require either. It does use other controllers and models to determine if a collision has occurred. If something was hit, a suitable sound is made, and an action is performed.

```
class CollisionController(object):
    def __init__(self, game, swarm, player, explosionController,
    playState):
        self.swarm = swarm
        self.player = player
        self.game = game
        self.BulletController = player.bullets
        self.EnemyBullets = swarm.bullets
        self.expCtrl = explosionController
        self.playGameState = playState
```

```
self.alienDeadSound = pygame.mixer.Sound('aliendie.wav')
self.playerDie = pygame.mixer.Sound('playerdie.wav')
```

The constructor for 'CollisionController' takes in the game, swarm controller, player controller, explosion controller instances, and the play game state. We also load a couple of sounds for when the player hits an alien ('aliendie.wav') or if an alien unfortunately hits the player ('playerdie.wav').

```
def update(self, gameTime):

    aliens = []
    bullets = []

    for b in self.BulletController.bullets:

        if (bullets.count(b)>0):
            continue

        for inv in self.swarm.invaders:
            if (inv.hit(b.x+3, b.y+3, 8, 12)):
                aliens.append(inv)
                bullets.append(b)
                break
```

Gather all the player's bullets and the aliens that have hit an invader.

```
    for b in bullets:
        self.BulletController.removeBullet(b)
```

Remove all the bullets that were found that hit an alien

```
    for inv in aliens:
        self.swarm.invaders.remove(inv)
        self.player.model.score += (10 * (inv.alientype + 1))
        self.expCtrl.list.add((inv.x, inv.y, 6, 50))
        self.alienDeadSound.play()
```

Remove all the aliens that have been hit by the player's bullets. This part also increments the player's score and plays the alien death sound.

```
playerHit = False

for b in self.EnemyBullets.bullets:
    if ( self.player.hit (b.x+3, b.y+3, 8, 12 ) ):
        self.player.model.lives -= 1
        playerHit = True
        break
```

Now we check the enemy bullets. If any one of them has hit the player, we set the 'playerHit' flag to 'True' and 'break' the for-loop. There is no need to continue searching through the bullets if we have already hit the player.

```
if ( playerHit ):
    self.EnemyBullets.clear()
    self.player.bullets.clear()

    if ( self.player.model.lives > 0 ):
        self.player.pause(True)
        getReadyState = InterstitialState( self.game,
        'Get Ready!', 2000, self.playGameState )
        self.expCtrl.list.add((self.player.model.x,
        self.player.model.y, 6, 50), getReadyState)

    self.playerDie.play()
```

If the player has been hit, we clear all the bullets from the game. If the player still has lives left, we pause the player and change the game state to the 'get ready' screen and add an explosion to show the player's tank destroyed. Remember: we can change the state after an explosion (see the 'ExplosionController' class) and that's what we're setting up here.

We're almost done! Two more files to go. These are the main program and the main game state.

The Main Program

The main program is a single file called 'invaders.py'. Create a new file called 'invaders.py' and enter the following code. The 'RaspberryPiGame' class that we created earlier is expecting an initial state. Our main program's function is to create the states used by the Finite State Machine (FSM) and set the initial state.

```
import pygame, os, sys
from pygame.locals import *
# Our imports
from raspigame import *
from interstitial import *
from menu import MainMenuState
from invadersgame import PlayGameState
```

Our usual imports for the OS and PyGame modules plus our own local modules. We're installing everything from 'raspigame.py' and 'interstitial.py' but only MainMenuState from 'menu.py' and PlayGameState from 'invadersgame.py'.

```
invadersGame = RaspberryPiGame("Invaders", 800, 600)
mainMenuState = MainMenuState( invadersGame )
gameOverState = InterstitialState( invadersGame, 'G A M E   O V
E R !', 5000, mainMenuState )
playGameState = PlayGameState( invadersGame, gameOverState )
getReadyState = InterstitialState( invadersGame, 'Get Ready!',
2000, playGameState )
mainMenuState.setPlayState( getReadyState )
```

Create instances of the states used in the game: main menu, game over, play game, and the get ready states.

```
invadersGame.run( mainMenuState )
```

Set the initial state of the game to be the main menu. And that's it – that's the main program. Its sole purpose is to create the links between the game states and to set the initial state, and it's all achieved in six lines of code.

Save this file. The last class that remains to do is the main game state.

The Main Game State

Create a new file called 'invadersgame.py'. Enter the following code:

```python
import pygame, os, sys
from pygame.locals import *
from raspigame import *
from swarm import *
from player import *
from collision import *
```

Module imports.

```python
class PlayGameState(GameState):
    def __init__(self, game, gameOverState):
        super(PlayGameState, self).__init__(game)
        self.controllers = None
        self.renderers = None
        self.player_controller = None
        self.swarm_controller = None
        self.swarmSpeed = 500
        self.gameOverState = gameOverState
        self.initialise()
```

Our 'PlayGameState' class derives from 'GameState' and so the constructor must call the base class' constructor. The fields for the controllers and the 'Game Over' state are initialized. To keep this method down to a bare minimum, the initialise() method is called.

```
def onEnter(self, previousState):
    self.player_controller.pause(False)
```

The onEnter() method is part of the GameState class. The only thing we need to do is tell the player controller that it is unpaused.

```
def initialise(self):
    self.swarm_controller = SwarmController(800, 48, self.
    swarmSpeed)
    swarm_renderer = InvaderView(self.swarm_controller,
    'invaders.png')

    self.player_controller = PlayerController(0, 540)
    player_renderer = PlayerView(self.player_controller,
    'ship.png')
    lives_renderer = PlayerLivesView(self.player_
    controller, 'ship.png')
    bullet_renderer = BulletView(self.player_controller.
    bullets, 'bullet.png')
    alienbullet_renderer = BulletView(self.swarm_
    controller.bullets, 'alienbullet.png')

    explosion_controller = ExplosionController(self.game)
    collision_controller = CollisionController(self.
    game, self.swarm_controller, self.player_controller,
    explosion_controller, self)

    explosion_view = ExplosionView(explosion_controller.
    list.explosions, 'explosion.png', 32, 32)
```

```
self.renderers = [ alienbullet_renderer, swarm_
renderer, bullet_renderer, player_renderer, lives_
renderer, explosion_view ]
self.controllers = [ self.swarm_controller, self.player_
controller, collision_controller, explosion_controller ]
```

The initialise() method contains the code that creates the instances of each of the controllers and renderers. These are then added to the 'renderers' and 'controllers' fields. Each of these fields is a list that we can iterate through in the update() and draw() methods.

```
def update(self, gameTime):
    for ctrl in self.controllers:
        ctrl.update(gameTime)
```

Loop through all of the controllers and call the update() method on each of them. Because we have stored the controllers in a list, updating each of them is a fairly trivial piece of code

```
if ( self.player_controller.model.lives == 0 ):
    self.game.changeState( self.gameOverState )
```

If the player has no more lives left, we change the state of the game to the "Game Over" state. As it stands, it doesn't matter what lines follow, but you may want to add a 'return' here to exit from the method.

```
if ( len(self.swarm_controller.invaders) == 0 ):
    self.swarmSpeed -= 50
    if ( self.swarmSpeed < 100 ):
        self.swarmSpeed = 100
```

If there are no more aliens left onscreen then we start a new level. The speed of the aliens is decreased; this means that the delta time between updates is decreased. This also means we get faster aliens.

```
            self.swarm_controller.reset(48, self.swarmSpeed)
            levelUpMessage = InterstitialState( invadersGame,
            'Congratulations! Level Up!', 2000, self )
            self.game.changeState ( levelUpMessage )
```

Now that we are starting a new board (swarm of aliens) we tell the swarm controller to reset to the new speed and change the state of the game to show the "Level Up" message.

```
    def draw(self, surface):
        for view in self.renderers:
            view.render(surface)
```

The last method draws all the objects on the screen.

Save the file. We're finished! You now have a fully working "Invaders" game.

Running the Game

To run the game, press F5 in the code editor for 'invaders.py' or type the following at the command prompt from within the 'pygamebook/projects/invaders' folder:

```
$ python ./invaders.py
```

Us the arrow keys to select the menu option and press space to select as shown in Figure 20-5. Have fun, you've earned it!

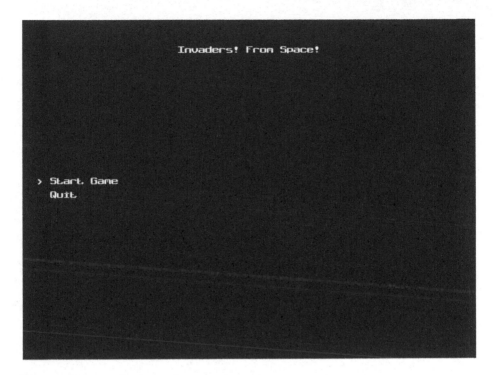

Figure 20-5. *The Invaders main menu*

Conclusion

We have built complex arcade-style games using our Raspberry Pi, Python, and PyGame. Using patterns like MVC (Model View Controller), our program classes can be kept relatively short and focused on doing one thing be it rendering sprites, controlling a character or being the data model.

In the last few chapters of the book we will combine what we have learned with Python and PyGame and create other interactions with our environment using the General Purpose Input/Output, or GPIO, pins of the Raspberry Pi to control LEDs and receive input from buttons.

CHAPTER 21

Simple Electronics with the GPIO Pins

Up until now we have seen the Raspberry Pi communicate with the keyboard and mouse as input devices and the display as an output. The Raspberry Pi can communicate with a wide variety of peripherals – a fancy name for things you can add on – as well as electronic components like Light Emitting Diodes (LEDs) or switches. This is achieved by attaching devices through the pins on the top of the Raspberry Pi. These pins are called the General Purpose Input/ Output pins or GPIOs for short.

There are 40 pins on a Raspberry Pi Model B+ as shown in Figure 21-1.

© Sloan Kelly 2019
S. Kelly, *Python, PyGame, and Raspberry Pi Game Development*,
https://doi.org/10.1007/978-1-4842-4533-0_21

General Purpose Input/ Output (GPIO) Pins

Figure 21-1. *The location of the General Purpose Input/Output (GPIO) pins on the Raspberry Pi board*

You should always be careful when attaching and detaching peripherals and should turn the power off when doing so. Keeping the power on and attaching devices may damage the computer.

Careful when plugging devices into the Raspberry Pi! Always turn off the machine before doing so!

Voltage, Current, and Resistance

Before we connect our components to the Raspberry Pi, we should take a step back and discuss some of the basics of electronics. An electronic circuit is formed when a path is created that allows free electrons to move along it. The continuous movement of these electrons is a *current*, think river. The force causing these electrons to flow is called *voltage* and is the measurement of potential energy between two points in the circuit.

Finally, there is resistance. No matter how well you plan your circuit, you will always get some resistance to the flow. This might be caused by imperfections in the wire, loss of energy because of heat loss, etc. You can even add imperfections by adding devices called *resistors* to lower the flow of current. In Figure 21-2 we see a circuit that contains an LED (a light) and a switch as well as a resistor. They are all connected to a battery. The circuit is completed because the two ends of the battery – the +ve and –ve ends – are connected through the resistor, switch, and LED. The circuit will be *complete*, that is, the electrons will be free to flow from +ve to –ve terminals of the battery when the switch is connected. This flow is called *conventional current*.

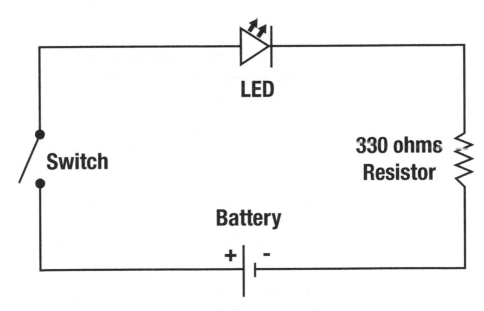

Figure 21-2. *A simple circuit that will illuminate the light when the switch on the left has been pressed*

This circuit will light the LED when the switch is pressed. Later in this chapter we will build this circuit using the components listed as follows.

What You Will Need

For the remaining projects in this book, you will need a few things before you can get started creating circuits with the Raspberry Pi. At the minimum you will need

- Breadboard

- A breakout board

- Jumper wires

- LEDs

- Resistors (330Ω will be fine)

- Switches

The Raspberry Pi can provide 3.3V power as well as ground. Again, be careful connecting and disconnecting wires. You can cause damage to your Raspberry Pi if you do not take care what pins you are connecting.

Breadboard

A breadboard is used to prototype electronic circuits. It allows for easy placement and removal of components like LEDs, wires and switches without having to solder or de-solder those components. As shown in Figure 21-2, the breadboard is covered in tiny connectors protected by a plastic shell. The tiny connectors are arranged in a very particular way.

On the top and bottom are two lines labeled + (positive) and – (negative). These are the power (3.3 volts) and ground (0 volt) lines. If you connect the Raspberry PI's 3.3V output to the + rail, *all the connectors* on that rail receive 3.3 volts. This makes attaching a component to the +ve (positive) and –ve (negative) rails easy.

The middle section is split down the middle and separates each row in half. The columns of each row section are connected. Again, this makes connecting multiple outputs to a single pin easier. Each row is not connected to the other. There is usually a numbering system on breadboards to make creating circuits easier. In the following example the columns are labeled 'a' through 'j' and the rows are numbered in intervals of 5: 1, 5, 10, 15, etc.

Breakout Board

A breakout board is a simple device that makes connecting a Raspberry Pi to a breadboard for prototyping easy. The device is placed on the breadboard as shown in Figure 21-3. The remaining columns in each row allow jumper wires or resistors to be connected to the associated pin on that row.

Figure 21-3. *A breadboard for prototyping electronic circuits*

The Raspberry Pi and the breadboard can then be connected using the supplied ribbon cable. Please read the instructions on how to connect the ribbon cable as it varies depending on the supplier and the model.

Most breakout boards come in the variety shown in Figure 21-3 but some are T-shaped to make connecting even easier.

Notice that the breakout board has the Raspberry Pi pins marked on the side. This makes pins easier to identify when placing jumper wires. Adafruit supplies a breakout board called the 'cobbler' for various Raspberry Pi models. See `www.adafruit.com/` for more details.

Jumper Wires

Jumper wires come in a variety of lengths as shapes as can be seen in Figures 21-4 and 21-5. Some are pre-packages in a box and others are random assortments inside a plastic bag. Either way they are usually a solid piece of wire that allow you to connect LEDs, switches, etc., to the Raspberry Pi pins.

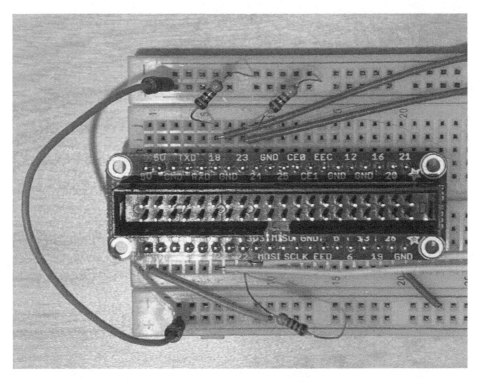

Figure 21-4. *A breakout board (middle of the picture) on a breadboard with jumper wires and resistors connected to the pins*

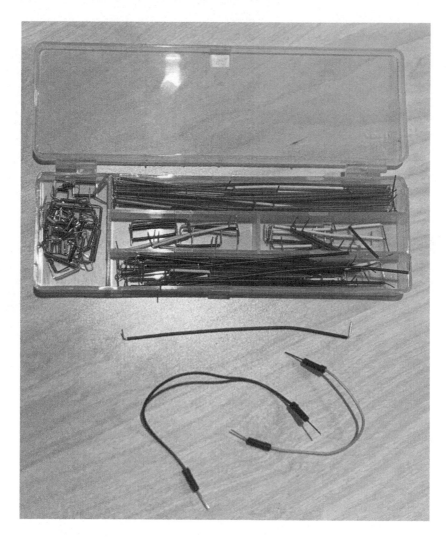

Figure 21-5. A selection of solid core wires

LEDs

Light Emitting Diodes (LEDs) allow an electric current to pass in one direction (that's the diode part) and emit light at the same time. It is used to provide cheap low-cost light and comes in a variety of packages. For most electronics, the familiar color domed version, as shown in Figure 21-6, is used.

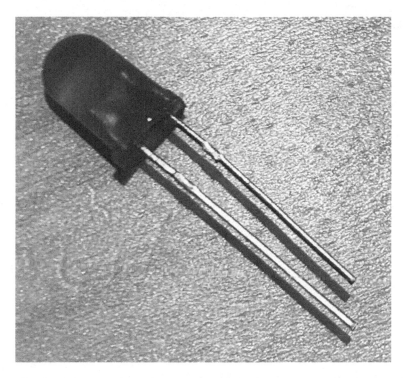

Figure 21-6. *An LED. Note that one leg is longer than the other. The longer leg is the anode and is always connected to the positive rail.*

You have probably noticed that one leg is longer than the other. This is called the anode and is always connected to the +ve (3.3V) rail. The shorter leg is called the cathode and is connected to the ground or 0V line. If you connect it the other way, the light will not illuminate. You won't break the light, it just won't light.

You will also need to attach a resistor to the circuit when using LEDs because they can draw more power from the Raspberry Pi which can then damage the computer.

Resistors

Resistors limit the amount of current traveling through a circuit. The measure of resistance is called an ohm (Ω) and the larger the resistance value, the more it limits the current. The formula for calculating voltages, current (measured in amps), and resistance (ohms) in a circuit is

V = IR

where V is the voltage, I is current, and R is resistance. If you want to calculate the current going through a 330Ω resistor at 3.3V, then it would be

V = IR

So, that means that I = V / R:

I = 3.3 / 330
I = 0.01 amps

If we increase that resistor to 470 Ω, it drops the amps from 0.01 amps to 0.006 amps, almost half of the original value, meaning that there is less current going through to the other side of the resistor.

A strip of resistors is shown in Figure 21-7. The value of the resistor has been written on the paper strip to make it easier to identify its value: 330Ω. The bands around the resistor indicate its value. There are between three and six colored bands, but the resistors I have use five as shown in Table 21-1:

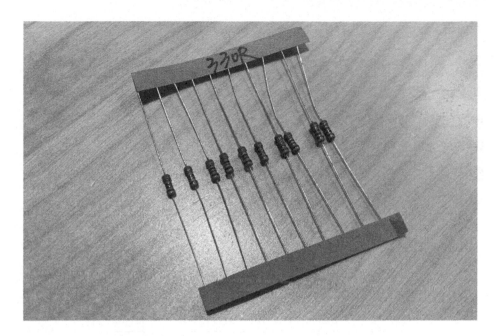

Figure 21-7. *A strip of resistors from a supplier with the value marked on the paper tape*

Table 21-1. *Resistor Color Band Positions and Meanings*

Color	First Band	Second Band	Third Band	Multiplier	Tolerance
Black	0	0	0	1Ω	
Brown	1	1	1	10Ω	± 1%
Red	2	2	2	1KΩ	± 2%
Orange	3	3	3	10KΩ	
Yellow	4	4	4	100KΩ	
Green	5	5	5	1MΩ	± 0.5%
Blue	6	6	6	10MΩ	± 0.25%

(continued)

Table 21-1. (*continued*)

Color	First Band	Second Band	Third Band	Multiplier	Tolerance
Violet	7	7	7	1GΩ	± 0.1%
Gray	8	8	8	0.1Ω	± 0.05%
White	9	9	9	0.01Ω	
Gold					± 5%
Silver					± 10%

The colors of the resistors I have are shown in Table 21-2.

Table 21-2. *Converting the Colored Bands to Determine the Value of the Resistor*

Color	Value
Orange	3
Orange	3
Black	0
Black	1 Ω
Gold	± 5%

This is $330 \times 1\ \Omega$ or $330\ \Omega$ with a tolerance of ± 5%.

It is important to use a resistor when placing a LED in your circuit. A LED will try to absorb as much current as possible and a resistor is a great way to limit that absorption. Resistors do not have directionality, unlike LEDs, so you can put them any way round you like, I'd recommend keeping them all facing the same direction for clarity.

Switches

Figure 21-8 shows a simple push-button tact switch. It contains four pins arranged in two pairs. Each pair is disconnected from the other. When the switch is depressed a contact inside the package completes the connection between the pairs.

Figure 21-8. *A simple push-button tact switch*

Building a Circuit

Now that we have learned the basics of electronic circuits, let's build a very simple one that requires no programming. We're going to recreate the circuit from Figure 21-1. For this we will need

- A breadboard

- A breakout board

- Three jumper wires

- A 330Ω resistor

- A tact switch

- An LED

Connecting the Breakout Board to the Raspberry Pi

Shut down the Raspberry Pi by clicking on the Raspberry Pi menu and choosing "Shutdown…" as shown in Figure 21-9.

Figure 21-9. *The shutdown menu item on the Raspberry Pi system menu*

Wait until the machine full shuts down. Don't disconnect the power! We need the power to build the circuit.

Connect the ribbon cable for the breakout board to the Raspberry Pi's GPIO pins. Be careful not to force it as this may bend the pins if the cable is not seated correctly.

There is usually a white wire on the ribbon cable. This indicates the first pin and is used to align the Raspberry Pi with the breakout board. Make sure that the white wire is nearest the top of the board, that is, further away from the USB and network ports as shown in Figure 21-10.

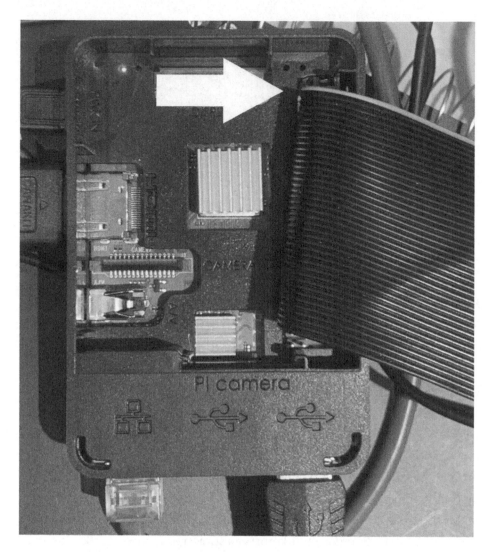

Figure 21-10. *The arrow indicates the location of the white wire on the cable. Notice the orientation of the board to the USB, network, and HDMI ports*

Insert the breakout board on the breadboard. The breakout board should straddle the middle trough of the breadboard as shown in Figure 21-4. Again, take care not to bend any of the pins.

Next, connect the other end of the ribbon cable to the breakout board. This is made easier by having a notch in the side of the breakout board and a raised section on the ribbon connector. It can only go in one way, but to be sure, the white wire on the cable should at the top of the board.

You should now have the Raspberry Pi connected to the breadboard. Even though the Raspberry Pi is off, the power is still connected to it. We can use this to power our circuit.

Providing Power and Ground

The first two jumper wires we will add are to the Raspberry Pi's 3.3V and ground pins. These are located near the top of the breakout board and are shown in Figure 21-11.

Figure 21-11. *The 3V3 pin and the ground pin wires*

Insert one end of a wire in the 3V3 (3.3 volt) pin row as shown in Figure 21-11. Place the other end in the +ve rail of the breadboard. This is our 3.3V line. Anything connected to that line – shown in red on the breadboard – will be connected to 3.3V.

Next take another wire and connect it to a row marked with a GND or ground. This will be our ground wire. We don't have a place to put that yet, so just leave it floating for now.

Adding the LED

Place an LED on the motherboard with the anode (the longer leg) on one row and the cathode (the shorter leg) on another. Don't place the pins on the same row or it won't work! In Figure 21-12 I show how I placed the LED. It doesn't matter which way round it is – the arrow indicates the anode – so long as you remember which way it is.

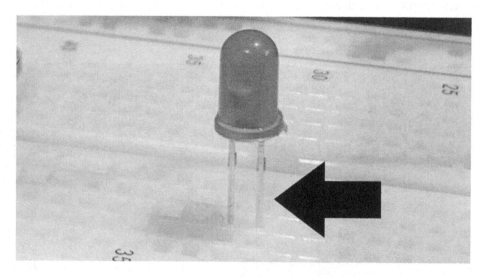

Figure 21-12. *The LED pins are placed on different rows. The arrow is pointing to the anode pin.*

To connect the LED to the 3.3V line, we will use a 330Ω resistor.

Remember! Always use a resistor with an LED!

Connect one end of a resistor to the same row as the anode and the other to the +ve rail as shown in Figure 21-13.

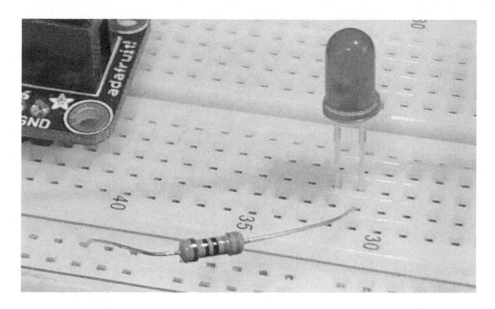

Figure 21-13. *Connecting the LED to the 3.3V line using a 330Ω resistor*

Completing the Circuit

We'll now complete the circuit by adding the tact switch and the jumper wires. Place a switch on the breadboard as shown in Figure 21-14.

Figure 21-14. *A tact switch straddling the trough in the middle of the breadboard*

I like to place it across the trough in the middle of the board, but you can place it any where you want. Remember that the switch has two pairs and the pins of each pair are connected to each other. This means that, as shown in Figure 21-14, we need to connect the wires to the top and bottom pins so that when the tact switch is pressed the circuit is completed. If we connected the two top pins or the two bottom pins, the circuit would complete.

Take the 0V (ground) wire that we left floating earlier and insert it into a connector on the same row as the top pin of the switch. Take another jumper wire and connect it to the same row as the bottom pin of the switch and to the cathode (short pin) of the LED.

You should now have a circuit that looks something like that shown in Figure 21-15.

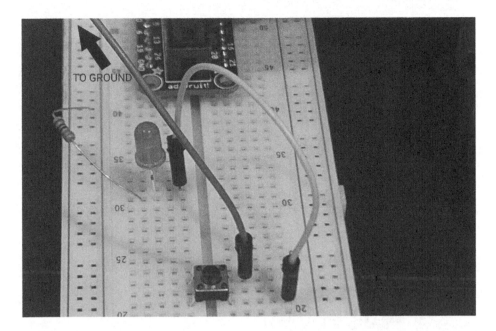

Figure 21-15. *The completed circuit. The breakout board is partially visible at the top of the picture.*

Testing the Circuit

The full circuit is shown in Figure 21-16. You should review the connections in that circuit against the physical circuit you have just made. Make sure all the connections match with the ones in the figure before pressing the tact switch.

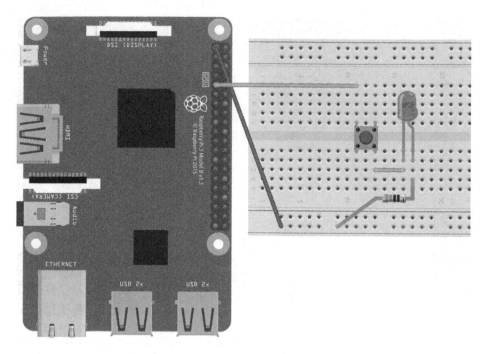

Figure 21-16. *The circuit diagram showing the connections between the Raspberry Pi and the breadboard. Use this diagram to ensure you have your circuit built correctly before pressing the tact switch.*

If everything is OK, press down on the tact switch and the circuit should light up! If it doesn't, check your wiring. If you disconnected the power from the Raspberry Pi – remember, we need that power for this circuit – you should re-connect the power. This will turn on your Raspberry Pi, but that's fine. For this exercise we only need the power from the pins.

Pin Meanings

Each pin has a specific purpose and the Raspberry Pi allows you to connect to peripherals using SPI (Serial Peripheral Interface), I2C (Inter-Integrated Circuit), or the GPIO pins directly. For the remainder of this book we will be concentrating on the GPIO pins themselves. We will see later that we must tell the Raspberry Pi how we will be using the GPIO pins, that is, what mode of operation. Figure 21-17 shows what the physical pins map to.

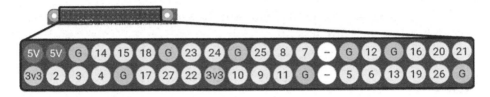

Figure 21-17. The position of each GPIO, voltage, and ground pins

The first thing you'll notice is that the numbered pins are not in sequence. These are the GPIO pins and are directly accessible through Python. You can connect switches, LEDs, etc., to these pins and have Python read their values or write values to them to turn on lights.

The 3v3 pins output 3.3 volts and the 5V pins output 5 volts. It is recommended that you stick to 3.3V lines unless the peripheral that you are trying to connect requires 5 volts. The ground pins are agnostic; it doesn't matter whether you are using 5 volts or 3.3, your circuit uses the same ground pins. The ground pins are marked 'G' in Figure 21-17.

The last two pins are pins 0 and 1 of the GPIO and are not accessible. You should NOT connect devices to these two pins. Those pins are marked '- -' in the diagram.

Let's rebuild the circuit and use Python to turn on the light.

The gpiozero Library

To 'talk' with the electronic components on the breadboard, we will use the gpiozero library. This is a set of utilities that make it easy to talk to and read data from components connected to the GPIO pins.

This book will only cover a very small part of the functionality that this library covers. If you want to attach motion sensors, temperature gauges, potentiometers, etc., then I recommend reading through the documentation at https://gpiozero.readthedocs.io.

The first program that we'll create with this library is one that turns an LED on for a second and then off.

The Circuit

The circuit, shown in Figure 21-18, connects the LED's anode (longer of the two pins) to the Raspberry Pi through GPIO pin 4. The resistor is connected to the cathode (shorter of the two pins) of the LED and in turn to one of the ground pins of the Raspberry Pi. Construct the circuit shown in Figure 21-18.

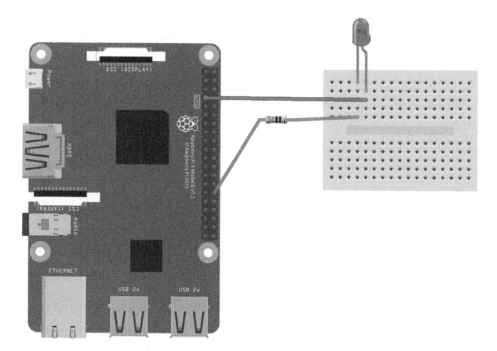

Figure 21-18. *The circuit for the Python controlled LED*

The LED should not be lit at this point. We're going to do that in code.

The Python Program

Open up the IDLE IDE and create a new file called 'ch21-1.py' and place it in a new folder called 'ch21' inside the 'pygamebook' folder. Inside the file, type the following:

```
from gpiozero import LED
from time import sleep
```

Import the gpiozero library to access the LED class. This wrapper class makes it easier to turn on and off LEDs. The second import is for the sleep() function. Sleep takes one parameter and that is the number of seconds that the computer should wait before executing the next statement

```
led = LED(4)
```

Create a LED object that is connected to a physical LED that is connected to GPIO pin 4.

```
led.on()
sleep(1)
```

Turn the LED on and wait for a second.

```
led.off()
sleep(1)
```

Turn the LED off and wait for a second.

Save and run the program. Observe what happens on the breadboard – the LED lights up for a second and then turns off!

Other Functions

The on() and off() functions are perfect for turning off and on the LED, but you can also toggle the state of the LED, so if the light is illuminated, calling toggle() will turn if off and vice versa. Lastly, blink() will do just that – it will blink the LED. You can specify the duration that the light is on, and the duration that the light is off.

319

Getting Button Input

As well as outputting values to a GPIO pin, the Raspberry Pi can read
values in. In this section we will add a button to the circuit and control the
blinking of the LED. The modified circuit is shown in Figure 21-19.

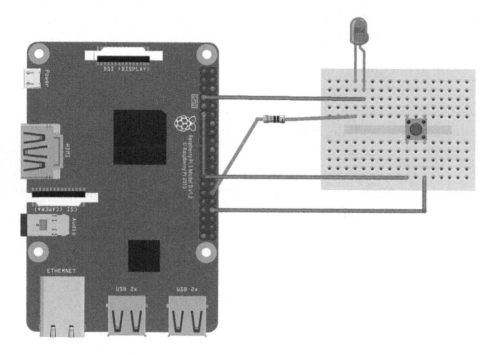

Figure 21-19.   *The circuit for the tact switch controlled LED*

The LED is still connected to GPIO pin 4 as it was in the previous
circuit. The switch is connected to GPIO 17 on one side and the other side
is tied to a ground pin on the Raspberry Pi. The Button object can be used
to make reading the state of the button (pressed, released) easy.

Reading Button Input in Python

Create a new file called 'ch21-2.py' in the same folder as the previous program. Enter the code exactly as written:

```
from gpiozero import LED, Button
```

Import both the LED and Button classes from the gpiozero library.

```
led = LED(4)
button = Button(17)
```

Create a LED object where the physical LED is connected to GPIO pin 4. Create a Button object where the physical tact switch is connected to GPIO pin 17.

```
ledOn = False
wasPressed = False
```

Flag to remember the state of the LED – ledOn. When the program starts it is off so 'ledOn' is set to False. Flag to remember the last state of the button – wasPressed. This will prevent the button from being pressed continually and flashing the LED off and on rapidly.

```
while True:
```

Keep the program running. To quit the program press Ctrl+C.

```
    if not button.is_pressed and wasPressed:
        ledOn = not ledOn
```

Toggle the state of the 'ledOn' variable if the button has been released, that is, if the button *was* pressed and is not *not* pressed.

```
    if ledOn:
        led.blink()
    else:
        led.off()
  wasPressed = button.is_pressed
```

If the LED should be on, set it to blink. Otherwise, it should be turned off. The 'state' variable is set to the current state of the button pressed.

Save and run the program.

Press the tact switch on the breadboard briefly. The LED will start to blink. Pressing the button again will stop the LED blinking. Press Ctrl+C on the keyboard to quit the program. You could add another button to the circuit board and query that button to determine if the program should stop. Sounds like an interesting exercise! How would you go about it?

Conclusion

The General Purpose Input/Output (GPIO) pins allow the Raspberry Pi to talk to electronic components like LEDs, switches, motion sensors, temperature gauges, etc. It has additional modes that allow you to connect to peripherals that support SPI or I2C standards.

Using the GPIO we can extend our programs by flashing LEDs or getting input from tact switches. In the next couple of chapters, we will see how we can use the GPIO for game input and output.

CHAPTER 22

Game Project: Memory

The game 'Memory' is the first GPIO project. The board is set up with two rows: one with four LEDs and the other with four buttons as shown in the finished board in Figure 22-1.

Figure 22-1. *The suggested layout of the breadboard with two rows: one with four LEDs and the other with four buttons*

© Sloan Kelly 2019
S. Kelly, *Python, PyGame, and Raspberry Pi Game Development*,
https://doi.org/10.1007/978-1-4842-4533-0_22

When the sequence plays on the LEDs, the player repeats the sequence by pressing the corresponding buttons on the row underneath the LEDs. The game starts with one LED being played but moves up to four LEDs as the game progresses.

Arranging the Breadboard

We will build the breadboard in a specific order: the row of LEDs, then the row of tact switches. After each row has been constructed, a small script is written to test the components and make sure the wiring is correct.

Placing the LEDs

Arrange the LEDs and tact switches as shown in Figure 22-1. The LEDs should be aligned so that the longer leg (the anode) is on the right-hand side. There is no technical reason for this, but it keeps the design consistent and ensures that the wires will be placed in the correct holes on the board. Figure 22-2 shows how the LEDs should be connected.

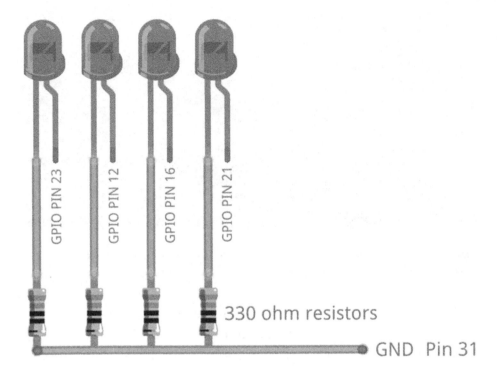

Figure 22-2. *The connections from the GPIO pins to the corresponding LEDs*

Each cathode (the shorter pin) is connected to ground pin 31 via a 330Ω resistor. The anode (the longer pin) is connected to a specific GPIO pin number as shown in the diagram. To make creating the circuit easier, I placed a small jumper – as shown in Figure 22-3 – from pin 31 (ground) to the –ve rail on the breadboard. Connecting the resistor to pin 31 then means connecting the resistor to the –ve rail.

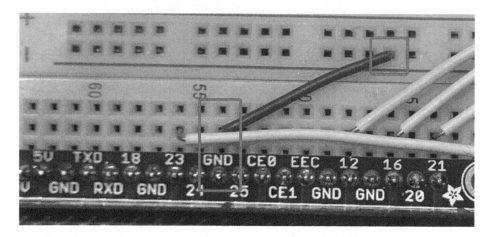

Figure 22-3. *Connecting ground pin 31 to the –ve rail makes connecting the resistors easier*

Notice in the taller box there are only three exposed holes in the breadboard that connect with pin 31 (ground). By making the –ve rail connect with pin 31, we effectively have approximately 50 holes connected, depending on the size of your breadboard.

As can be seen in Figure 22-3, the lighter wires are connecting to pins 23, 12, 16, and 21.

Testing the Circuit

To test the circuit we will write a small Python script to turn on and off the LEDs in sequence. Create a new folder inside the 'projects' folder inside 'pygamebook' called 'memory.' Inside this folder create a new Python script called 'ledtest.py'. It is a very short program that turns each LED on in turn for half a second and then moves onto the next one.

```
from gpiozero import LED
from time import sleep
```

Import the gpiozero library to access the LED class. Import time for the sleep function.

```
leds = [ LED(23), LED(12), LED(16), LED(21) ]
```

Create an array of LED objects. Notice that the numbers are in the order the LEDs appear from left to right.

```
while True:
    for led in leds:
        led.on()
        sleep(0.5)
        led.off()
```

The loop will keep the program running, cycling through all the lights, turning them on then off one after the other. Save and run the program. To exit the program, press Ctrl+C.

If there are any problems, check the wiring and which pins are connected to the LEDs.

Placing the Tact Switches

The buttons, or tact switches, are placed on the board and attached to the GPIO pins and ground as shown in the (simplified) diagram shown in Figure 22-4.

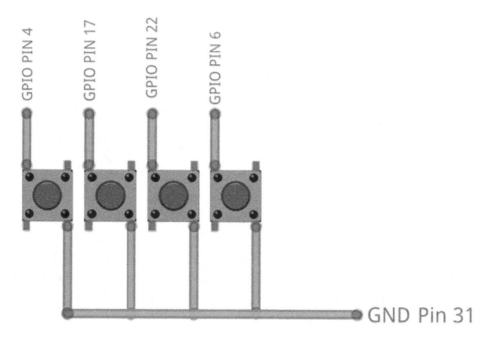

Figure 22-4. *The tact switch connections to the GPIO pins and ground*

The wires connecting to Pin 31 (ground) can be done by placing wires from the switches to the –ve rail as we did previously for the LEDs.

Testing the Button Circuit

For this test, we will write a script to turn on the corresponding LED when a switch has been pressed. From a logical point of view, the button on GPIO 4 will turn on the LED connected to GPIO 23, the button on GPIO 17 will turn on the LED connected to GPIO 12, and so on.

Our program will use tuples of LED and Button classes.

Create a new script called 'buttontest.py' inside the 'memory' folder and enter the following code:

```
from gpiozero import LED, Button
from time import sleep
```

Imports for the program. gpiozero for LED and Button classes and time for the sleep function.

```
pair1 = (LED(23), Button(4))
pair2 = (LED(12), Button(17))
pair3 = (LED(16), Button(22))
pair4 = (LED(21), Button(6))
```

The pairings match each LED with a corresponding button. The zeroth element of the tuple is the LED and the first element of the tuple is the button. Remember: we can use integer index values to access tuple parts.

```
pairs = [ pair1, pair2, pair3, pair4 ]
```

To make our program short, we will use a list of the pairs and loop through them.

```
while True:
    for pair in pairs:
        if pair[1].is_pressed:
            pair[0].on()
        else:
            pair[0].off()
```

The loop keeps the program running while we test the buttons. Each pair in the list is looped through. The button's 'is_pressed' property is tested and if the button is pressed, the corresponding LED is illuminated. Otherwise, the LED is turned off.

Save the program and run it. Press and hold each switch in turn. The corresponding LED should illuminate. If it does not, check your wiring and try again.

The full wiring for the circuit is shown in Figure 22-5.

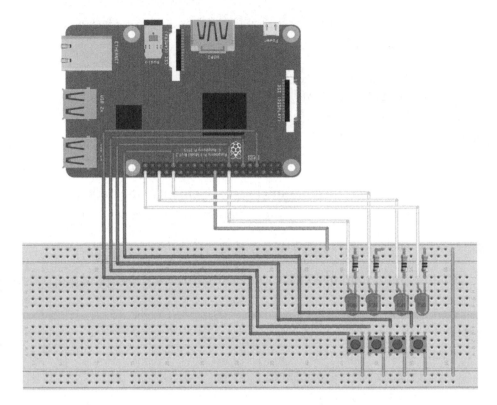

Figure 22-5. *The game's completed diagram showing all the connections*

Now that we have built and tested the circuit, we can make the game.

The Memory Game

The basic algorithm of the program is this:

- Choose one, then two, then three, then four LEDs in a random order

- Play the sequence of LEDs

- Wait for the player to input the sequence back

- Display congratulations/bad luck message (in the console)

- Continue with the next sequence

Start a new Python script file inside 'memory' called 'buttonled.py'. This will contain two helper classes for our project. The first helper class is a LED/Button aggregate class and the second is a collection of instances of this class that will handle choosing the random sequences.

The ButtonLED and ButtonLEDCollection Classes

Enter the following code:

```
from gpiozero import LED, Button
import random
```

Imports for the ButtonLED and ButtonLEDCollection classes. gpiozero is imported for the LED and Button classes and random is imported because of our need to randomly shuffle the list of LEDs to make the game different each time it is played.

```
class ButtonLED(object):
    def __init__(self, ledPin, buttonPin):
        self.led = LED(ledPin)
        self.button = Button(buttonPin)
```

Constructor takes two arguments: the GPIO pin number connected to the LED and the GPIO pin number connected to the tact switch.

```
    def on(self):
        self.led.on()
```

Turn the LED on.

```
    def off(self):
        self.led.off()
```

Turn the LED off.

```
def wait(self, timeout):
    self.button.wait_for_press(timeout)
    return self.button.is_pressed
```

The wait() method will wait, stop program execution, until the button has been pressed. If the button has not been pressed after the 'timeout' value (in seconds) then the program will resume. The button's current pressed state is returned to the caller. The method will be used by the program to determine if the player has clicked the button in the correct sequence in the main program.

```
class ButtonLEDCollection(object):
    def __init__(self):
        led1 = ButtonLED(23, 4)
        led2 = ButtonLED(12, 17)
        led3 = ButtonLED(16, 22)
        led4 = ButtonLED(21, 6)
        self.items = [ led1, led2, led3, led4 ]
```

The constructor creates ButtonLED objects and adds them to an internal list called 'items.'

```
def pick(self, count):
    leds = self.items
    random.shuffle(leds)
    picked = []
    for n in range(0, count):
        picked.append(leds[n])
    return picked
```

The pick() method shuffles the LEDs and chooses the first 'count' items. Let's say the initial sequence points to GPIO pins 6, 7, 8, and 9. After shuffling it might be 7, 6, 9, and 8. Choosing the first three would return 7, 6, and 9 meaning the second, first, and fourth LEDs. This method is the heart of creating a random sequence of LEDs for the Memory game.

```
def waitForClick(self):
    isPressed = False
    while not isPressed:
        for led in self.items:
            isPressed = isPressed or led.button.is_pressed
```

This waits for the player to press any of the tact switches. This is a blocking call and the program will not be able to proceed until a button has been pressed.

```
if __name__=='__main__':
    from time import sleep
    collection = ButtonLEDCollection()
    leds = collection.pick(4)
    for led in leds:
        led.on()
        sleep(1)
        led.off()
```

To test the classes and make sure everything is working, a small test-stub has been created. It creates an instance of the ButtonLEDCollection class and picks four LEDs turning them on and off one by one. Save and run the script. If you don't see the four LEDs flash in a random order, you should check the program and the wiring to make sure you have everything wired and coded correctly. Do this before proceeding to the main program.

The Main Program

The main program is a new file called 'memorygame.py'. Create this new file and enter the following code:

```
#!/usr/bin/python3
import sys
from time import sleep
from buttonled import ButtonLEDCollection
```

The imports for the game include the 'buttonled.py' file created in the previous part. There are only two classes imported, we could have used *, but I chose to explicitly name ButtonLEDCollection in this instance because it is the only class needed.

```
collection = ButtonLEDCollection()
```

Create an instance of the ButtonLEDCollection class.

```
print ("Welcome to the Game of Memory!")
print ("A sequence of LEDs will flash, ")
print ("you will be asked to repeat the")
print ("pattern. Press any button to start")
```

Display a welcome message to the player. Even though most of the action happens on the breadboard, some information on the console is helpful.

```
collection.waitForClick()
```

Wait for the player to press any of the tact switches.

```
for n in range(1, 5):
```

Remember that although the range value is from 1 to n, the values actually go 1 to n-1 which means that this will loop through the numbers 1-4.

```
leds = collection.pick(n)
print ("Remember this sequence")
for led in leds:
    led.on()
    sleep(1)
    led.off()
```

Pick a random sequence of LEDs. Flash the sequence and tell the player they need to memorize the sequence.

```
print("Your turn!")
for led in leds:
    if led.wait(1):
        led.on()
        sleep(0.5)
        led.off()
    else:
        print ("Missed! Game Over!")
        sys.exit()
```

It is now the players turn. The led objects are looped through again – remember, those are LED/Button aggregate objects – and the button is tested. If it has been pressed within the given time of 1 second, then the next led object is chosen. Otherwise, it is game over.

```
print ("Congratulations!")
```

Display a congratulatory message if the player correctly remembers all four sequences. Save the file.

Run the program by typing:

```
$ python3 memorygame.py
```

Or, change the execution mode of the script and run it by itself:

```
$ chmod +x memorygame.py
$ ./memorygame.py
```

The game will begin and you will be presented with sequences of one, two, three, and finally four random LEDs. Good luck!

Full Listing buttonled.py

The full listing of buttonled.py has been included to help debug any issues you may encounter:

```
from gpiozero import LED, Button
import random

class ButtonLED(object):
    def __init__(self, ledPin, buttonPin):
        self.led = LED(ledPin)
        self.button = Button(buttonPin)

    def on(self):
        self.led.on()

    def off(self):
        self.led.off()

    def wait(self, timeout):
        self.button.wait_for_press(timeout)
        return self.button.is_pressed
```

```python
class ButtonLEDCollection(object):
    def __init__(self):
        led1 = ButtonLED(23, 4)
        led2 = ButtonLED(12, 17)
        led3 = ButtonLED(16, 22)
        led4 = ButtonLED(21, 6)

        self.items = [ led1, led2, led3, led4 ]

    def pick(self, count):
        leds = self.items
        random.shuffle(leds)
        picked = []
        for n in range(0, count):
            picked.append(leds[n])
        return picked

    def waitForClick(self):
        isPressed = False
        while not isPressed:
            for led in self.items:
                isPressed = isPressed or led.button.is_pressed

if __name__=='__main__':
    from time import sleep
    collection = ButtonLEDCollection()

    leds = collection.pick(4)
    for led in leds:
        led.on()
        sleep(1)
        led.off()
```

Full Listing memorygame.py

The full listing of memorygame.py has been included to help debug any issues you may encounter:

```
#!/usr/bin/python3

import sys
from time import sleep
from buttonled import ButtonLED, ButtonLEDCollection

collection = ButtonLEDCollection()

print ("Welcome to the Game of Memory!")
print ("A sequence of LEDs will flash, ")
print ("you will be asked to repeat the")
print ("pattern. Press any button to start")

collection.waitForClick()

for n in range(1, 5):
    leds = collection.pick(n)
    print ("Remember this sequence")
    for led in leds:
        led.on()
        sleep(1)
        led.off()
    print("Your turn!")
    for led in leds:
        if led.wait(1):
            led.on()
            sleep(0.5)
            led.off()
```

```
    else:
        print ("Missed! Game Over!")
        sys.exit()

print ("Congratulations!")
```

Conclusion

This was a fun little game to get you used to coding up a hardware game with the Raspberry Pi and Python. The gpiozero library makes accessing the GPIO pins very easy.

I would always recommend creating test programs for your circuits to prove that they work before setting about writing your actual games. In fact, writing tests is really important, the more tests you can write the better you can prove that your program will do what it is setting out to achieve.

To enhance the memory game you could have a dedicated start button to begin the sequence rather than the four play buttons. In addition, you could let the player choose their skill level. The timeout value passed to the wait() method could be altered; 1.5 seconds for easy, 1 second for normal, and 0.5 seconds for hard.

CHAPTER 23

Game Project: Quiz

The last project of this book is a couch quiz game for two players. Players are presented with a series of multiple-choice questions and must decide the correct answer. The game uses a mix of PyGame and electronics; the questions are displayed on the monitor and all the input comes from two pairs of three tact switches. Some of the game screens are shown in Figure 23-1.

Figure 23-1. *Screens from the Quiz game: splash, get ready, the question, and score screens*

Create a new folder inside the 'pygamebook' 'projects' folder called 'quiz.' This is where all the scripts we will write for this project will be located.

The Electronics

For this game's circuit you will need the following:

- A breadboard

- Six tact switches

- Various lengths of wire

© Sloan Kelly 2019
S. Kelly, *Python, PyGame, and Raspberry Pi Game Development,*
https://doi.org/10.1007/978-1-4842-4533-0_23

Figure 23-2 shows the circuit diagram for the project. It consists of two pairs of three tact switches. Each tact switch is connected to ground using Pin 31 on the Raspberry Pi. Player 1's buttons are connected to GPIO pins 4, 17, and 22, and Player 2's buttons are connected to GPIO pins 5, 6, and 13.

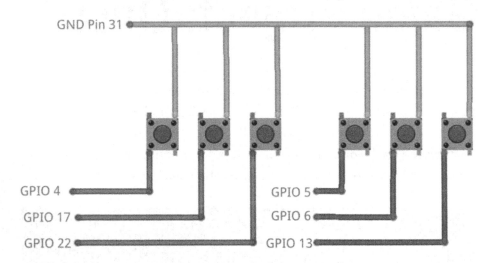

Figure 23-2. *The circuit diagram for the quiz game showing the two sets of tact switches*

Once the circuit has been built on the breadboard and attached to the Raspberry Pi, we will use a short program to test the buttons. To do this, our program will light up an onscreen display using PyGame.

Testing the Buttons

The test program, shown in Figure 23-3, displays two groups of three circles. When a tact switch is depressed, the circle 'lights up,' that is, the red dot appears as a brighter color.

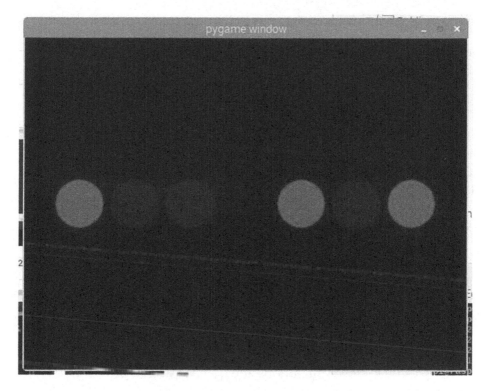

Figure 23-3. *The test program running showing that three tact switches have been depressed*

Create a new script inside the 'quiz' folder called 'buttontest.py' and enter the following:

```
#!/usr/bin/python3
import pygame, os, sys
from pygame.locals import *
from gpiozero import Button
```

Standard imports for PyGame as well as the gpiozero library.

```
def drawButtonState(surface, button, pos):
    color = 32
    if button.is_pressed:
        color = 192
    pygame.draw.circle(surface, (color, 0, 0), pos, 35)
```

Draw the state of the button. If the button is pressed, a bright circle is displayed.

```
def drawPlayerState(surface, buttons, startx):
    x = startx
    for b in buttons:
        drawButtonState(surface, b, (x, 240))
        x = x + 80

    return x
```

Loop through the given buttons and detect if each is pressed. Calls drawButtonState.

```
pygame.init()
fpsClock = pygame.time.Clock()
surface = pygame.display.set_mode((640, 480))
```

Initialize PyGame and create a screen and clock.

```
player1 = [ Button(4), Button(17), Button(22) ]
player2 = [ Button(5), Button(6), Button(13) ]
```

Create two lists of buttons. Each button is connected to the tact switch on the specified GPIO pin.

```
background = (0, 0, 0) # Black

while True:
    surface.fill(background)
```

```
for event in pygame.event.get():
    if event.type == QUIT:
        pygame.quit()
        sys.exit()

x = 80
x = drawPlayerState(surface, player1, x)
x = x + 80
drawPlayerState(surface, player2, x)

pygame.display.update()
fpsClock.tick(30)
```

Save and run the program. Press and hold each of the tact switches. The colored circles onscreen should 'light up' when the switch is depressed. If that is not the case, check the circuit and try the program again.

If the circuit is working correctly, we can move onto the visual part of the project. This will require us to create a state machine.

The Finite State Machine

There is a total of five states in the game and their transitions are shown in Figure 23-4. The five states are

- Splash screen – Shows a welcome message

- Get ready – Shows a 'Get Ready' message

- Choose question – Chooses a new question from the list

- Show question – Displays the question, the three choices, and a countdown

- Show score – Displays the current scores for both players

- Game over – This is the same state as 'show score' but contains an indicator showing who won the overall game

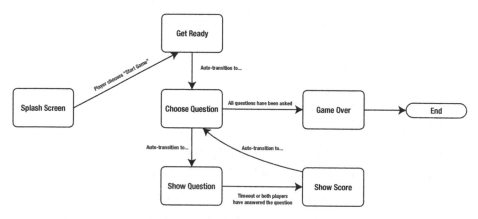

Figure 23-4. *The Finite State Machine (FSM) for the quiz game*

Because "Show Score" and "Game Over" are very similar, we will only need to create one class for both of those states, as well as the "Get Ready" and "Splash Screen" states. The rules for moving, also called state transformations, between states are shown in Table 23-1.

Table 23-1. *The Game States, Their Transition Rules, and Classes*

State	Next State	Class	Transform Condition
Splash Screen	Get Ready	HeaderTextScreen	One of the players presses a tact switch
Get Ready	Choose Question	HeaderTextScreen	Automatically moves to the next state after a certain duration
Choose Question	Show Question or Game Over	ChooseQuestion	Automatically moves to the next state. If there are no more questions, the next state is "Game Over"
Show Question	Show Score	ShowQuestion	Automatically moves to the next state after the time limit (countdown) has reached zero, or both players have chosen their answer
Show Score	Choose Question	ShowScore	Automatically moves to the next state after a certain duration
Game Over	None – Game ends	ShowScore	No condition. Game ends

Making the Game

There are some additional classes that need to be built in addition to the states mentioned earlier. These are

- Question deserialization

- The base state class

- The game runner

- UI helper classes

We will look at each of these in turn.

The Questions

The questions for the quiz were sourced from Pub Quiz Questions HQ (https://pubquizquestionshq.com/) which is a free and open resource for questions. The questions are formatted on a web page so I took some time to organize them into a JSON file. The resulting data file should be saved as 'questions.json' to the 'quiz' folder:

```
{
    "questions":
    [
        {
            "question": "New York City Hall is in which
                        Borough?",
            "answer": "Manhattan",
            "answers": [
                "Queens",
                "Brooklyn"
            ]
        },
        {
            "question": "Which was the first baseball team
                        in Texas to make it to the World
                        Series?",
            "answer": "Houston Astros",
            "answers": [
                "Houston Oilers",
                "Texas Rangers"
            ]
        },
```

```
{

    "question": "Dwight D. Eisenhower was
                President from 1953 to 1961, but
                who was his Vice President?",
    "answer": "Richard Nixon",
    "answers": [
        "John Kennedy",
        "Lyndon Johnson"
    ]
},
{

    "question": "Which was the most successful NFL
                team of the decade beginning in
                Jan 2000 with 4 Super Bowl wins?",
    "answer": "New England Patriots",
    "answers": [
        "Buffalo Bills",
        "San Diego Chargers"
    ]
},
{

    "question": "Why was there no World Series
                played in 1994?",
    "answer": "Player's strike",
    "answers": [
        "No one bought tickets",
        "Ban on baseballs"
    ]
},
```

```
    {
        "question": "Lansing is the state capital of
                    which northern state in America?",
        "answer": "Michigan",
        "answers": [
            "Ilinois",
            "Wisconsin"
        ]
    },
    {

        "question": "As of 2013 the most widely
                    circulated newspaper in the USA
                    was The Wall Street Journal.
                    Which company owns it?",
        "answer": "News Corporation
        "answers": [
            "Chicago Tribune",
            "Conde Nast"
        ]
    },
    {

        "question": "Out of which city were Aerosmith
                    formed?",
        "answer": "Boston",
        "answers": [
            "New York",
            "Los Angeles"
        ]
    },
```

```
    {
            "question": "Which future president gained
                         national fame through his role in
                         the War of 1812, most famously
                         where he won a decisive victory at
                         the Battle of New Orleans?",
            "answer": "Andrew Jackson",
            "answers": [
                  "George Washington",
                  "Abraham Lincoln"
            ]
    },
    {
            "question": "Born in Massachusetts, which
                         painter's most famous work is
                         'Arrangement in Grey and Black
                         No.1'?",
            "answer": "James Abbott McNeill Whistler",
            "answers": [
                  "Andy Warhol",
                  "Phillipe Stark"
            ]
    }
    ]
}
```

The JSON file is formatted as an object with a list property called "questions." Each object in the array has the following properties:

- Question – The text of the question
- Answer – The correct answer for the question
- Answers – A list of incorrect answers

I chose to use a function to create an array of questions. This function loads in the questions from the 'questions.json' file and fills a list of 'Question' objects.

Create a new file called 'questions.py' and enter the following:

```python
#!/usr/bin/python3
import json
import random
```

Imports for JSON serialization/deserialization. The random import will be used to randomize the order of the questions and the answers

```python
class Question(object):
    def __init__(self, jsonQuestion):
        self.question = jsonQuestion['question']
        self.answers = jsonQuestion['answers']
        self.answer = jsonQuestion['answer']
        self.answers.append(jsonQuestion['answer'])
        random.shuffle(self.answers)
        index = 0
        for a in self.answers:
            if a == jsonQuestion['answer']:
                self.answerIndex = index
            index = index + 1
```

The 'Question' class is used to store the question text, the correct answer, and the other suggestions. The index of the correct answer is also stored. This will make determining whether a player has chosen the correct answer a little easier; the first button is mapped to the first choice and so on. To make it interesting, each time the game is played the answers are shuffled using the 'random.shuffle()' method. This handy method scrambles the elements of a list. We'll see it be used in the following 'loadQuestions()' function.

```
def loadQuestions(filename):
    f = open(filename)
    questionFile = json.load(f)
    f.close()
```

Load the entire contents of the question file into memory.

```
questions = []
for q in questionFile['questions']:
    questions.append(Question(q))
```

For each question in the file, create a new instance of the 'Question' class and append it to the 'questions' list.

```
random.shuffle(questions)
return questions
```

Once all the questions have been added to the list, the 'random. shuffle()' method is used again to re-order the questions so that no two games are identical.

```
if __name__ == '__main__':
    questions = loadQuestions("questions.json")
    for q in questions:
        print(q.question)
        print("Answer index %d" % q.answerIndex)
        for a in q.answers:
            if a == q.answer:
                print("\t* %s" % a)
            else:
                print("\t%s" % a)
```

To test that the code runs, I added a test stub to the bottom of the file. It loads in the 'questions.json' file and displays the question and answers. The correct answer is marked with an asterisk (*).

Save the file and run it. You will have to add the execution bit before you can run it:

```
$ chmod +x questions.py
$ ./questions.py
```

You should see a list of questions displayed onscreen. If you don't, please check the code.

UI Helper Classes

The UI helper classes are contained within a single file. The classes are

- Text – Basic text component

- Question – Displays the question and answers

- Countdown – Displays a progress bar that counts down from 30 seconds to 0

Create a new file called 'ui.py' and enter the following text:

```
import pygame
from pygame.locals import *
```

Import the PyGame modules.

```
class Text(object):
    def __init__(self, size, colour):
        self.size = size
        self.colour = colour
        self.font = pygame.font.Font(None, size)

    def draw(self, surface, msg, pos, centred = False):
        x, y = pos
        tempSurface = self.font.render(msg, True, self.colour)
```

```
if centred:
    x = x - tempSurface.get_width() / 2
    y = y + tempSurface.get_height() / 4
    pos = (x, y)
surface.blit(tempSurface, pos)
```

The Text class is a wrapper around the existing PyGame Font class. It makes positioning the text easier onscreen and provides a handy way to draw text centered to a particular point.

```
class QuestionText(object):
    def __init__(self):
        self.questionText = Text(32, (255, 255, 0))
        self.answerText = Text(32, (255, 255, 255))
        self.disabledText = Text(32, (56, 56, 56))
```

Constructor for the QuestionText class. This creates three separate Text instances: one for the question text, one for the answer text, and one for the disabled state. When the round is over, the correct answer is highlighted. The disabled text is used to draw the two incorrect answers.

```
def draw(self, surface, question, answer, answers,
showAnswer = False):
    y = 64
    maxWidth = 60
    lineHeight = 32
    if len(question) > maxWidth:
        question.split(" ")
        temp = ""
        for word in question:
            temp = temp + word
```

```
            if len(temp) > maxWidth:
                pos = (400, y)
                self.questionText.draw(surface, temp, pos,
                True)
                temp = ""
                y = y + lineHeight
        self.questionText.draw(surface, temp, (400, y), True)
    else:
        self.questionText.draw(surface, question, (400, y),
        True)
```

If the question text is longer than the screen width, it is split into separate words. Each word is added to a list until the maximum width has been reached. That text is then drawn to the screen. The remaining text is then processed until the entire question has been displayed. If the question text is less than the width of the screen it is displayed normally.

```
y = y + lineHeight * 2
label = "A"
for a in answers:
    font = self.answerText
    if showAnswer and a != answer:
        font = self.disabledText

    font.draw(surface, "%s. %s" % (label, a), (100, y),
    False)
    labelChar = ord(label)
    labelChar = labelChar + 1
    label = chr(labelChar)
    y = y + 40
```

Each answer is displayed with A, B, or C prefixed to it. In order to achieve this 'effect,' we must first convert the current label to a number – this is what the 'ord()' function does. It looks up the ASCII (American Standard Code for Information Interchange) table and returns a number based on the character. The first time the loop is run, label = 'A' and so ord() will return 65 because 'A' is at position 65 of the ASCII table. The value is incremented to get to the next character so 65 would become 66 and this is converted to a character using the 'chr()' function. 66 in ASCII is 'B'.

```
class Countdown(object):
    def __init__(self, seconds, pos, width, height,
    innerColour, borderColour, text):
        self.maxSeconds = seconds
        self.seconds = seconds
        self.pos = pos
        self.width = width
        self.height = height
        self.finished = False
        self.text = text
        self.innerColour = innerColour
        self.borderColour = borderColour
        self.fullRect = Rect(pos, (width, height))
        self.rect = Rect(pos, (width, height))
```

That's quite a long constructor! These parameters will be used to draw the countdown meter that takes the shape of a progress bar that gets shorter the longer it remains onscreen.

```
    def draw(self, surface):
        pygame.draw.rect(surface, self.innerColour, self.rect)
        pygame.draw.rect(surface, self.borderColour, self.
        fullRect, 2)
```

To draw the progress bar, we'll use the 'draw.rect()' method provided by PyGame. It can be drawn in one of two ways: filled or with a border. The 'inside' of the progress bar will be drawn as a filled rectangle and the 'outside' of the progress bar will be drawn with a border.

The current size of the countdown is drawn from 'self.rect' and the full rectangle 'self.fullRect' is drawn over the top as shown in Figure 23-5.

27

Figure 23-5. *The progress bar for the quiz game*

```
x, y = self.pos
x = x + self.width / 2
pos = (x, y)
self.text.draw(surface, "%02d" % self.seconds, pos, True)
```

The seconds remaining is drawn on top of the progress bar.

```
def reset(self):
    self.finished = False
    self.seconds = self.maxSeconds
```

Reset the countdown each time we display the question.

```
def update(self, deltaTime):
    if self.seconds == 0:
        return

    self.seconds = self.seconds - deltaTime
    if self.seconds < 0:
        self.seconds = 0
        self.finished = True
    progressWidth = self.width * (self.seconds / self.
    maxSeconds)
    self.rect = Rect(self.pos, (progressWidth, self.height))
```

Update the countdown by decrementing the current seconds count in 'self.seconds'. If seconds reaches 0 then we don't update. If the timer reaches zero, 'self.finished' is set to True. Finally the current width of the inner part of the progress bar is calculated and stored for the 'draw()' method.

Save the file.

The Game Runner and Base State Class

The game runner is a very basic framework class that will allow the game to transition between states. To create an interface to program to, a base state class needs to be created. This will also be used as the basis for all other state classes.

The 'NullState' class will provide the basis for the other states in the game's FSM. The 'GameRunner' class will

- Initialize PyGame

- Update the current state

- Draw the current state

The game update method will also transition between the various states too. We will write a main entry point to the program later that will create an instance of the 'GameRunner' class.

Create a new file called 'gamerunner.py' and enter the following:

```python
import pygame
from pygame.locals import *
```

Imports for PyGame.

```python
class NullState(object):
    def update(self, deltaTime):
        return None
```

```
def draw(self, surface):
    pass

def onEnter(self):
    pass

def onExit(self):
    pass
```

The 'NullState' class is the basis for the other states in the game. It contains four methods that are used to

- Update

- Draw

- Inform the state that it is being entered

- Inform the state that it is being transitioned out

```
class GameRunner(object):
    def __init__(self, dimensions, title, backColour,
    initialState):
        self.state = initialState
        self.clock = pygame.time.Clock()
        self.backColour = backColour
        self.surface = pygame.display.set_mode(dimensions)
        pygame.display.set_caption(title)
```

Initialize PyGame and create a clock. This creates the display and sets the caption of the window.

```
def update(self):
    deltaTime = self.clock.tick(30) / 1000.0
    if self.state != None:
        self.state = self.state.update(deltaTime)

    return self.state
```

The time between the last time this method was run and now is calculated and stored in 'deltaTime.' The time is in milliseconds so to get it into seconds we divide by 1000. The current state's 'update()' method is called. The state's 'update()' method returns the next state to transition to. The current state is returned to the caller. The caller will be the main program that we will write later.

```
def draw(self):
    self.surface.fill(self.backColour)
    if self.state != None:
        self.state.draw(self.surface)

    pygame.display.update()
```

This clears the main surface and gets the current state to draw itself on top and then updates the display.

Save the file.

Player Input

Without player input we would be making movies! For this game the player input is captured using the 'PlayerController' class. This class also contains the player's current score. Create a new file called 'playercontroller.py' and enter the following text:

```
from gpiozero import Button
```

The import for the gpiozero library.

```
class PlayerController(object):
    def __init__(self, pins):
        self.buttons = []
        self.score = 0
        for pin in pins:
            self.buttons.append(Button(pin))
```

Constructor for the 'PlayerController' class. Notice that it creates a list of buttons from the 'pins' list that is passed to it.

```python
def anyButton(self):
    for button in self.buttons:
        if button.is_pressed:
            return True

    return False
```

Method to determine if any button has been pressed.

```python
def playerChoice(self):
    index = 0
    for button in self.buttons:
        if button.is_pressed:
            return index
        index = index + 1

    return -1
```

Method to determine the player's answer selection. This method returns –1 if the player has not made a selection, or the index in the 'self.buttons' list of the button that the player pressed.

The State Classes

The following classes will be created for the states in the game:

- ChooseQuestion
- HeaderTextScreen
- ShowQuestion
- ShowScore

Each game state is *re-entrant*. This means that the state can be run any number of times during program execution. Each state is told when they are entered by calling the 'onEnter()' method and when they are no longer the current state by calling the 'onExit()' method.

When you are making your own states, setup code for states should be performed in the 'onEnter()' method and tear down (clean up) actions should be performed in the 'onExit()' method.

Separating Class from State

The state of a finite state machine (FSM) is *an instance of a class*. There is no need to create multiple classes that perform the same or similar operations just because they represent a different state. In this game there are two uses where the same classes are used:

- HeaderTextScreen – Used by the 'Get Ready' and 'Splash Screen' states

- ShowScore – Used by the 'Show Score' and 'Game Over' states

This topic will be revisited when we create the main file.

Maintaining Game State

The game's current state is in two parts: the action currently being performed and the data that action is processing. The data is stored in the current question and in each of the player's controllers. We already have separate classes for the players ('PlayerController') but we need one for the current question. Create a new file called 'currentquestion.py'. Inside this file will be a class definition for the currently displayed question. This information will be altered by the 'ChooseQuestion' state and displayed by the 'ShowQuestion' state.

It should be noted as we will see later that the other states *do not need to know about the current question* and are therefore not given this data.

Enter the following code in 'currentquestion.py':

```python
class CurrentQuestion(object):
    def __init__(self):
        self.question = ""
        self.answer = ""
        self.answerIndex = -1
        self.answers = []
```

And that's it; it's just the information for the current question. Save the file.

ChooseQuestion Class

The 'ChooseQuestion' state picks Create a new file called 'choosequestion. py'. This class will be used to choose the current question from the list of questions.

```python
from gamerunner import NullState
```

The 'ChooseQuestion' class extends 'NullState' and so we must import 'NullState' into this file.

```python
class ChooseQuestion(NullState):
    def __init__(self, nextState, gameOverState,
    currentQuestion, questions):
        self.questions = questions
        self.nextState = nextState
        self.gameOverState = gameOverState
        self.current = -1
        self.currentQuestion = currentQuestion
```

The constructor takes four parameters. The first is the default game state to transition to if there is another question. As we see from Table 23-1, this would normally be the 'Show Question' state. However, if the 'end of game' condition is reached, the game will transition to the 'gameOverState' state.

'currentQuestion' is the instance of the game state talked about in *Maintaining Game State*. The final parameter is the list of 'Question' instances loaded from the JSON file containing the questions.

```
def update(self, deltaTime):
    self.current = self.current + 1
    if self.current == len(self.questions):
        self.currentQuestion.question = "
        self.currentQuestion.answer = "
        self.currentQuestion.answerIndex = -1
        self.currentQuestion.answers = []
        return self.gameOverState
    else:
        question = self.questions[self.current]
        self.currentQuestion.question = question.question
        self.currentQuestion.answer = question.answer
        self.currentQuestion.answers = question.answers
        self.currentQuestion.answerIndex = question.
        answerIndex
    return self.nextState
```

The index 'self.current' is incremented. If the value is equal to the length of 'self.questions', it is game over. Otherwise the current question's data is set and the 'nextState' is returned.

The 'ChooseQuestion' class doesn't have a 'draw()' method so we don't need to add an override method for it here; 'NullState' already provides a basic 'draw()' method. Save the file.

HeaderTextScreen Class

The HeaderTextScreen is used by both the 'Splash Screen' and 'Get Ready'
states to display informative text to the players. In the case of the splash
screen, the name of the game is displayed along with "Press any button"
to continue. With 'Get Ready' the text "Get Ready" is displayed. The
difference between the two states is that the splash screen requires input
from the player whereas the 'get ready' instance automatically transitions
to the next state after a set duration.

Create a new file called 'headertextscreen.py' and enter the following
text:

```
from ui import *
from playercontroller import *
from gamerunner import NullState
```

Required imports.

```
class HeaderTextScreen(NullState):
    def __init__(self, nextState, player1, player2, waitTime = 0):
        self.nextState = nextState
        self.player1 = player1
        self.player2 = player2
        self.big = Text(128, (255, 192, 0))
        self.small = Text(36, (255, 255, 255))
        self.waitTime = waitTime
        self.currentTime = 0
        self.header = ""
        self.subHeader = ""
```

The constructor takes four parameters: the next state, the player
controllers, and the wait time. If the wait time is zero then it is assumed
that some player interaction is required, that is, one of the players has to
press a button to move to the next state.

```
def setHeader(self, header):
    self.header = header
```

Set the heading text.

```
def setSub(self, subHeader):
    self.subHeader = subHeader
```

Set the subheading text.

```
def setNextState(self, nextState):
    self.nextState = nextState
```

Set the next state.

```
def update(self, deltaTime):
    if self.waitTime > 0:
        self.currentTime = self.currentTime + deltaTime
        if self.currentTime >= self.waitTime:
            return self.nextState
    elif self.player1.anyButton() or self.player2.anyButton():
        return self.nextState
    return self
```

This performs the state transition. If 'self.waitTime' is greater than zero then it is the automatic countdown version, otherwise it is the user-controlled version of the state.

```
def draw(self, surface):
    self.big.draw(surface, self.header, (400, 200), True)
    self.small.draw(surface, self.subHeader, (400, 300), True)
```

Save the file.

ShowQuestion Class

The 'Show Question' state displays the current question, the answers, and a countdown. When the countdown reaches 0 (from 30 seconds) or both players have made their selection the state transitions to the next state. The state makes use of the 'PlayerController'; one for each player as well as the 'CurrentQuestion' instance.

Create a new file called 'showquestion.py' and enter the following text:

```python
from gamerunner import NullState
from ui import Text, QuestionText, Countdown
```

Importing the 'gamerunner' file for the 'NullState' class. This class uses the 'Text,' 'Countdown,' and 'QuestionText' classes from 'ui.'

```python
class ShowQuestion(NullState):
    def __init__(self, nextState, currentQuestion, player1,
    player2):
        self.nextState = nextState
        self.player1 = player1
        self.player2 = player2
        self.player1Choice = -1
        self.player2Choice = -1
        self.currentQuestion = currentQuestion
        self.showAnswer = False
        self.endCount = 3
        self.questionText = QuestionText()

        text = Text(32, (255, 255, 255))
        self.countdown = Countdown(30, (80, 560), 640, 32,
        (128, 0, 0), (255, 0, 0), text)
```

The constructor for ShowQuestion takes four parameters: the next state to transition to, the current question instance, and the two player controllers to get input from them.

```
def calcScore(self):
    if self.player1Choice == self.currentQuestion.answerIndex:
        self.player1.score = self.player1.score + 1
    if self.player2Choice == self.currentQuestion.answerIndex:
        self.player2.score = self.player2.score + 1
```

Helper function to calculate the players' scores.

```
def update(self, deltaTime):
    if self.player1Choice == -1:
        p1 = self.player1.playerChoice()
        if p1 >= 0:
            self.player1Choice = p1

    if self.player2Choice == -1:
        p2 = self.player2.playerChoice()
        if p2 >= 0:
            self.player2Choice = p2

    if self.player1Choice >= 0 and self.player2Choice >= 0:
        self.showAnswer = True

    if not self.showAnswer:
        self.countdown.update(deltaTime)
        if self.countdown.finished:
            self.showAnswer = True
    else:
        self.endCount = self.endCount - deltaTime
        if self.endCount <= 0:
            self.calcScore()
            return self.nextState

    return self
```

The update method ticks the countdown timer if 'self.showAnswer' is False. When the countdown timer reaches zero or both players have made their selection 'self.showAnswer' is set to True. Once a player has selected an answer, they cannot change it.

```
def draw(self, surface):
    self.questionText.draw(surface, self.currentQuestion.
    question, self.currentQuestion.answer, self.
    currentQuestion.answers, self.showAnswer)
    if not self.showAnswer:
        self.countdown.draw(surface)
```

Draw the question and answers, the 'self.showAnswer' field value is passed to the questionText's 'draw()' method to highlight the correct answer. If the countdown is active, show it.

```
def onExit(self):
    self.endCount = 3
    self.showAnswer = False
    self.countdown.reset()
```

Clean up the current state on exit.

```
def onEnter(self):
    self.player1Choice = -1
    self.player2Choice = -1
```

Set up the player data on entry to the state.
Save the file.

ShowScore Class

The 'Show Score' and 'Game Over' states both share this class. In between each question, the players' scores are shown. When the 'Game Over' screen is shown, the scores and "Winner" or "Tie" is displayed. The "Winner" tag is shown under the player who won the game.

For this file I created a simple test stub to verify the positions of the onscreen text.

Create a new file called 'showscore.py' and enter the following text:

```
#!/usr/bin/python3

import pygame
from pygame.locals import *
from gamerunner import NullState
from ui import Text
```

Imports required by the 'ShowScore' class.

```
class ShowScore(NullState):

    def __init__(self, nextState, player1, player2, showWinner
    = False):
        self.nextState = nextState
        self.player1 = player1
        self.player2 = player2
        self.counter = 3
        self.showWinner = showWinner
        self.scoreText = Text(300, (255, 255, 0))
        self.playerText = Text(128, (255, 255, 255))
```

The 'ShowScore' constructor takes four parameters. The first is the next state to transition to, the next are the controllers for the first and second player. These are required for the 'score' field on the 'PlayerController' class. Finally, the 'showWinner' parameter is used to display either "Winner" or "Tie" depending on the end state of the game when all the questions have been asked.

```
def update(self, deltaTime):
    self.counter = self.counter - deltaTime
    if self.counter <= 0:
        return self.nextState

    return self
```

The score screen only shows for a specific amount of time. Once that time expires, the state transitions to the next.

```
def draw(self, surface):
    self.playerText.draw(surface, "Player 1", (200, 85), True)
    self.playerText.draw(surface, "Player 2", (600, 85), True)

    self.scoreText.draw(surface, str(self.player1.score),
    (200, 150), True)
    self.scoreText.draw(surface, str(self.player2.score),
    (600, 150), True)

    if self.showWinner:
        winner = "WINNER!"
        pos = 200
        if self.player1.score == self.player2.score:
            winner = "TIE!"
            pos = 400
        elif self.player2.score > self.player1.score:
            pos = 600
        self.playerText.draw(surface, winner, (pos, 400), True)
```

Draw the screen.

```
def onEnter(self):
    self.counter = 3
```

When entering the state, set the current counter to 3 seconds.

```
if __name__ == '__main__':
    import sys
    class P(object):
        def __init__(self, s):
            self.score = s

    pygame.init()
    fpsClock = pygame.time.Clock()
    surface = pygame.display.set_mode((800, 600))

    score = ShowScore(None, P(55), P(10), True)

    background = (0, 0, 0) # Black

    while True:
        surface.fill(background)
        for event in pygame.event.get():
            if event.type == QUIT:
                pygame.quit()
                sys.exit()

        deltaTime = fpsClock.tick(30) / 1000.0
        score.draw(surface)
        pygame.display.update()
```

Test stub. This will display a 'Game Over' state. Save and run the file to see. If you want to see a 'Show Score' screen, change this line:

```
score = ShowScore(None, P(55), P(10), True)
```

to

```
score = ShowScore(None, P(55), P(10))
```

The Main File

The main file is actually only a few lines of code and most of that is setting up the Finite State Machine. Create a new file called 'quiz.py' and enter the following text:

```
#!/usr/bin/python3
```

```python
import pygame
from gamerunner import GameRunner
from questions import *
from headertextscreen import HeaderTextScreen
from choosequestion import ChooseQuestion
from playercontroller import PlayerController
from showquestion import ShowQuestion
from showscore import ShowScore
from currentquestion import CurrentQuestion
```

All the imports for the program.

```python
pygame.init()
```

```python
player1 = PlayerController([4, 17, 22])
player2 = PlayerController([5, 6, 13])
currentQuestion = CurrentQuestion()
```

Initialize PyGame and set up the game state data that is stored in the 'PlayerController' instances as well as the 'CurrentQuestion' instance.

```python
questions = loadQuestions("questions.json")
```

Load the questions from the JSON file.

```python
showQuestion = ShowQuestion(None, currentQuestion, player1,
player2)
gameOver = ShowScore(None, player1, player2, True)
```

```
chooseQuestion = ChooseQuestion(showQuestion, gameOver,
currentQuestion, questions)
showScore = ShowScore(chooseQuestion, player1, player2)
showQuestion.nextState = showScore
```

The 'ShowQuestion,' 'ShowScore,' and 'ChooseQuestion' classes are used to build some of the states used in the game. Because of the creation of the states it wasn't possible to set the initial state for the 'ShowQuestion,' instead the 'showQuestion' instance's 'nextState' was set manually and None was passed to the constructor of 'ShowQuestion.'

```
interstitial = HeaderTextScreen(chooseQuestion, player1,
player2, 3)
interstitial.setHeader("Get Ready!")
interstitial.setSub("")
splashScreen = HeaderTextScreen(interstitial, player1, player2)
splashScreen.setHeader("QUIZ!")
splashScreen.setSub("Press any button to start")
```

The interstitial (in between game play) screens for "Get Ready!" and the splash screen. Notice that we didn't create a separate class for the splash screen and for "Get Ready!", it just uses two separate instances of 'HeaderTextScreen.'

When we transition from one state to another, we transition from one *instance* of a class to another. So there is no need to write completely separate classes for each state.

```
game = GameRunner((800, 600), "Quiz", (0, 0, 0), splashScreen)
```

The instance of the game runner is being set to a 800×600 sized window with a black (0, 0, 0) background and the initial state to the splash screen instance 'splashScreen.'

```
lastState = None
while game.state != None:
    nextState = game.update()
    if nextState != lastState:
        if game.state != None:
            game.state.onExit()
        if nextState != None:
            nextState.onEnter()
        lastState = nextState
    game.draw()

pygame.quit()
```

The main program loop consists of calling the game's 'update()' and 'draw()' methods. It could be argued that this loop be placed in a 'run()' method of 'GameRunner,' I mean it is in the name. I will leave that as an exercise for you the reader; create a method called 'run()' on 'GameRunner' that runs the loop.

Save the file.

Playing the Game

To play the game you will need an opponent; it's a couch-based quiz game after all. Position yourselves on the couch and run the 'quiz.py' file. You will need to set the execution bit for the file:

```
$ chmod +x quiz.py
```

And then run it:

```
$ ./quiz.py
```

Once the game starts, one of you presses a button on the breadboard to start the quiz. Try to answer each question as it appears. If you don't answer within the 30 second timeout, you forfeit the point. The winner is the person with the most points at the end of the game. Good luck!

Conclusion

That was a fun game that showed how you can build PyGame-based games that interact with electronic components. You could rewrite the input routines of the earlier projects like Brick, Snake, and Invaders to use tact switches for input instead of computer keys.

CHAPTER 24

Conclusion

By now, you should have a good understanding of the Python language as well as the PyGame library. With the games included in this text, you should have a good understanding of what goes into creating a video game. Indeed, armed with a good idea, you should have enough knowledge to make a game on your own! In this book we've covered player input, displaying graphics, playing sounds, and moving characters about the screen as well as alternative forms of input and output in the form of reading and writing to the GPIO pins.

In addition to the games, we also looked at Object-Oriented Programming and some associated design patterns such as Finite State Machines (FSMs) and Model View Controllers (MVCs). These will help you in the construction of your own games, and if you wanted to take it further, a possible career in the games industry.

Hopefully by this stage you should have a good understanding of the Python language itself and PyGame. Due to the three games included in this text (Bricks, Snake, and Invaders), you have an understand what goes into making a video game. With everything in here, you should have enough to create your own. All it takes is a great idea!

Where to now? Now that you have the programming bug (pardon the pun), the sky is the limit. Perhaps you want to learn C++ and do some 3D games.

© Sloan Kelly 2019
S. Kelly, *Python, PyGame, and Raspberry Pi Game Development*,
https://doi.org/10.1007/978-1-4842-4533-0_24

If you want to read more about Python you should head over to `https://docs.python.org/`. PyGame has full documentation too at `www.pygame.org/wiki/index`.

Even if you don't decide to take up programming as a full-time job, making games for a hobby is still great fun.

Consider taking part in a game jam like Ludum Dare (`https://ldjam.com`) or others listed at `https://itch.io/jams`. It's great fun to work on a game for a short time period, usually over a weekend. You can even bring in friends to help you make it. Who knows, you might even create the next "Nuclear Throne," "Super Meat Boy," or "Stardew Valley."

I hope that you have enjoyed this book and whatever you choose to do I hope you have fun doing it.

Happy coding!

Index

A

Abstraction, 155

Aggregation, 179–180

Algorithm, 2

Alien Swarm classes

    alien types, 276

    BulletController class, 277

    current shooter, 280

    flipframe() method, 276

    framecount, 278

    getarea() method, 279

    PyGame libraries, 275

    ronder method, 281

    reset method, 278

    SwarmController class, 276

    view class, 281

American Standard Code for
Information Interchange
(ASCII), 260, 357

And statement, 50

Anti-aliasing, 194

append() method, 67

Arithmetic operators, 26

Artificial intelligence (AI), 241

Audio

    playing sound, 234–235

    play/pause music, 236–238

        playsong.py output, 239

    pygame.mixer.fadeout(), 235

    pygame.mixer.unpause(), 237

    Sound.set_volume(), 238–239

    pygame.mixer.get_busy(), 233

    pygame.mixer.init(), 233

    pygame.mixer.quit(), 233

B

Ball update() method, 161

BatImage/BatSprite, 111

Bitmap font class

    ASCII character, 260

    centre() method, 263

    ord() function, 263

    sprite sheet, 259

    toIndex() method, 261

blit() method, 194, 196

Blocks, 44–45

Boolean logic, 50–52

Breadboard, 298–299

Breakout board, 299–300

Bricks, 137

Bullet classes

    bullet controller, 270

    bullet view, 270

    countdown variable, 268

    killList, 269

    update() method, 267

© Sloan Kelly 2019

S. Kelly, *Python, PyGame, and Raspberry Pi Game Development*,
https://doi.org/10.1007/978-1-4842-4533-0

Made in the USA
Columbia, SC
14 December 2019

84910778R00228